THE GREENING OF PSYCHOLOGY

The Vegetable World in Myth, Dream, and Healing

To Howard Shapiro
thanks for the stories.
— Peter Bishop

PETER BISHOP

Spring Publications, Inc.
Dallas, Texas

First printing 1991. Text printed on acidfree paper
Printed in the United States of America
Published by Spring Publications, Inc.; P.O. Box 222069;
Dallas TX 75222. Cover illustration, design, and
production, as well as interior art, by Margot McLean

Library of Congress Cataloging-in-Publication Data

Bishop, Peter, 1946–
The greening of psychology : the vegetable world in myth, dream, and healing / Peter Bishop.
p. cm.
Includes bibliographical references and index.
ISBN 0–88214–345–X (pbk. : alk. paper)
1. Symbolism (Psychology) 2. Vegetables—Psychological aspects.
3. Plants—Psychological aspects. 4. Psychoanalysis. I. Title.
BF175.5.S95B57 1991
154.6'3—dc20 90–27418
CIP

For Louise

CONTENTS

ACKNOWLEDGMENTS

I wish to thank all of those people who have told me their vegetable thoughts and especially their dreams. I am also most grateful for the editorial thoroughness of Mary Helen Sullivan. Part of this material appeared in a different form in "The Vegetable Soul," *Spring: A Journal of Archetype and Culture 1988:* 73–90. Lines from I. Sinclair's *Lud Heat* are reproduced by kind permission of Goldmark Press. Quotations from the *Collected Works* of C. G. Jung (Bollingen Series XX), translated by R. F. C. Hull, edited by H. Read, M. Fordham, G. Adler, and Wm. McGuire are by kind permission of Princeton University Press.

PROLOGUE
Toward a Green Psychology

Recent years have witnessed a surge of concern about the ecological fate of the Earth. Perhaps as never before, Western civilization sees its future as being inescapably interconnected to that of all life on the planet. Side by side with an acceleration of ecological degradation, there has therefore emerged a growing *ecological identity*, both individual and social. This sense of identity includes not just personal biography, family history, or ethnic and cultural values, but also the sense of ourselves as members of a species within a complex ecology.

The most far-reaching attempt to revision our relationship to the natural world is called "Deep Ecology."[1] Unlike most other ecological approaches, which seek only to control the environmental effects of industrialism and to reform, or modify, individual attitudes, "Deep Ecology" insists upon a total transformation: of the way that society is organized and how it interacts with the "natural" world, of individual attitudes and values, but—most importantly—of our very *identity*, both as individuals and as a species. Deep Ecology insists that the world's fauna and flora should be respected not just because of their usefulness to humanity (a usefulness estimated variously in terms of environmental, aesthetic, spiritual, psychological, scientific, or economic needs), but due to their *inherent* value.

In other words, they have a right to exist, and it is humanity's task to bring its consciousness into a rapport with that of the world's other species. Instead of an I–It relationship to the world, there is a desire for one that is more I–Thou. All fauna and flora are assumed to occupy a unique place in the ecological totality; as well, each possesses a complex consciousness, perhaps even a vision of the world, that is no less indispensable and of equal consideration and value to that of humans. The perspectives of myriad creatures are therefore not just to be understood or empathized with, but moved toward. Deep Ecology calls for a complete shift both in the quality and in the center of gravity of what has hitherto been called consciousness.

What are the implications for an imaginal psychology of this radical revisioning? First of all, it is important to remember that the dynamic psychologies present not literal truths but healing fictions. They have consistently drawn their metaphorical soils from other areas: both Sigmund Freud and C. G. Jung, for example, derived the psychic energy model from physics, especially thermodynamics; they also used images drawn from biology, with its study of nerve and brain physiology; similarly, both borrowed extensively from archeology, anthropology, philosophy, the study of the classics, of comparative mythology and religion. These other fields of inquiry were not used simply for their ideas but for their metaphorical power. I believe that a fundamental remetaphorizing is required, that an ecological image of psyche should complement the images based on the aforementioned disciplines.

In addition, imaginal psychology can provide a "deep" ecology with an essential poetic middle ground, the *metaxy* between philosophical abstraction and direct action. It helps to sustain the metaphorical nature of this ecological vision, which otherwise can so easily congeal into another literalism, another image-phobic fundamentalism. We need to assert paradox and contradiction in the face of an urgency and desperation that cry out for more muscular action, that want to simplify the contemporary ecological dilemma, that insist there is no time for psyche, for the awkward indirection, clumsy hesitation, and depressive moodiness, as well as joy and pleasure, that accompany so much soulwork.

The idea of *ecology*—no matter how sophisticated, how pertinent and "right" it seems for these desperate times—is an imaginal fiction. Nevertheless, the creation of such a fiction, such an important symbol, is a major psychological event. Through this symbol, concern for images of the *Other* is becoming more important than concern for images of *Self.*[2]

Many now grieve for the wrongs against the symbolic "Mother" and blame the "Father," but such a mythic formula is too simple. Words such as *natural*, *bio-*, *organic*, *growth* have become leitmotifs of a new quest, a new hope. Yet all too often, the complex material world of *things* gets left behind as optimistic belief skims across the surface in search of a new fundamental truth. Perhaps the most common of these new ecological ideas is that of a "greening." "Green Spirituality," "Green Politics," "Green Consumerism," "Green Economics": every day we are confronted by yet another "Green" label, as politicians, manufacturers, retailers, energy producers, activists, dietitians, rock stars, and numerous others compete with each other to establish their environmental respectability—their "green" credentials.

The adjective *green* has moved rapidly from being a radical source of hope, renewal, and harmony into becoming a meaningless haven for opportunism and cliché. Already the freshness of "green" is becoming rotten—green around the gills. On a metaphorical level, we have moved quickly from the green bud to the green of decay without experiencing ripeness in-between. A cynicism is already apparent, as the popular press mockingly contrasts those people who are "pale green" with those who are "dark green"; many on the political left insist that this so-called radical greening is merely a bourgeois ploy to make the middle classes feel nice.[3] The rapid corruption of this "greening" is blamed on the dubious ability of consumer capitalism to appropriate *any* idealism and to market it as a product or is seen as an indication of the political naiveté and shallowness of the "Green" movement itself.

Whatever the truth in these arguments, I want to suggest

that this almost simultaneous appearance of growth and decay, hope and despair, idealism and cynicism, enthusiasm and opportunism is inherent in the metaphor *green*. Above all, it is time to de-naturalize "Green" and at the same time to de-green "Nature." "Green" is not simply a color and especially not the quintessential color of "Nature" or the "natural" world. It is a root metaphor of *a* way the world is experienced, valued, and perceived, as well as of *a* way that the world presents itself.

In his seminal studies on the colors white and blue, James Hillman writes: "All whites are not the same white. . . ."[4] This dictum applies equally to green. Olive, emerald, moss, leaf, myrtle, ivy, avocado, lime, spinach, sage, lettuce, marjoram, sea, mold, and slime present us with both radically different hues and sharply contrasting metaphors. One large manufacturer of embroidery thread alone markets eighty-one different greens. To green's spectral position we need also add saturation or intensity (chroma), as well as brightness or brilliance (value). The ready availability to the eye, on even the shortest stroll through Nature, of a multitude of subtle varieties of green is a crucial aspect of its metaphorical power and richness,[5] echoing the bewildering plenitude and extraordinary subtlety of the vegetal world.

Like other colors, green usually presents itself as an attribute of a particular *thing*—dragon, lion, bird, frog, dress, eyes, hair—which also radically affects its metaphoricity. Many cultures have no separate word for *green*. This does not mean they cannot see green but rather that it has not been abstracted, and generalized as a category, from specific objects: grasses, bushes, underwater algae, leeks.[6] In addition, green generally finds itself in the company of other colors: blue, red, black, yellow, white. Its relationship to these colors profoundly modifies its imaginal sense.

The way we symbolically "read" green depends to a significant extent on the psycho-cultural template that we impose upon it.[7] For example, our interpretation of green varies according to whether we see it from within a kind of psycho-biological system—such as Jung's schema of the four functions where green is identified with sensation and placed oppositionally to intuition imagined as yellow; or from within the myth of the hero's struggle against matter and Nature (green as the maternal unconscious origins); or from within a fantasy of alchemical stages, enroute from the *prima materia* to gold, from the *massa confusa* to the *mysterium coniunctionis*; or from within a fantasy of harmony and balance, much akin to the system of humors, temperaments, and cosmic correspondences developed by Marsilio Ficino, in which, for example, the green of Venus tempers the red heat of Mars.[8]

But even from within these overall fantasies, our approach to green will vary according to which archetype or color governs our perception. We cannot, for example, simply assign green to Venus: Saturn, Mars, Mercury, Dionysus, Apollo, Artemis, Demeter, Persephone, and so on all have their own relationship to Nature and to their own green(s). Through the eyes of Demeter, green is part of the "whole-Earth" fantasy: back to nature, bio-, organic, natural; green is healing, bounteous, trustworthy, a datum of simple truths in a complex, destructive, and deceitful world. On the other hand, the story of Persephone casts a dark shadow over this naive green; the presence of the underworld Goddess Hekate confirms the essential presence of blackness within it. There is danger in the fantasy of "pure" green or greenness. Sometimes a blackening, or a whitening, or a blueing, or a reddening may be appropriate.

Nevertheless, as we shall see, from within this bewildering complexity there arises a kind of green-consensus. Time and again we keep returning to similar themes, hearing the green echoes of an archetypal metaphoricity. Certainly, while all colors have a vegetable aspect, green refers to the *blood* of the vegetable world.[9] Indeed, chlorophyll and sap-flow have much in common with hemoglobin and the circulation of the blood. In classical Greek poetry, we find references to "green blood," as well as to "green" honey, dew, and tears. The basic meaning of the word *chloron* seems to have been moisture, liquidity, fluidity, with their connotations of life and youth. Even in connection with trees, the word *green* seems to refer more to *sap* rather than to the presence of leaves or greenery.[10]

GATHERING THE GREEN

Rural Green

Following Hillman's lead with white and blue, we must know where we can find this green or greenness. The anima has long been associated with green, and green is often referred to as the color of soul, even of the World Soul—"green is the color of the heart and of the vitality of the heart."[11] So we can look to our moods, to our aesthetic perceptions, and soulful experiences to find our greens. As with the poet Andrew Marvell, this experience may be one of solitary repose in a bower or glade of healing innocence, a sacred benevolence, lush coolness, and amorous abundance: "Annihilating all that's made/ To a green thought in a green shade."[12]

There are also times when such a green-proliferation seems entangling, overwhelming, suffocating. Jung recounts a case where a woman patient suddenly begins noticing "that green things are growing all about" an important male figure in her dreams. Jung suggests that this indicates a fear that the woman's animus, her interior masculine, "will be swallowed up, dissolved by nature, and she feels the necessity of freeing him, protecting him from complete dissolution in nature."[13] On the other hand, we may have an imaginal "green thumb," a ready knack at promoting "growth" and fertility, either within our own lives or round about us.

Sometimes we may find ourselves on "the village green," viewing the world from a "country" innocence: either a basic earthiness or an idealized notion of the "rural"—harmony, community, tradition, a place outside the mess and alienation of modern urban life. Alternatively, as health-conscious adults, we may insist upon trying to redeem our childhood dislikes by compulsively "eating our greens," doing what's said to be "good" for us despite disliking the taste.

Fresh Green

There are situations which expose us to our lack of experience, situations when we are "green." Less fresh than a "fresher": clumsy, unripe, awkward. There is a kind of virginal greenness—raw, easily hurt, like a sensitive green blush before the full impact of spring. The tender fragility of fresh green shoots—lettuce, barley, fennel, wheat—was associated by the Greeks with the lack of vital force, impotence, and death of Adonis.[14]

The green lion was often a synonym for the unicorn, with its close association with virgins in general, as well as with the Virgin Mary.[15] Jung refers to the laurel, which—as an evergreen and believed to be unharmed by either lightning or cold (*intacta triumphat*)—symbolized the Virgin Mary.[16] From the wound in the side of the green lion or unicorn, which is often shown in alchemy as being held in a virgin's lap, flows the blood that brings new life.[17] When our wounded sulfurous enthusiasms or hurt pride are calmly held by, and united with, a receptive innocence, then the everyday world becomes animated and nourished with spirit, revegetated.[18] In Homer the word *chloron* (a kind of green/yellow) meant fresh, as of vegetation, but also as applied to honey: a smooth, sweet freshness.[19]

On the other hand, green has also been associated with bitterness. Jakob Boehme envisioned angels in terms of the colors of their spirituality. One was "like a green precious stone" that had a strong bitterness within it.[20] The vitriolic, biting intensity of alchemy's "Green Lion," the *aqua fortis*, even dissolves gold: our triumphs and insights lose their fixity and certainty in the green light of a corrosive, raw acidity.[21] Our green, unripe moments can therefore have a certain astringent sharpness about them, leaving an invigorating—albeit bitter—taste. Or when encountering such a greenness in others, we can experience a tangy, intoxicating freshness that clears the soul of its weighty greys and dark blues.

Green Passion

Under the signs of Venus or Dionysus, we meet a green passion: an eruption of spring, a sulfurous green, a "green lizard." Jung refers to a "green bird and bronze and sulphur. . . . In the sphere of Christian psychology, green has a spermatic, procreative quality, and for this reason it is the color attributed to the Holy Ghost as the creative principle."[22] According to the fifth-century Syrian mystic Dionysus the Areopagite, green is the color of youth and vigor.[23]

In modern color therapy, green has been used to treat both fatigue and insomnia. It "lowers the blood pressure but dilates the capillaries . . . the weary are, so to speak, advised to lay themselves down in green pastures (*se mettre au vert*)."[24] On the other hand, Vincent Van Gogh advised using green (as well as the expected red) "in painting terrible human passions."[25] This vegetable passion, like a Dionysian frenzy of the sap, can have a fearful madness about it: "The force that through the green fuse drives the flower/ Drives my green age. . ." writes Dylan Thomas.[26] Contrasting with this green spermaticism is the slow but inexorable oceanic greenness of vegetable expansion and proliferation, as expressed by Marvell in terms of his boundless "vegetable love."[27]

Green Hope

Green is the color of life and hope, of rebirth and resurrection, a new awakening after the long nights of our winter moods and black experiences. Jung refers to the "blessed greenness, which givest birth to all things. . . ."[28] He writes: "For the thing that has never been seen or accepted, that has never lived, is as green and fresh as spring."[29] In the Philippine Hanunoo island culture greenness is associated with a fresh succulence. It represents one side of a more general opposition between wetness and dessication which is fundamental to the way the Hanunoo view the world.[30] This opposition was also fundamental in classical Greece, where life, youth, and moisture were contrasted with death, old age, and dryness. Jung similarly referred to a dry, sapless existence, one that lacked the vital moisture of a vegetative anima.[31]

Greenness was seen to be the result of the Holy Spirit infusing things with light, bringing warmth, breathing into them "a kind of germination, which is the viridescence. . . . The earth sweats out greenness."[32] This is the color of Wilhelm Reich's vegetative healing, the invigorating release of stale, repressed, unlived vegetable energy; a reunion with the "natural" God; an orgonic re-vegetation.[33]

Following the symbolism of Kundalini Yoga, Jung identifies green with "Shiva in the dormant condition."[34] He writes: "In Kundalini yoga the 'green womb' is a name for Ishvara (Shiva) emerging from his latent condition."[35]

Deathly Green

However, green is also the color of decay, mold, slime. These are our moments of rotting stuckness, or of over-ripeness, which have no option but to pass into total putrescence or else to remain like an ever present mildew around the edges of our lives. There are also times when we are sick, nauseous, "green around the gills." Yet, as it has been said in alchemy, this "leprous" greenness contains a kind of "perfection . . . because that greenness is straightway changed by our magistery into our most true gold."[36] Our nausea, by its very intensity, can disturb and overwhelm mundane reality, thereby providing, as in Jean-Paul Sartre's classic novel, a direct and immediate access to the deeper, darker regions of soul.[37] Contemporary "green" awareness has similarly come through the back doors of our consciousness, through extreme distress and despair, pulling us on a terrifying descent into the psyche.

Green has long been associated with death.[38] In Anglo-Celtic tradition, green is the color of the small people from the other realm, the underworld. Virtually all the elfin folk dress in green. In the famous otherworldly tale of "Gawain and the Green Knight," the latter's face, hair, coat, and mantle—even his horse—

are green.[39] In "Thomas Rymer" the protagonist wears a green costume while living in the fairy realm. Even his shoes are of "velvet green."[40] We read of green ghosts and green dwarfs, green dogs and a "grass-green horn." Fairies are dressed in "robes of green," some with skirts of "the grass-green silk" and mantles "of velvet green."[41]

In British folksong, green was often considered to be unlucky, an "ill omen." It was frequently connected to death or with the dead and was a trait of supernatural beings. In one tale, dreaming of "pulling green heather, green apples, or green 'birk' is premonitory of death."[42] There are gruesome stories of green ladies dancing "in a basin of blood; or Jenny Greenteeth, an evil water spirit; there is . . . *Jenny Jo*, a singing game in which green is the colour of grief."[43] "Death is greener than the grass" goes one riddle; "and poyson is greener than the grass" goes the reply.

One folktale tells of ghost-sons leading their mother along a green road—"the greenest that ever was seen." We read of ghosts vanishing into green forests, of graves of "gravel and green." In certain prehistoric funeral practices green stones were placed in the mouth of the corpse to symbolize life.[44]

Green eyes have long been associated with mystery and an otherworldly fascination. Jung relates green eyes to Dionysus and Pan.[45] How often are we curious about "what's behind the Green Door? What's that secret you're keeping?"

Green Envy

The association of green with Venus/Aphrodite should also alert us to the other side of love and desire—when one is green with envy. Aphrodite's attitude to Psyche, or to Helen, shows the archetypal nature of jealousy's greenness. Just as green is related to Venus, so it is also to Mercurius with whom one can experience a wet, slippery, evergreen trickiness.[46] A green intolerance can be found in the determined purity and spiritual aloofness of Apollo and his sister, Artemis.

One could read the whole of the Trojan War through a green eye: beginning with the green envy of Aphrodite; the jealousy of Menelaus; the sacrifice of Iphigenia to Artemis; the raw enthusiasms of the young warriors; the bleeding sap of the freshly cut-down youths; the vast, vegetable love and patience of Penelope; the virile, evergreen determination of Odysseus and his constant help from Athene with the sea-green or olive-green eyes (*glaukopis*).[47]

WHITENING THE GREEN

There are many intensities of green: the lion represents a *hot* green ("wild, rampant, . . . penetrating"); the Holy Ghost a *warm* green ("fostering warmth"); laurel a *cool* green.[48] But even more important are the relationships between green and other "colors."

Although the main stages in the alchemical opus were characterized by the colors black (nigredo), white (albedo), red (rubedo), and then gold (citrinitas), green was often seen as marking an intermediary stage between the nigredo and the albedo.[49] As we have seen, green is one of the colors of the alchemical sulfur: "Everything that suddenly lights up, draws our joy, flares with beauty—each bush a God burning: this is the alchemical sulphur, the flammable face of the world . . . its aureole of desire. . . ."[50]

But just as sulfur "conflates, it also coagulates. . . . Desire and object become indistinguishable."[51] In order to modify this compulsive, erotic literalism, to free the objective, aesthetic sensibility of the heart (*himma*) from identifying with the objects of its desire, the heart needs to be whitened, the green lion chastened. Hillman continues: "One well-known method cuts off the green lion's paws, depriving it of its reach into the world. Yet it stays alive as a *succus vitae* in the heart."[52] This literalizing, "smokey" green can also be illuminated through the whitening of reflection.[53] Especially important are the moments of weakness, failure, cowardice or when the heart finds itself yearning "for loveliness, wanting grace. . . ." Hillman suggests "these can be indicators of the lion's taming with virgin's milk."[54]

BLACKENING THE GREEN

Green must sometimes be blackened. For example, when fresh, naive enthusiasms are blackened with melancholy, with doubt, or by failure, they once more find their roots in the earth. Without such roots they either live parasitically suspended around any convenient host—enthusiasm for its own sake, poised like mistletoe between heaven and earth but touching neither—or else for want of nourishment and roots they soon wither and die. Hillman writes of the ancient belief that silver comes from "a forest fire, a holocaust. A gigantic fire rages through a forest, charring the greenwood, decimating nature, and after that ruin a thin stream of silver emerges."[55] In this way silvery reflection can come from burnout, but "only after the woody bowers of protective naturalism have been totally blackened."

Although death is a painful truth, it must be admitted into the green garden of innocence. Wallace Stevens laments: "At the sight of blackbirds/ Flying in a green light,/ Even the bawds of euphony/ Would cry out sharply."[56] "Black mortality," writes Kessler, "is inextricably a part of life's evergreens; it sits 'in' them not 'on' them."[57] As if to underscore this truth, Stevens writes: "I saw how the night came . . ./ Came striding like the color of the heavy hemlocks. . . ."[58]

Conversely, blackness must sometimes be greened. Jung writes of a woman's vision of herself "clothed in black, shot through with veins of green."[59] Deep in earth, she is "at the beginning of spring, . . . in the muladhara, which is the darkness where things begin." Ficino, ever alert about the dangers of too much thick black bile—its propensity for drying out, for cooling and coagulating the soul, for engendering a state of excess melancholy—advises that it be thinned by some greening: Saturn tempered by Venus and by venereal things. He considered this to be especially important advice for old people. "Venus . . . sends nature, with its green things, to bloom everywhere, not just to make us alive, but younger, giving us our healthy humor back, and making us overflow with a lively spirit."[60]

He ponders the reasons for the healing property of green: "why it delights us so wholesomely, . . . though it is fickle and easily dissolves away?"[61] Green, although "afraid of darkness," is by nature a temperate, diffusing, mediating color that stops a cramped, coagulating literalism, one that brings one's view into a too "narrow focus."[62] Green gathers and spreads "the animal spirit, even brightening it. . . ."[63] By the use of certain "cordials" made of select spices, a person can become refreshed "as if a greenness has come over his eyes." It keeps a person "in a natural state of greenness, as if he were a laurel tree, an olive or a pine, still green in winter."[64]

"But under my blackness I have hidden the fairest green," exclaims the rejected Shulamite of Cabalistic legend.[65] This state of blackness, infused with an as-yet-unseen greenness, is like the moment just prior to achieving a long-awaited goal. This time can frequently be one, not just of anxious impatience, but of a "hidden happiness," a delicious sense of expectancy, made all the more intense because of its hidden, secret intimacy and the close anticipation of fulfillment.

THE PURPLING OF GREEN

Related to this blackening of the green is a purpling. In alchemy, during a process of gentle heating, liquefaction, and sublimation, known as the regimen of Venus, the green color associated with that Goddess would gradually change into a "livid purple" from which "the philosophical tree will blossom."[66] Jung writes that this livid purple "has something deathly about it." It parallels the mystery of Christ's passion, his death and resurrection.[67] This purpling of the green is experienced as a death by the naturalistic attitude which prefers to remain in the realm of tangible, sensual nature. Yet its concrete green literalisms, its simple direct truths must be dissolved and sublimated to some extent before psychological and spiritual reflection can begin.

THE BLUEING OF GREEN

In the work of the poet Wallace Stevens, easily the most dominant colors are green and blue.[68] Stevens associates blue with imagination, reason, reflection, while green is the color of the vital force of Nature, "the reality outside the mind." Green has the power either to revitalize human culture, ideas, and reflections or to overwhelm, destroy, and negate them. Stevens was deeply concerned with a reconciliation between these forces, without which creative and meaningful life isn't possible. So, by slightly blueing or whitening the green, tinging physical contact with a touch of reflection or idealism, one can awaken the imagination of the sensual world.

Stevens felt that the "green" world holds the secret of life, that it is the *actual*, the *real*, and that without it the blueness of reflection drifts into mere abstraction and empty speculation. But without blue we are lost in a monotonous, meaningless—albeit innocent, even blissful—instinctuality, discrimination gone.

Stevens constantly searched for the greenness of *things* and of language itself, not just of literal vegetation. Yet even the most successful blueing of primal greenness will bring with it a sense of loss, the direct truths of paradise gone forever in the sophisticated blue light of reflection. In his poem "The Man with the Blue Guitar" he writes: "the day was green/ . . . things as they are/ Are changed upon the blue guitar." Yet despite the blues of this sad but necessary transformation, green inevitably persists through both inner and outer worlds as a mediating continuum, what he calls the "fluent mundo."

Since we always exist within *both* green *and* blue, the task is to reconcile them within consciousness. Although Stevens attempts this by imagining green–blue and blue–green, the result is unsatisfactory: "the colors (as they embrace concepts) can never be blended."

REDDENING THE GREEN

Red and green are closely related alchemically through their common association with sulfur and with Venus. The "red" lion and the "orgiastic" Venus are images of a "red balsam," of the "burning water" or red sulfur that burns away impurities.[69] Robert Grinnell correlates the affect of the red balsam with a "soothing activity in the neuro-vegetative nervous system."[70] This is a cool, red vegetable heat that arises through brooding, cooking, self-heating, and finally an assimilation of unconscious emotionality. Grinnell terms it the "red feeling in its moist earthy aspect. . . ."[71] When greenness is reddened in this way, a passive attitude of "it's only natural"—or of things being in a state of "somnambulist vegetative grace"—is energized; moods are acknowledged and confronted directly.[72] This reddening brings us back into contact with "disruptive human problems"; it moves us away from the escapism that can be associated with the "green shade" of Marvell's garden.[73] Stevens writes of a "Fat cat, red tongue, green mind . . ." in an attempt to reconcile aggressive instinctuality with calm, almost lazy serenity.[74]

YELLOWING THE GREEN

As we have seen with the Greek word *chloron*, green and yellow have an affinity. But we have also seen how, in Jung's functional approach, they are imagined oppositionally. This yellow/green has been associated with bile, with fear, with a sickly pallor—surely an appropriate response to the doom that seems to threaten this planet.[75] But the yellow/green conjunction also has links with Hermes-Mercurius and suggests an imaginative mobility, sorely lacking in contemporary environmental debates, but crucial if paradox and opposition are to be sustained, endured, and insighted.[76] Yellow is also affiliated with stains: a yellowing of the green suggests a tempering of pure green idealism with the mess and unsatisfactoriness of daily life. In many ways yellow is the color most suited to highlighting green's green shadow: its all-embracing naturalism that lends quiet but absolute authority to any position adopted in its name.

GREEN CONSCIOUSNESS

For some alchemists green, not black, was the color of the prima materia and hence marked the beginning of the work. But elsewhere we find references to the green lion as equivalent to the goal, to the gold itself. Alternatively, green has been viewed as marking the stage immediately before the final achievement of gold.[77] However, rather than identifying the color green with any single one mineral, or planet, or stage, we can see it as "the desirability of the world which appears as sulphur, as lion, as Venus, etc."[78] This green desirability is constantly present throughout the opus although manifesting differently according to circumstances. Not being a primary color allows green to act as a bridge or intermediary between the "warm, 'advancing' colours (red, orange, yellow, white) and the cold, 'retreating' colours" (blue, indigo, violet, and black).[79] Green also mediates between the "black" of the mineral kingdom and the "red" of the animal world. These are not so much developmental stages as layers in an imaginal deepening, always present at any moment.

"Green" can also be taken as a cosmos within itself, a lens through which other "colors" of the world are perceived. In much the same way that an individual's psychological life may well be overdetermined by a particular archetype, so the life of other colors could be bounded by a particular imaginal "color." This specific "coloring" of their life does not preclude imaginal complexity or soul-work. In other words, we should not immediately judge it in terms of being stuck. It is possible, shall we say, to be a servant to "green," to imagine a "green" alchemy, or psychology, replete with its unique paradoxes, questions, resolutions, pathologies, and so on.

The life and work of the English painter John Constable can be read as a study in such a green alchemy. His sensual devotion to the color itself, its myriad nuances, hues, tones, and textures, its embodiment within an intense particularity of forms—these were echoed throughout his life and opus by his spiritual, psychological, and social concerns. In Constable's paintings can be seen his struggle with a nostalgia for the green of his childhood: "Willows, old rotten banks, slimy posts. . . ." His biographer and friend, Leslie, tried to portray Constable only in the green light of his enthusiasms, idealisms, and love of nature and to omit reference to the green envies, moodiness, and depressions.[80]

The low impact of green, both as a color and a metaphor, also hindered the acceptance of Constable's work in his own time. An influential contemporary described one of Constable's paintings as "that nasty green thing." It was felt that such "natural" greens, just on their own, lacked spirit, were too melancholy. Subsequently, Constable's paintings became a symbol for a quintessential Englishness, the green and pleasant fields, with all the associated, mainly conservative, nostalgia. Radicals, no less nostalgic in their own way, pour the green scorn of youthful idealism on such patriotic greenness: "Green . . . is suddenly a world in itself; people walk around and stand on it . . . 'green' becomes the very ground of an England of the mind. . . . It is the 'green' of imagined turf rather than any literal grass. . . ."[81]

Certainly, not all greens are the philosopher's green, the sacred viridescence, the blessed greenness. Constable's intense struggle to connect soul with mundane things of the natural world, to "discover" the blessed greenness, is frequently reduced to a quest for a realistic naturalism, or to an ideological coverup of prevailing social conditions, or to an attempted reconciliation of his Oedipal complex, or to an exemplary portrayal of "Englishness." Even his close friends, such as Dr. Fisher, thought Constable a bit stuck with his themes. They failed to see in Constable's constant preparatory sketches, repeated drawings of identical scenes, and seemingly endless obsession with a tiny area of countryside the *reiteratio*, the alchemical repetition, distillation, the reworking and deepening.

CONCLUSIONS

As we approach the fin de siècle, indeed the fin de millennium, Western culture appears to be in an acute and decadent decline. Its values, philosophies, and morals seem either green with mold and decay or dried-up with misspent old age. In either case, the appeal of a fresh greening is all too clear. But as the Greek word *chloron* suggested, green is not just sap and dew. It also refers to tears and bile. A greening of psychology is not just a rejuvenation of a tired, slightly putrescent orthodoxy. Nor does it mean a literal environmentalism. This greening will come from an imaginal descent into "greenness," into the interior alchemy of "green."

Hillman writes of restoring to the world "its multicolored soul."[82] Certainly, the *greening of psychology* is not just a matter of Demeter's horizontal fields, or of Artemisian wildernesses, or of Venusian bowers. As we have seen, "Green" is a whole world, filled with subtlety, contrast, and paradox.

CHAPTER ONE
The Vegetable Soul

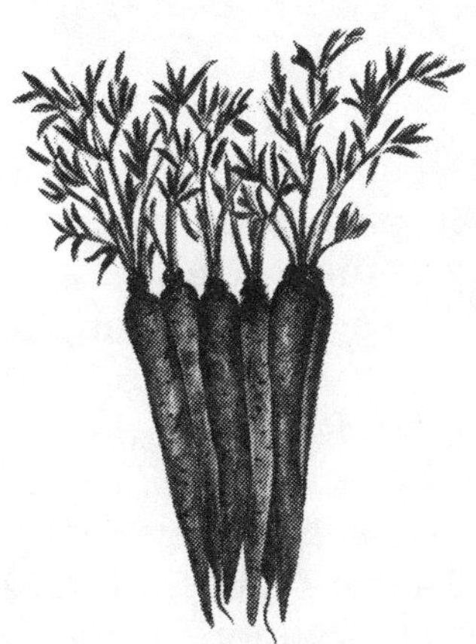

In the opening pages of his bizarre modern classic *Perfume*, Patrick Suskind recounts how the book's protagonist was abandoned as a baby and how this infant, scarcely conscious, made the decision to survive: "he did not decide this as an adult. . . . But he did decide vegetatively, as a bean when tossed aside must decide whether it ought to germinate or had better let things be."[1] The notion of a vegetative psyche is a much ignored root metaphor in Western culture; yet it is central to any ecological revisioning, to any *greening* of psychology. This metaphor can be traced back to ideas about the "vegetable soul" so popular in the Middle Ages and the Renaissance (although owing their genesis to Plato and Aristotle). It can also be found in the ideas of Freud and Jung in the twentieth century. The "vegetotherapy" of Wilhelm Reich and therapeutic concerns about "diet," or "body," or "place" can all be seen as attempts to reach and influence this "vegetable soul." This metaphor indicates a region of psychic functioning that is extraordinarily difficult for the conscious, rational mind to imagine, let alone to connect with.

The idea of a vegetable soul draws us into the twilight zone that imaginatively separates soul and body, psyche and soma, mind and matter. Nowhere is this more apparent than in the history of the "discovery" of the nervous system, concerned as it was with locating the seat of the soul (or of mind or consciousness) *within* the body. The autonomic, or vegetative, nervous system has been called the most ancient, the most basic aspect of this mysterious apparatus.

In this long historical project, scientificity and metaphoricity have rarely been far apart. Ideas about soul, mind, and imagination have consistently intertwined with those of brain and bodily functions. Such common phrases as "loss of nerve" or "nervous breakdown" reveal the metaphorical power of this nervous fantasy and echo depth psychology's origins within the study of nervous disorders.

At the same time, following the historical trace of this vegetative metaphor takes us far from the body–mind of the isolated individual, evoking the mystery of humanity's place within the macrocosm of planetary life: from ideas of a "Great Chain of Being," to those of an evolutionary continuum, to the modern formulations of holism and ecology. Such reflections continually return to the borderland between mind and matter: from the ancient idea of the World Soul, or *Anima Mundi*, to a neo-Romantic life-force, from Reich's "Orgone Energy" to contemporary notions of "Deep Ecology."

Depth psychology is the most recent representative of a Western tradition that stretches back to the ancient Greeks, a tradition which insists that psyche, or soul, is not confined within the human body, that psychic interiority does not literally refer to a location *inside* the human body or brain. Innerness is a mode of perception that sees the interiority of things. Anything can be a vessel for psyche, even a vegetable:

> Inside of one potato
> There are rivers and mountains.[2]

Alchemists considered the greater part of soul to lie *outside* the human body. To the friends who hesitated to enter his kitchen, Heraclitus cried: "Come in, come in! The Gods are here too!"[3]

I am not suggesting that we go back to the Greeks or to the Italian Renaissance in order to find a lost key, an ancient truth, but rather to reestablish a metaphoricity that promised, however imperfectly, to sustain an intimate imaginal relationship between humanity and the wider world. This metaphor constantly locates itself at and questions a series of well-entrenched imaginal interfaces: body/psyche, interior/exterior, private/public, individual/social, nature/culture, science/poetry. Through this metaphor the whole question of identity can be seen in a green light and reimagined.[4]

A PLURALITY OF SOULS

Perhaps the most comprehensive formulation of the vegetable soul is in Robert Burton's Renaissance classic *The Anatomy of Melancholy.*[5] This enormously popular work, first published in 1621, imagines the soul in three parts: the vegetal, the sensitive, and the rational. Here is a hierarchy of souls, where the higher cannot exist without the lower. Therefore, humans possess all three parts, while animals have two (the sensitive and vegetal) and plants only one (the vegetal). Symbolically and imaginatively, the vegetable kingdom stands as a link between the mineral and animal worlds.

The genealogy of a tripartite classification of souls starts with Plato and Aristotle. Imagining soul, or life-force, to be present differently in plants, animals, and humans, Aristotle associated the animation of plants with the processes of nutrition and reproduction.[6] For Plato, the soul's three parts were appetite, spirit, and reason. He believed each part had its own "motion" or logic.[7]

These classifications were taken up by the great Medieval Arab philosopher Averroes, who systematically developed ideas about the *anima composita*, or composite soul.[8] Averroes' work was extremely influential, and the concept of the vegetable soul entered the mainstream both of Medieval philosophizing and of science.[9]

The relationships between the various classes of life-form—the human, animal, and vegetable, and even the mineral—were frequently imagined as a continuum rather than as absolutely separate categories. Thomas Aquinas, for example, saw a gradation among minerals from the lowest forms up to gold, the highest. Similarly, he imagined gradations in the vegetable kingdom: the highest for him were types of perfect trees. The animal kingdom graduated up to the human species.[10] Much earlier Aristotle had written that Nature

> passes so gradually from the inanimate to the animate that their [life-forms'] continuity renders the boundary between them indistinguishable. . . . For plants come immediately after inanimate things; and plants differ from one another in the degree in which they appear to participate in life. . . . And the transition from plants to animals is continuous; for one might question whether some marine forms are animals or plants, since many of them are attached to the rock and perish if they are separated from it.[11]

In much the same way, the sheer plenitude of life-forms seemed to demand a plurality of souls. For example, Averroes exclaimed: "Why did God create more than one sort of vegetative and animal souls?"[12]

It was such ideas as these that fed directly into the Renaissance, with its emphasis on the *Anima Mundi*, on the animation of all things, and on a mutual, sympathetic relationship between them.[13] In particular, the extensive work by the Italian philosopher Marsilio Ficino in Florence was both formative and decisive. In his *Theologica Platonica de Immortalitate Animorum* (1482), Ficino developed and systematized extant ideas about the nature of the soul and its tripartite division into vegetative, sensible, and rational souls.[14]

Ficino's influence is evident in the works of subsequent Hermetic philosophers, including Pico della Mirandola, Henry Cornelius Agrippa, Paracelsus, Giordano Bruno, and the Englishman John Dee. Pico, for example, wrote: "It is a commonplace of the schools that man [*sic*] is a little world, in which we may discern a body mingled of earthy elements, and ethereal breath, and the vegetable life of plants. . . ."[15] Of course, during this long span of time there were innumerable shifts of interest, debates, disagreements, and controversies. Nevertheless, the *Anima Mundi* and the *anima composita* formed a fairly consistent and coherent body of ideas whose influence, as we shall see, can be found in poetry, drama, theology, medicine, gardening, magic, and science. For example, in 1574 Southwell wrote: "As Thou are one in essence, so is my soul, containing all the powers, with a vegetary, sensible and reasonable life." One hundred years later, Joannes Amos Comenius, in his classic school text *Orbis Sensualium Pictus*, continued to suggest that the human soul consisted of vegetative, sensitive, and rational aspects.[16]

Burton imagined the vegetable soul to be a fundamental part of human existence. It is "the substantial act of an organic body by which it is nourished, augmented and begets another like unto itself."[17] This statement can be read variously: bodily, as part of an archetypal medicine and anatomy, or as an alchemical psychology, a vegetative way of working with images. This nutritional, digestive process can also be seen as a cosmic reverie, drawing sustenance from an earthy rootedness while being open to the stars. "The lower man is nought but a fair plant," wrote Henry Moore.[18] He understood that the vegetative aspect of the individual soul derived its energy from the far more expansive World Soul, the *Anima Mundi:*

> that vitality,
> That doth extend this great Universall,
> And move th'inert materiality
> Of great and little worlds.[19]

This lower, or vegetative, aspect of the individual soul was imagined to be in *direct* and *intimate* connection with the World Soul.

Moore and Burton differed over whether in fact there were three souls (Burton) or, rather, just three aspects of the one soul (Moore). For Moore, these aspects were like three "essences" or "vehicles." The close relationship between the vegetative soul and the common or material world made it vulnerable to injury and sickness. But the vegetable aspect could be healed by means of its relation to the higher part of the soul, which in its turn was envisaged as being directly connected with "The ever-live-Idees, the lamping of fire/ Of lasting Intellect."[20] The soul's vegetative essence could be healed by an archetypal reflection from above, as it were. However, Burton, from within his deep acceptance and even celebration of melancholy, was less spiritually inclined than Moore and saw the reflection and healing as possibly occurring from within the vegetable soul itself.[21]

In Burton's schema, nutrition is more important than the other two functions of the vegetable soul: augmentation and generation. After identifying this nutrient function with the liver in animals and humans and with the roots and sap in plants, he subdivided it into four parts:

1. Attraction: Nourishment is drawn up from the depths by the root system. Imaginally this can be viewed as the connection with our earliest beginnings: personal childhood, ancestral, evolutionary, primal. Attraction relates to our sense of being *placed*, of being grounded.
2. Retention: The nourishment drawn from the imaginal ground, whether physical or psychic, individual or collective, has to be held until it can be concocted, used, absorbed. There has to be an adequately sealed container for soul-work.
3. Digestion: In many ways this seems to be crucial. As Ficino had warned: "Nothing is more harmful than indigestion"; "digestion is the root of life"; "take care of digestion before anything else."[22] He particularly warned scholars and contemplatives about neglecting their bodies and the body of the world, about their preoccupation with incorporeal things, about their neglect of the material imagination.[23]
4. Expulsion: The superfluous waste must be expelled by purging, vomiting, spitting, sweating, urinating, and so on, lest it poison the system.

There is clearly a pathological dimension to these functions: times of rootlessness when the imaginal life seems unable to draw sustenance from the "ground," moments of barren placelessness. Or times when even a rich imaginal stream flows too quickly through an inadequate vessel—times when images cannot be held, cooked, absorbed. Then there are moments of imaginal indigestion, times when the gross materiality of imaginative life has been neglected.

One can readily see the parallel between the functions attributed to the vegetable soul and those attributed to the vegetative, or autonomic, nervous system: the functioning of the entire alimentary tract, from lips through intestines and colon to the anus; heart rate; blood sugar levels; sleep; temperature homeostasis; emotions; and so on. The importance of the vegetable soul in reimagining such modern disorders as "stress" need hardly be emphasized. The metaphor of "stress," for example, is a product of metallurgy in an industrial culture that is almost completely dissociated from the vegetative world.[24] But the idea of the nervous system is too metaphorically impoverished, despite being extended into government, communications (e.g., "nerve center"), or character analysis (e.g., "nerveless").

Burton then quickly discussed the remaining two functions of the vegetable soul: augmentation (an appropriate increase in proportion, shape, and quantity) and generation (which includes life and death, birth and old age). But it is the nutrient function, particularly the digestive aspect, which lies at the heart of the vegetable soul. Indeed, digestion is so important that Burton subdivided it even further:

i) Maturation: ripening, the opposite of which is crudity. By this last term Burton meant a lack of natural heat for want of exercise. This is the fate of those who are either idle or gluttonous. It can also refer to being choked as when too much wood puts out a fire.

ii) Elixation: a seething, cooking, or boiling.

iii) Assation: a breaking down and assimilation, either by chewing it over, or by letting it sit in the stomach, or by transforming it in the liver into blood, or by allowing it to be absorbed throughout the body.

The word *digestion* comes from the Latin *gerund* meaning "to bear" or "to carry." The *geste* (ME) of di-gestion refers to a deed, an exploit, a tale; other derivatives include gestate as in a womb; gesticulate and gesture as a signaling or display; jest as a joke or prank; register as an account or list; suggest as in a hint or association. To digest clearly implies a taking apart, a separating, and arranging. It appears to be an orderly process that takes time, that involves display, story, and also, sometimes, humor.[25]

Digestion is essentially a process of dissolution, an alchemical *dissolutio*, with all the connotations of decay and death. *The Tibetan Book of the Dead* describes death as an orderly process: the various elemental components, plus the gross and subtle levels of consciousness, dissolve and are absorbed back into the primeval emptiness and chaotic plenitude of Śunyata.[26] Death is here imagined as a kind of ultimate digestion by the World Soul. The vegetative aspect is part of the *matter* of soul—part of the body's imagination.

Perhaps unlike the two other souls in Burton's schema, the vegetable soul offers no hope to fantasies of individual salvation or immortality, except to become part of the ancestral earth. The Islamic mystic Shaikh Ahmad Ahsa'I wrote: "The vegetable soul in man—when separated [in death] returns to its origin, there to blend and be lost, not to survive there autonomously."[27] Through the vegetative way into the imaginal world, we are brought to face the *materiality* of death. Perhaps here lies a reason for humanity's ancient, melancholy fear of vegetating, a fear of being drawn into the earthy, material depths. But we are only nourished, physically and psychically, by the death of things.

Not only is Burton's work invaluable due to the comprehensive way that it treats the vegetable soul, it also directs our attention to the importance of the Renaissance for Archetypal Psychology. James Hillman has articulately called for us to return to the Renaissance as psychologists searching for a "vision of psyche which might also provide a background for a re-vision of psychology."[28] By virtue of its position midway between the ancient and the modern, its intense pathologizing, its deep concern with reimagining the wisdom of the ancients—particularly with regard to myth, soul, and imagination—and because of its seminal position in the formation of all humanistic disciplines, the Renaissance offers us an Archimedean point by which to shrug off the encrusted literalisms stifling modern psychology's sense of soul and imagination.

The metaphorical ground of Burton's psychological schema is melancholy, not sexuality, or libido, or psychic energy, or even meaning. His was not the psychology *of* melancholy any more than Freud's was the psychology *of* sexuality. Melancholy provided his psychology with its logos, its basic dynamic and coherence. As we shall see, melancholy is fundamental to the vegetable soul. Human vegetativeness is therefore integral not just to Burton's schema but to Renaissance psychology in general with its deep appreciation of melancholy. After Burton this view was quickly lost as the West celebrated human rationality, technological progress, and the domination over Nature both "out there" and "in here." Humanity's grounding in the two "lower" souls was forgotten until the revolutions marked by Darwin, Freud, and Jung moved the West to begin to reembrace the *sensible soul,* our psycho-biological kinship with the animal kingdom. The fundamental and elemental foundation of human soulfulness in vegetative life still awaits full recognition, although its voice can be heard from within movements as diverse as depth psychology and Deep Ecology.

THE VEGETABLENESS OF THE VEGETABLE SOUL

Though the Earth be not animated with a Sensible soul, yet it is possible that it may be a great, Immortal Vegetable.

M. Hale (1677)

At this point we could trace the images associated with the vegetable soul by following two directions. One way lies the psycho-physiological explorations of human individuals, particularly the "discovery" of the autonomic, or vegetative, nervous system. But this route leads directly into the dynamic psychologies of the twentieth century and is better dealt with in the next chapter. The other way keeps us close to the ground of the metaphor itself, the vegetableness of the vegetable soul. By following this latter path, we can reanimate the metaphor and feel its substance before entering the sometimes austere abstractions of psychology. In the remainder of this chapter, I will focus primarily on the vegetable kingdom in human fantasy. Paralleling the unfolding of philosophical ideas about the vegetative life have been cultural attitudes toward the vegetable kingdom.

I prefer not to begin with fruits, trees, or flowers, which can too easily be made into transcendental symbols, doorways to the spirit or to fantasies of wholeness and wellness, thereby losing touch with the darker, earthy, downward regions of soul. Nor do I wish to begin with so-called "exotics"—the vegetable inhabitants of swamps, rainforests, or jungles; or obscure fungi eking out their livelihood in the dark, damp places of the Earth—which can distract us from our purposes. Nor do I want to focus upon the ocean's vegetation—the algaes and seaweeds. Apart from among isolated communities on the fringes of modern Western culture, these sea-plants are now generally associated with macrobiotics, health, or Japanese cuisine. No, I wish to concentrate, at least initially, on the most mundane plants of our culture, those least capable of being spiritualized or holized: the cabbage, the potato, and the other *vegetables* of the vegetable kingdom.

How can we respond to and enter the vegetable world? Our way of listening should stay as close as possible to the things themselves. We need to hear the vegetable at work in the imagination—a vegetable way into the imagination. Definitions of the word *vegetable* reflect its common usage: unconscious life, inactivity, immobility, a person incapable of normal intellectual activity, someone living an uneventful and monotonous life. This negative usage is not recent. For example, in 1626 someone wrote, "A great number of men are now a dayes vegetals, that is to say, who so live, as if they had no other soule but the vegetative, as plantes, and lead the very life of the mushroom."[29] Such an estimation often carried critical, or even despairing, judgments: "He is in what his doctor calls a vegetative state, and incapable of connecting two ideas together" (1893); "Idiots of vegetative grade" (1899); "In short, we rather vegetated than lived" (1777).[30]

In modern parlance, a "cabbage" is a person who is inactive or lacks interest. To be called a vegetable is an insult. It suggests inertia in much the same way that being called an animal implies uncontrolled savagery. In both cases the respective "kingdom," or soul, is sorely misrepresented. While most nations have national flowers, few have a vegetable as their emblem. Vegetables are frequently pejorative terms: Spud-Murphy for the Irish, Swedebashers for the Cornish. Even the mineral kingdom comes off better than vegetables in human fantasy. Teaching a stone to talk (the title of a recent meditative book on nature) seems better, more "zen," more spiritual than teaching, say, a cabbage to talk. It's nearly always the philosopher's stone, never the philosopher's cabbage, although alchemy did imagine and create the vegetable stone, the *lapis vegetabilis,* the *quinta essentia.*[31]

Part of the human, or dayworld, aversion to the vegetable soul involves its supposed lack of will, or low intelligence, or apparent immobility. Hence the appellation *vegetable* applied to people in a coma or severely incapacitated. But the apparent immobility of vegetables is not a pathology. It is their defining characteristic, their mode of being. As the French poet Francis Ponge says of plants and vegetables: "To their immobility they owe their perfection."[32] A vegetable-like immobility is not simply the *absence* of an animal-like activity. Within it there can be a repose for the soul. "Vegetable permanence," writes Gaston Bachelard, "what an *anima* truth, what a symbol for a soul's repose in a world worthy of dreams. . . !"[33]

Studies show how physical immobility can deepen imaginal reverie. Indeed, most contemplative traditions encourage a great measure of physical quiescense, from the yogic postures of meditation to the supine state on the analyst's couch. Even the whirling dance of the Sufis keeps the adept grounded to one spot. Robert Sardello, while commenting on the weariness often associated with cancer and other illnesses, writes: "The fatigue of the natural body, its apparent loss of animation, calls for a different kind of engagement with the world, one sensing everything in the world as alive, as image, as autonomously animated. Only in our fatigue can the world's animation begin to show."[34] As Patricia Berry insists, "stopping" can be a "mode of animation."[35] Vegetable repose evokes a different imagination of time and place than that of creatures, for whom time invariably means movement *through* and *across* space. Ponge puts it succinctly: "Time among plants is expressed in terms of their space."[36] Time as an unfolding into their shape, time as shaping.

In addition to immobility, the slow downwardness of the vegetable soul awakens fear in rational consciousness. Cabbages, according to Burton, cause troublesome dreams, send black vapors up to the brain, and hence are especially to be avoided. Galen condemned the cabbage of all the vegetables, claiming that it brought heaviness to the soul. Some Renaissance thinkers felt that *all* raw vegetables (except lettuce which was then considered an herb) bred melancholic, vegetable blood: inert, still, without heat. Ficino wrote that black bile, which causes a drying-out and encourages Saturnian depression, is made worse by cabbages, radishes, garlic, onions, leeks, and carrots. He cautioned against eating too many fresh vegetables.[37] Indeed, most vegetables were traditionally associated in Europe with melancholy and depression, provoking the fear of the loss of rationality and will.

In fact, however, the word *vegetable* comes from a root that means the very opposite of immobile, passive, dull, or uneventful. *Vegere* (ML) means to animate, enliven, invigorate, arouse. *Vegete* (E) means to grow, to be refreshing, to vivify, animate. From these roots come words such as vigil, vigilant, and vigor, with all their connotations of being wide-awake, alert, of keeping watch. "The understanding . . . was vegete, quick, and lively," observed one critic in 1662.[38] In 1609 Ben Johnstone described what he saw as desirable characteristics in a woman: "faire, yong, and vegetous."[39] Such respect for the vegetable soul was not confined merely to a robust sensual life, but extended into the religious dimension. "Man is righteous in his Vegetated Spectre," proclaimed Blake when commenting about the beliefs of the ancient Druids.[40] Elsewhere it was insisted that "A vegetous faith is able to say unto a mountain, Be removed into the sea."[41]

The downward pull of vegetables, of the vegetable soul,

has also provided exemplary images of being placed, of being grounded, and of having roots. For example, Jung said, "I am fully committed to the idea that human existence should be rooted in the earth." He bemoaned modern culture's lack of earth-based ancestral connections.[42] As Henry Corbin put it, the past is not behind us, but beneath our feet.[43] What better way to touch the ground than through cabbages, which the poet Robert Bly says "love the earth." The word *root* comes from the Indo-European root *ra*, meaning to derive, to grow out of. To be "radical" is to get back to the roots. *Radish* stems from the same etymological roots.[44]

The metaphor of vegetability therefore contains a profound ambivalence. On the one hand, it signifies dullness, monotony, and so on, while on the other it stands for vigor and growth. Respect for the vitality and energy of the vegetable soul has all but vanished in the shadow of the West's worship of the rational soul, especially its abstracting, achieving, and controlling aspects. This disregard can be seen as part of Western culture's denial of death, its intolerance of depression, its fear of the depths, of going down.

While many people now seek for roots, few can face the depths of the psyche into which such a search invariably leads. Such an aversion is echoed in the related metaphoricity of the vegetative nervous system. Plants are characterized by a *lack* of nerves: they have no nervous system. To be called nerveless suggests a lack of courage or will. But as one professor of physiology put it, "It is a sobering thought that the intellectual activity of the best of us is very much at the mercy of his gastro-intestinal tract. . . . The vegetative functions of the body simply cannot be ignored. They provide a background rhythm to the business of living."[45] Like the vegetable soul, the fantasy of "nerves" is the site of a profound ambivalence: force and will on the one hand, weakness and cowardice on the other.

THE FATE OF VEGETABLES IN THE WORLD

Not to be confused with a literal, spatial location inside the individual, "innerness" is a mode of perception. Our fantasies shape the world as much as the world shapes our fantasies. We do not only need to look at someone's dreams but also at how they treat vegetables. Their sensitivity to the carrot displays their ability to allow their own vegetableness to deepen, to articulate itself. Similarly, we need to reflect on the fate of vegetables in the world.

The Neolithic revolution, commencing about ten thousand years ago, involved "taming" both animals and vegetables. The Celts, for example, domesticated the ancestral wild cabbage, bringing it with them to Europe during the second millennium B.C.[46] But with human intervention came selection, cross-breeding, the elimination of certain types of vegetables, and the global transportation of others. The imaginal significance of these events was immense: vegetables as discoveries, inventions, artifacts. The Neolithic, or agricultural, revolution also introduced a vast store of new metaphors about life, death, soul, and spirit. From patterns in art to structures in mythology, new rhythms emerged with a radically different relationship to the seasons, to the earth, heavens, the animal and vegetable kingdoms.

When travelers came home, they brought with them not only goods and stories but also plants and seeds. Returning crusaders carried the cos lettuce to Northern Europe from the Greek island of Kos; the carrot didn't appear in England until the fifteenth century, and then only as a novelty. (There were then four kinds: purple, yellow, white, and orange.) Early travelers told of fabulous plants, like vegetable bestiaries. For example, there was the mandrake, a human-shaped root that screamed when pulled from the earth; there were "vegetable lambs": Tartarian sheep growing upon stems in the earth and devouring all vegetables that came within their reach; there was a lamb in the eastern part of Tartary that was furnished with thick tubers surrounded on all sides by yellow wool and that was raised so high that its roots resembled legs.[47] Many people have experienced the wonder of exotic vegetables and have imaginatively traveled on the backs of their images to distant, marvelous places. Perhaps, like the people in Stuart England, we too have used carrot-tops to decorate hats, or as brooches, or as ornamental gardens? In those days the carrot was regarded much as an avocado was in 1960s Britain.

But the great post-Columbian exchange of vegetables produced a revolution, not only in eating habits, but also in the vegetable imagination of the world.[48] To the Americas from Europe went wheat, olives, chickpeas, melons, onions, radishes, salad greens, vines. In the other direction came potatoes, various beans—the lima, stick, scarlet runner. Also to Europe came peanuts, tomatoes, avocados and, of course, maize or corn. This last grain was then introduced into China, where it sustained a massive population explosion between the sixteenth and seventeenth centuries. The ancient food staples suddenly began to lose their privileged positions in the habits, folkways, and imaginations of many cultures.

In Europe, the introduction of the potato had far-reaching consequences. Brought from America by Francis Drake, planted in Ireland, the potato took a long time to be accepted: over one hundred years in Britain and not until 1800 in Germany. It was feared by the Puritans because the Bible failed to mention it. Once it was thought a prized delicacy: "These potatoes be the most delicate rootes that may be eaten, and doe far exceede our passeneps or carets," exclaimed Hawkins in 1565.[49] Indeed, among the Incas it was worshiped as a treasure; units of time were measured by how long it took to cook one. (The sweet potato or yam has, of course, wide-ranging spiritual significance from Africa to the Pacific. The yam dance of the Aboriginal women of Central Australia is just one example.)

Potatoes were as vital to culture as the wheel. It has been said that the industrial revolution in Germany would have been impossible without them. They supplied concentrated energy and were rugged and easy to grow in the small, backyard plots into which the former peasants of Europe were being squeezed.

The potato traveled from the Andes mountains to the backdoor of the industrial revolution, from archaic divinity to contemporary mundanity.

Throughout the nineteenth century, Westerners came into contact with the prolific variety of all three kingdoms: animal, vegetable, and mineral. Zoos and botanical gardens were set up, geological societies founded. The importance of botanical gardens early in the century has been compared with the vital role chemical laboratories were to play at the century's end. Gardens encouraged and facilitated plant transfers which had enormous impact in those parts of the world subject to Western hegemony: tea in India, Africa, and Ceylon; rubber in Asia; sugar in the Caribbean and Australia; wheat in Canada and Australia; coffee in Africa and Latin America.[50]

These were tremendous shifts in the *Anima Mundi*, as indeed was the simultaneous massive degradation of other, supposedly non-profitable, aspects of the vegetable kingdom: forests, grasslands, wetlands, etc.[51] There were furious debates about the purpose of the botanical gardens themselves. Should they be economic/scientific laboratories or playgrounds for the promenading bourgeoisie? How should the vegetable kingdom be imagined, how displayed, how placed? What was the *topos* of these fascinating new images? What was humanity's relation to the vegetable kingdom and the vegetative life? Out of this tumultuous and scientifically arrogant milieu were born both Darwinism and the dynamic psychologies.

These transcontinental movements and totemic changes must be seen imaginally and the soulfulness of vegetable history reclaimed from both scientific abstraction and everyday mundanity. The consequences of living among vegetables imagined as inert and soul-less have been profound, as the present ecological crisis bears witness. Ninety-five percent of plant food for the entire human race now comes from only thirty species, with just three (wheat, rice, and maize) being especially vital. It has been estimated that prehistoric cultures, by comparison, used about five hundred species. Today, crops are designed for responsiveness to artificial fertilizers, pesticides, simultaneous ripening, machine harvesting, transportation, factory processing, and maximum yield.

The Florida MH-1 tomato can withstand a fall of six feet at a speed of 13.4 miles per hour (which is two and a half times the impact resistance for United States car bumper standards).[52] Everyone knows the modern tomato is tasteless; that lost voluptuousness still eludes horticultural scientists preoccupied with mass production.[53]

The European Economic Community prohibits marketing any vegetable that isn't registered—a long and expensive business. Vegetables of limited appeal are in great risk of extinction. Vegetable sanctuaries have sprung up to save types and seeds; seed banks precariously attempt to save varieties in deep freeze.[54] Many vegetables have vanished, and it is possible that three-quarters of Europe's vegetable varieties will be extinct in the very near future. The situation is exacerbated by the patenting of seeds, especially by multinational industries. Many new crops are lower in protein than the earlier versions. For example, potatoes now have about two percent of protein, whereas in their traditional South American form they had three times as much.[55]

This may all seem a long way from psychology and its concerns. The threat to our vegetable imaginings can seem remote and diffuse despite our constant involvement with them. But the daily disappearance of numerous vegetable species and the homogenization of form and taste limit the possible plurality and variety of vegetable imaginings, showing a scorn and indifference toward the vegetable soul.

We have seen how the vegetable soul was traditionally connected to the idea of being grounded, of having roots. In contemporary Western societies there has been a loss of seasonal eating. I am not referring here to the occasional exotic delicacy but to the basic, staple diet. The advent of freezing, processing, and international marketing has had undeniable benefits (and I have no wish to sentimentalize the hardships of our ancestors), but it has also broken the direct and fundamental connection between our vegetable-eating and the place where we live, its rhythms and seasons—a direct involvement with *Anima Mundi*.[56] To the modern city-dweller such earthy, grounded reminders of Nature's cycles are few. I am not denigrating the value of an attempted redistribution of global wealth by massive food shipments to the Third World, nor the value of relieving the monotony of diet in harsh and remote habitations. Those cultures have enough reminders of place and season. But when in London one's potatoes, lettuces, tomatoes, onions, apples, etc., come from all parts of Europe and America, vegetables cease to ground the soul in the seasonal place. Instead, they ground one in a homogenized, global cosmopolitanism. The "market" rhythms of corporate capitalism replace the rhythms of the *vegetable market*, further adding to stress and dis-location. Losing its vegetative ground, soulful orientation yields to an organization by the abstracted, depersonalized machinations of politics and big business.

Vegetables are becoming completely separated from their vegetableness. Now falsely mobile, they, too, are becoming rootless and placeless. Even in the nineteenth century, many emigrants from Northern Europe to the United States were suspicious of fresh vegetables. Concerned with disease, they only trusted tinned and processed food.[57] In 1940, fifty percent of the flour in the United States went directly to home kitchens; now scarcely eleven percent finds its way there—and seldom in its basic, unrefined form. Much of the flour bought by householders in Australia, Europe, and the United States is many years old, having been chemically preserved to ensure steady market availability, pricing, and so on. There has been a shift of taste: it is now conditioned by machines and marketability rather than by the vegetables themselves.

One of the worst hit casualties has been peas. Traces of these ancient vegetables have been found in Burma and dated back to 9,750 B.C. They contain more protein and dietary fiber than most other vegetables. But their prized characteristic is their sweet, succulent flavor. The fact that this tastiness deteriorates rapidly after picking has traditionally made fresh peas a delicacy. Freezing has supposedly made this delicacy available all the year round. Peas must now be one of the most commonly eaten "green" vegetables in the Western world, but they are no longer signifiers of season. The great majority are purchased frozen, as rituals of picking and shelling have faded from most households.

HUMANS AND VEGETABLES

The relation between humans and vegetables has been imagined in many ways. These are the schema we use in our psychological amplifications, the alchemy of our vegetable imaginings, our vegetable metaphysics, and the ancestral roots of our vegetable reveries.

Classifying

The clearest expression of the perennial need for humans to feel involved with the vegetable kingdom is through naming. As Hillman writes: "The name bespeaks an image."[58] To name a thing is to relate it to an imaginal ground. The earliest classification of plants was always in terms of their usefulness to humans—whether edible, or of medicinal value, or of allegorical importance, and so on.[59] In the medieval era the world was viewed as a cryptogram, full of hidden meanings awaiting decipherment. The first important modern classification system was proposed by Linnaeus in the middle of the eighteenth century. It used sex as its basic metaphor—sex not as an object to be studied but as a mode of imagining. Elizabeth Sewell claims Linnaeus as an Orphic namer: he wanted to know things, to recognize their marks, to affix to every object its proper name, to determine the "Great Alphabet" of Nature.[60]

Linnaeus's system still used human, social metaphors. The vegetable kingdom was divided into "tribes" and "nations": grasses were "plebians"—"the more they are taxed and trodden upon, the more they multiply"; fungi were "vagabonds"—"barbarous, naked, putrescent, rapacious, voracious."[61] Linnaeus was a mixture of scientist and poet. Here was a desire to feel the natural and psychological worlds as interpenetrating, coexisting, and, perhaps, as being identical. But Orphic namers are not concerned with mere abstraction and nominal classification; they want to hold science and poetry together. After Linnaeus, both Goethe and Erasmus Darwin struggled to achieve such a goal, but their ideas were moved backstage. Science lost its poetry; poetry became alienated from science and from its observational rigor.[62]

By the close of the eighteenth century, formal classification and a new Latin terminology had become firmly established. The vegetable soul lay all but forgotten beneath the arid orderliness of abstraction. Poets complained, but their cries were epitaphs for the old order. As Keith Thomas writes: "In place of a natural world redolent with human analogy and symbolic meaning . . . they constructed a detached natural scene to be viewed and studied by the observer from the outside."[63] Nevertheless, this abstract, senex imagining lured the committed attention and desire of scientists into the vegetable world. The ground plans of our naming, whether abstract or poetic, are always mythic. It is not always necessary to invent new names or to return to old ones, but to insight *both*, imaginally.

Throughout the nineteenth century, attempts were made to reconnect observation and imagination, science with poetry; to create an overtly imaginal aesthetics; to move psychological reflection into the vegetable world. John Ruskin succinctly described the difference between the scientific and poetic approach to plants:

> The one counts the stamens, and affixes a name, and is content; the other observes every character of its attributes as an element of expression, he seizes on its lines of grace or energy, rigidity or repose . . . he associates it in his mind with all the features of the situation it inhabits, and the ministering agencies necessary to its support. In this way the plant becomes a living creature.[64]

Vegetarianism

In Western culture vegetarianism has moved in and out of popularity since ancient times.[65] But its arguments are primarily based upon questions about the relation between humans and animals, rather than with vegetables. Especially important are issues of animal intelligence, feeling, and will—whose absence is used to define the vegetable soul. Indeed, in this debate very little is said about vegetables at all, except in relation to human health and spiritual well-being. Vegetarianism is perhaps a negation of the vegetable soul by default. In the understandable urge to criticize the effects of meat eating (ecological, individual health, concern for animal life, etc.), vegetarianism can propagate a too onesidedly nice, or spiritual, view of both itself and of vegetables. Most of the literature has little to say about the vegetable soul, its dark downwardness, its association with melancholy and depression. Indeed, the digestive, putrefying aspect of the vegetable soul becomes cleaned up, neutralized.[66] The presence of death in the vegetable diet can be obscured by an emphasis on cycles of fertility and the fantasy of growth. Vegetarianism has also been recontextualized within the recent upsurge of interest in "diets" and its significance reshaped by the place of diets in the post-modern world.[67]

Nevertheless, vegetarianism has occasionally contributed to fantasies about the vegetable soul. The Manichaes, for example, believed that they could obtain spiritual power by eating vegetables rather than meat; Pythagoras believed that after death the human soul could transmute into beans and so forbade his followers' eating them. Vegetarianism contains both an upward and a downward transcendental fantasy. In the former, eating vegetables is imagined to bestow spiritual purity and simplicity, fineness of mind and blood, a non-violent and peaceful disposition, as contrasted with meat eating. Ficino asked, how could blood that had gorged itself on too much fat engage with heavenly things? Paralleling this upward move is a back-to-the-earth philosophy: vegetable gardens as part of the recreation of Paradise. A medieval fantasy saw "Adam and Eve sent out of Eden with hoes." Gardening was a monastic ideal. St. Jerome advised a young novice in the fourth century: "Hoe your ground, set out cabbages, convey water to the conduits." Cabbages as monks, monks as cabbages in God's garden: basic, simple, undemanding, unprepossessing, receptive to Him, contemplative. This is the wisdom of the gardener: "the answer lies in the soil." Jung was said to have consulted his gardener about important political issues in Switzerland; recall the wisdom/simplicity of the gardener in the film and book *Being There.*[68]

These vegetable fantasies clearly echo the dual movement of the vegetable soul: an upward opening to the imaginal heavens, the sky, the sun, moon, and stars, plus a downward deepening into the imaginal earth. But both moves can become too literal and easily lose touch with a melancholic materiality.

Vegetable Feelings

There has also been an attempt to animate vegetables by endowing them *directly* with feelings, intelligence, and will. Like vegetarianism, the fantasies found in books such as *The Secret Life of Plants* or *Supernature* have an ancient pedigree. In 1661, one author in England wrote: "Plants, herbs and trees have their passions and affections, their sorrow in pining and withering, their joy in blossom and flowering." At one point in the late eighteenth century it was suggested that plants be treated more humanely. William Wordsworth wrote: "And 'tis my faith that every flower enjoys the air it breathes. . . . I would not strike a flower as many a man would strike his horse."[69] Also considered in this fantasy are relations *between* vegetables. So, beans and peas are imagined to be inimical to the onion family but to enjoy growing next to carrots, beetroots, and cauliflowers. Pumpkins and marrows, cabbages and dill are the best of friends, while potatoes and onions are not at all on good terms. Burton quotes Claudian:

> Trees are influenced by love,
> and every flourishing tree in turn feels the passion;
> palms nod mutual vows,
> poplar sighs to poplar,
> plane to plane
> and alder breathes to alder.[70]

These ideas, however "unpsychological" they may seem, draw us into the soul of the vegetable world. But care must be taken not to simply draw them, tamed and sentimentalized, into *our* world. Animating vegetables by imputing human-like feelings, will, and intelligence runs the risk of refusing the essential vegetating downwardness of the vegetable soul. Such an animation denies that region of the psyche where human intentionality, purpose, and feeling are entirely absent—that region where an entirely different order of life holds sway. Such an anthropomorphizing move also reinforces the prevalent notion that psyche and imagination are concerned solely with feelings and experiences, rather than with aesthetics and display.[71]

Evolution

Rather than attempting an imaginal animation through an anthropomorphic fantasy, we can make a more subtle reconnection between humans and vegetables through botanical and ecological studies. Animals and plants are here imagined to share the same evolutionary roots. "Is this world animal or vegetable?" asks the poet Robert Bly. Charles Darwin wrote in his diary: "Prove animals like plants."[72] Of course, the evolutionary schema places plants at an earlier stage and hence at a lower level than human life; yet in a sense, Darwin drew us into a new dreaming with an unbroken continuity between animal, vegetable, and mineral—a process rather than a fixed "chain of being." Vegetables became part of our imaginal archeology, rather than just part of a fixed psychic structure or imaginal anatomy, as Burton imagined. This phylogenic fantasy of our earliest plant origins has become imbedded into the individual as an imaginal layering, either physically, as in the vegetative nervous system, or psychologically, as in Reich's "vegetotherapy" which seeks to act through the body directly on the deepest layers of the unconscious.[73]

But one does not have to literally embrace such a hierarchical topography of souls in order to imagine vegetableness as a particular quality of psychological life, a particular region of the psyche. Jung, for example, while often succumbing to the hierarchical view, also called Mercurius the "*spiritus vegetativus*," a unique archetypal aspect that was basic without being at a lower level. For Bachelard too, vegetableness is an elemental poetic force, a fundamental state of permanence, of repose, of animated materiality, and, especially, of childhood: "The vegetable force of childhood subsists within us throughout our lives. Therein lies the secret of our profound vegetalism."[74]

Rather than restrain our fantasy to levels, we can instead allow an imaginal resonance to be set up between the vegetable and animal kingdoms. This sustains difference without losing relationship. In Andrew Marvell's well-known poem "To His Coy Mistress," he urges haste in the consummation of their passion, contrasting this with the much slower, albeit far more expansive, growth of their "vegetable love." Dylan Thomas is less convinced of this vegetable calm and focuses instead on the dynamics of vegetable vigor—a kind of Dionysian frenzy, a virility of the rising sap: "The force that through the green fuse drives the flower/ Drives my green age. . . ."[75] Science has followed a similar parallelism between the kingdoms: the discovery of the circulation of the blood led to that of sap movement; the chlorophyll molecule closely resembles that of hemoglobin; one of the ways animals manufacture the "hem" of hemoglobin is the same as that used by plants to produce chlorophyll.[76] Vegetables even have cycoplasts which function like eyes—as light-sensitive areas. The important word here is *like*. Archetypal psychology is not concerned with literal botany and biology but with the fantasies they embody, express, reveal, sustain. Bachelard writes of a lake as "a large tranquil eye."[77] Science, by another route, has led us to a vegetable eye. The question now is how to recover our own vegetable eye.

Totemism

Another animation of the vegetable kingdom can be found in traditional cultures under the broad heading of "totemism."[78] Like other "things," vegetables *gather* the world or—as Martin Heidegger put it—Earth and sky, humans and Gods.[79] Vegetable totems, such as the yam, rice-plant, corn, wheat, coconut, taro, and breadfruit, gather and organize social, spiritual, individual, and collective identities. They also express difference: this clan is the yam, that one the taro. How these vegetables are placed in Nature imaginatively echoes how and where the clan is placed in the world. Vegetables are imagined to be vessels both for the Gods and for the ancestors. There is a mutual listening and response between vegetable and clan.[80] In modern Japan the radish lies at the center of numerous rituals, especially Buddhist ones marking the close of the year. For the Hopi Indians few rituals are conceivable without the presence of maize.[81]

In our own society vegetables are similarly the gathering point for a complexity of imaginings, although less consciously celebrated as such. Our vegetables too have their stories to tell, their "jests" and "*gestes*," which help us to "digest." Many Western cities are now filled with the "exotic" vegetables of recent immigrants, vegetable reminders of a colonial past which have their place in gathering together the various communities and subcultures. The Christian Harvest Festival and the enlistment of vegetable help from the Devas at places such as Findhorn gather together communities, Earth and Gods. There is a dark side to such gathering: who could doubt the place of the potato in the *memoria* of the Irish or that of the varied plantation crops—sugar, coffee, cotton, rubber—in the memory of countless exploited peoples?

Within such a fantasy, therapy becomes an initiation into vegetable stories and reflections, a process of reclaiming this imaginative complexity, of listening to the gathering power of vegetables in dreams and fantasies, of following the way vegetables, each in its own specific way, gather the dreams around themselves.

Vegetable Spirits

In Western folk culture, no less than in other traditional cultures, vegetables are animated by their association with "the small people." For example, in Russian tales we may hear of the "polevik" (field elves who protect bean fields), the "pilwize" (who live among rye and oats), and the "pavaro" (who live only among broad beans). There are also the ubiquitous tree elves, wood trolls, and moss-people. Generations of English children loved the "flower-pot men," whereas in Australia there were the frightening "banksia-men" and the friendly "gum-nut" people.[82] Every culture has such vegetable dwellers. These creatures are less spiritual, more personal and close, more mischievous than either the totemic Gods and ancestors or the cosmic correspondences of vegetable mysticism. They introduce us to a personification of the vegetable soul. Instead of functions and systems, instead of asking "what," this perspective asks "who": "*Who* is the Earth? *Who* are the waters, the plants, the mountains? or, *to whom* do they correspond?"[83]

Vegetables and Gods

The complex relations between vegetables and archetypal powers, as personified in the deities of ancient cultures, embrace most of the fantasies expressed above. These mythic and astrological correspondences are extensive: peas have been associated with the Great Mother, radishes with Mars, mushrooms with Mercury, onions and peppers with Mars, lettuce with the Moon, as are pumpkins and cucumbers; cabbages align themselves with the Sun, carrots with Mercury, beans with Demeter, and so on. The danger here is a recipe-book approach, an over-systematization of correspondences. In its own way, this approach can be a form of abstraction, using the deities as categories rather than as invitations to a deep, pluralistic appreciation of the vegetable soul.

This approach can also reach great sophistication and, by reconnecting vegetables with their ancestral "*gestes*," or stories, avoid the aridity of the recipe book. Fennel, for example, has been associated with Mercury under the sign of Virgo. Its resulting antipathy to Pisces has been used to explain its capacity to consume the phlegmatic humor experienced when eating fish. Prometheus carried the stolen fire in a giant fennel stalk, and these stalks have been used, ritually, to carry sacred fire. Asparagus has been linked with Aphrodite and sexuality. Plutarch is reputed to have commented that a veil of asparagus was appropriate for brides as it had rough spines but was pleasant to eat! Also associated with Aphrodite, the artichoke is claimed to incite lust. Hesiod wrote that, at the flowering of the artichoke in June, the goats are plumpest, the wine sweetest, and the women most wanton. The Adonis garden was created from short-lived plants, especially lettuce and fennel. These were grown quickly, being tended only eight days, then were allowed to wither before being thrown into the sea with an image of Adonis at his fertility festival.

This imaginal placing, as seen in the case of the Adonis garden, was not just a matter of story but frequently involved rituals, many of which have survived as planting lore. In medieval times sowing on saints' days was common: beans and peas on St. David's (1 March) and St. Benedict's (21 March), potatoes on Good Friday (the dead tubers laid in the ground in imitation of Christ's resurrection).[84]

Planting by zodiacal signs has generated systems of extraordinary complexity: Aries governs the head and so favors the planting of vegetables that are head-shaped, such as cabbage, turnip, and swede; Taurus favors earthy root vegetables, such as peanuts and potatoes, or through association with bull's blood it favors dark beets. Planting by the light of the sun benefits crops that grow above ground: cabbages, peas, beans. Those that grow below ground—potatoes, carrots, parsnips—should be planted in moonlight.

Such systems draw attention to the aesthetics both of vegetables and their contexts. Aesthetic resonances have been used by homeopathy through the ages: yellow sap cures jaundice; rough surfaces heal skin problems; red roses stop nose bleeding; walnuts are imagined as being good for the brain; the potato, due to its phallic shape (sweet potato) or testes shape (ordinary potato), has been suggested as an aphrodisiac. Gardeners' chants offer an aesthetic encouragement: "As round as my head/and as big as my butt!" went an old Illinois song to cabbage seed as it was being sown; "As round as my head/and as big as my thigh" for turnips; or a daily call to parsnips: "As long as my arm/as thick as my wrist."[85]

Naturally, both prayers *for* plants, addressed to higher powers, and prayers *to* plants as manifestations of higher powers have been common in most cultures throughout history. Paracelsus, for example, as a vegetable mystic, wrote: "each plant is a terrestrial star and each star a spiritualized plant."[86]

CONCLUSIONS

We have seen how vegetables have been imagined as divine reflections; or as corresponding to some transcendental power; as gathering points for social organization and as part of a line of ancestral continuity; as containing a power available to humans through ritual mastery; as being directly endowed with emotions and a quasi-human intelligence; as permanent homes of small beings who embody an essential folk relationship between humans and the vegetable kingdom; as part of an inter-related imaginal ecology; or as manifestations of a plurality of supreme, divine figures. Here is a rich field of associations. These are ways in which humans have sought to understand and communicate with vegetative life, whereby they have tried to locate themselves within it, to participate, intervene, and perhaps even control the vegetable soul both within themselves and within the wider world, the *Anima Mundi*.

As a foundation for healing, the image of the vegetable soul offers both a profound metaphoricity and an ability to synthesize an extremely diverse range of ideas. As a background for imaginal reflection, it leads us into the depths of our cultural past and into the depths of the world. There is an absurdity, a whimsy, about it that nicely balances the profundity of its archaic origins, an earthy substantiality that complements its cosmic, spiritual overtones. The vegetable soul fills the world with a complex green light, a viridescence, a green consciousness.

CHAPTER TWO
The Vegetable Soul in Depth Psychology

By the beginning of the eighteenth century, the explicit idea of the vegetable soul had all but disappeared from the worlds of science, philosophy, and theology. But the image of a tripartite soul—rational, sensible, vegetable—left a firm mark on subsequent formulations about human identity, consciousness, and well-being. This chapter will explore the fate of the vegetable soul both as it moved backstage during the past two hundred years and in its reformulation within the world of modern dynamic psychologies. The idea of a vegetable soul has persisted in depth psychology, although its metaphoricity has often been obscured beneath abstraction and scientificity.[1]

We have seen how the idea of a vegetative soul can be traced back to classical Greece and how it was sustained and developed through the medieval period until it found its most receptive home in the Renaissance tradition of Hermetic-Alchemical philosophy as exemplified by Ficino. The coherence of this ancient body of knowledge was gradually eroded throughout the course of the eighteenth century by the emergence and development of modern science.[2]

Experimentation, new observational techniques, plus the rise of quantitative measurement quickly moved to the leading edge of the West's attempts to understand both the human and the natural worlds.[3] One branch of the "Occult" or "Hermetic" tradition totally abandoned close observation of physical nature and spiraled off into speculative philosophy.[4] But another small, but influential, section refused to surrender the empirical observation of Nature to the mechanism and atomism of the new sciences and resisted succumbing to baseless speculation. Following on from Paracelsus and van Helmont, the mystical and psychologically inclined Goethe and Swedenborg successfully developed their own approaches to observation and experimentation. For example, Goethe's work on color and Swedenborg's pioneering discovery of the neuron early in the eighteenth century lay ignored and almost forgotten by the scientific establishment until the recent, more sympathetic attitude toward a "holistic" science.[5]

However, loosely clustered around the new observational sciences, attracted to their rigor and to the exciting discoveries opened up by anatomical dissection, by measurement, by optics (telescope and microscope), by the new chemistry (especially the study of gases), and by physics (especially machines, magnetism, and electricity), there persisted the essence of the old Hermetic tradition: a belief in the inter-relatedness of microcosm and macrocosm, the animation and soulfulness of the world, the interpenetration of imagination and matter. In some cases, for example in Mesmer's work on hypnosis, the marriage between Hermetic and natural sciences was fairly explicit. In other cases, for example with Newton, the two interests coexisted separately and uneasily. On the one hand lay his studies in gravity, optics, and mathematics, while on the other were his extensive alchemical experimentations. But in many cases—as with Hooke, Boyle, Harvey—one must search the underlying root metaphors of their scientific work to find the Hermetic dreams.[6] Reclaiming the root metaphors underlying scientific ideas and practices is fundamental to a reanimation of the modern world view, to a reconciliation with the *Anima Mundi*.[7]

As reason increased in prestige and became firmly located in the head, at the very highest part of the human anatomy, the two "lower" souls, the sensible and vegetal, became increasingly materialized, dissected, and rationally observed. The imaginative powers and divinity of these "lower" souls became lost in descriptions of anatomical systems.[8] From a psychological perspective, the most important of these was the nervous system. Within its new scientificity lingered the ancient tripartite description of soul, especially in the overt labeling of the autonomic nervous system as the "vegetable" or "vegetative" and perhaps in the more recent notion of the tripartite division of the brain.[9]

The long history of the "discovery" of the nervous system has unfolded, at least in part, within the context of the old Hermetic philosophy. Within this Neo-Platonic penumbra, the distinction between the "nerves" as physical anatomy or as psychological metaphor has always been flexible. This penumbra was one of the key regions from which modern depth psychology was born. As we shall see, from Mesmer to Freud and Reich, from Carus to Jung and Neumann, a nerve-mythology has hung like a cloud: now thick and dense as with Reich or vaporous as with Jung, as a kind of psycho-physical substratum in the case of the early Jung, or a delayed promise of true scientificity in the case of Freud.[10]

As the vegetable soul became reduced to bodily functions and to nervous systems within the individual, it simultaneously became "botanized" or de-souled in the natural world. A split occurred in natural science between the human world and the vegetable kingdom. But in the same way that a "Hermetic" sensibility continued to linger around scientific investigations into the nervous system, it also refused to relinquish the study of the world's fauna and flora to the abstractions of modern science. Throughout the nineteenth century, there was a continued insistence, albeit among a minority, that the natural world was ensouled and that the human psyche or soul was somehow intimately connected to the soul of the world. The dynamic psychologies of Freud and Jung emerged from both the study of "nervous" disorders and this sense of a macrocosm–microcosm interconnection.

THE NERVOUS SYSTEM AND THE WORLD SOUL

The term *neurology*, from which comes *neurosis*, was first coined by William Thomas (1621–1675), although classificatory terms such as *neurasthenia* had to wait until the second half of the nineteenth century.[11] The term *hypnotism* was first used in the 1840s by a Manchester physician called Braid, who also called it "neuro-hypnotism" or "nervous sleep."[12] Study of the brain and nervous system grew out of an ancient debate about the bodily location of the human soul, a debate which can be traced back to Plato and Aristotle.[13]

The Paracelsian van Helmont (1579–1644) made a detailed study of such nervous phenomena as clonic and tonic contraction, which he related to the action of the "vegetative centres."[14] He saw a close relationship between brain and stomach, between nightmares and colic, or indigestion. On the other hand, Descartes concluded "that the blood and animal spirits were the sole principles of movement and life. No allowance was made to the vegetative and sensitive souls to enter the body machine."[15] Throughout the eighteenth century, it was widely believed that a nervous "fluid," a *succus nerveus*, carried the nerve impulses. This substance, this nerve-sap, was variously imagined as animal spirits, a fire or light, a juice, an ether, oxygen, magnetism, or electricity.[16]

Mesmer's theories (1734–1815) were a crucial link between the development of ideas on the nervous system and those on the psyche. His theories have been summarized by Henri Ellenberger. (1) There is a subtle physical fluid that fills the universe and forms a connecting medium between humans, as well as between them and the earth and the heavenly bodies. (2) Disease is caused by an unequal distribution of this fluid. Healing occurs when equilibrium is restored. (3) By means of certain techniques this medium can be stored and transmitted to other people. (4) In this manner "crises" can be provoked and hence diseases cured.[17]

Mesmer described his fluid in terms of the recent discoveries in electricity: poles, streams, discharges, conductors, etc. Quite clearly, Mesmer's universal "fluid" had a direct affinity with Renaissance notions of a World Soul, albeit in a materialist guise. It takes its place in a tradition that includes Newton's ideas about an all-pervading "ether." But Mesmer's fluid, with its attendant notions of disequilibrium and cathartic healing, was also a precursor of twentieth-century ideas about nervous, or psychic, energy, libido, and orgone energy. Mesmer and his followers believed that a "somnambulic lucidity," rather than heightened consciousness, would reopen communication between the human mind and the soul of the world.[18] Such fluidic ideas coexisted with psychological theories through much of the nineteenth century.

Mesmer was really a child of the Enlightenment, and in many ways his ideas lost favor because they failed to dovetail with the Romantic ethos coloring the whole of the nineteenth century. Simple materialism and reason were no longer sufficient. The era demanded a place for feeling, beauty, intuition, history, an inner life and rapport both with other people and especially with Nature. The Romantic movement in Germany looked to theorists such as Goethe for inspiration, especially his studies in the metamorphosis of plant life. On the other hand, there was an unwillingness to sacrifice the scientific advances made through the course of the previous century. Gotthilf von Schubert (1780–1860) was in some ways typical of the era; both in his work and in that of Carl Gustav Carus (1789–1869), we can begin to see the gradual emancipation of truly psychological ideas from purely physical or mental ones.

Carus was one of the first to clearly formulate the idea of the unconscious and to correlate it with the nature of the soul.[19] In his model of the unconscious one can detect a psycho-physical parallelism, whereby certain bodily functions, such as blood circulation and liver activity, are associated with corresponding emotional states. He believed there were three kinds of dreams, each belonging to either the mineral, vegetal, or animal *Lebenskeise*, or "life circles."

Despite the decline in the popularity of Romanticism in the second half of the nineteenth century, its ideas continued to exert their influence. One key figure was Gustav Theodor Fechner (1801–1887). Initially a professor of experimental physics, he underwent a sea change of attitudes after a serious illness and three years of acute depression. On his recovery he wrote a book, *Nanna, or the Soul of Plants*. His influence was widespread, and Freud quoted him in *The Interpretation of Dreams, Jokes and the Unconscious*, and *Beyond the Pleasure Principle*, calling him the "great" Fechner. As Ellenberger points out, from Fechner Freud borrowed "the concept of mental energy, the 'topographical' concept of the mind, the principle of pleasure–unpleasure, the principle of constancy, and the principle of repetition."[20]

Fechner's work was also praised by William James (1842–1910) in his seminal book *A Pluralistic Universe*.[21] For Fechner the entire Earth had its own collective consciousness. He treated this earth-soul as the special guardian angel of humanity. The consciousnesses of the human, animal, and vegetable kingdoms were considered to combine in the soul of the Earth, which in its turn was merely part of the universal consciousness of the entire cosmos.

What appealed to James was the materiality of Fechner's vision, "the profuseness of his concrete imagination." Such a vision found its subsequent echo in the seminal works of Olaf Stapledon, or Teilhard de Chardin, or in Gaston Bachelard's insistence on both cosmic reverie and a material imagination. This concrete imagination was a direct precursor of such recent ideas as the "Gaia Hypothesis" or "Deep Ecology."[22] James also admired Fechner's description of a truly pluralistic consciousness—a conclusion of critical importance in the field of Archetypal Psychology with its insistence upon a radical polytheism. Jung, for example, referred to Fechner's ideas on a plurality of consciousness.[23] For James, reality took the form "not of an all but of a set of eaches. . . ." This perspective sustains the relative autonomy of the vegetable soul. Fechner believed that, although plants lacked a nervous system, they had another type of consciousness that included a heightened awareness of the functions of nutrition, respiration, and propagation, functions of which humans were usually unconscious. Similarly, merely because plants could not share a similar feeling life to humans did not mean that they had no feeling life at all. As James writes, Fechner's universe was "thickly alive."[24]

Meanwhile, scientific research into the nervous system of the individual grew in intensity throughout the nineteenth century. In addition to studying the expansive ideas of people such as Fechner, both Freud and Jung were also curious about hypnosis and neurology. The attempt to correlate psychological functions with anatomy, particularly brain structure, was well developed by the end of the century, but it was one of Freud's teachers, Theodor Meynert (1833–1892), who consolidated it. As one author put it, Meynert "paved the road to a classification of mental disorders on neuroanatomical, that is on spacial grounds."[25]

This correlation between mental disorders and brain diseases, as formulated by researchers such as Wernicke and Meynert, came to dominate psychiatry. But it was frequently the case that objective findings were unconsciously overlaid with more far-ranging psychological hypothesizing, thus creating an imaginary anatomy of the nerves and brain. This came to be known as *Hirnmythologie*, or brain mythology.[26]

Hence two very different groups gathered around the study of the nervous system and its relation to psychological states. On the one hand, there were those, like Freud and Jung, who grew up with a scientific neurological background but who either abandoned it or else were more interested in "brain mythologizing." On the other hand, there were those for whom psychological states were directly reducible to neurological physiology. While this chapter is primarily concerned with the former, it is worth pausing to outline some of the conclusions of the latter, particularly how they relate to the vegetative aspects of the nervous system.

The vegetative nervous system is thought to be, phylogenetically, the oldest part of the nervous hierarchy, initially evolving to serve the gut. Indeed, the parasympathetic nerves, which regulate the muscle of the alimentary tract and the secretions of the gland concerned with digestion, are the oldest part of the whole autonomic nervous system. As we shall see, such archaic layering and fundamentally deep, unconscious bodily functioning are crucial to the place assigned the vegetative nervous system in the mythology of depth psychology. Hillman has shown how there has been a close correlation made between the emotions and the autonomic nervous system. He quotes one author: "Vegetative processes are not open to 'psychic' influences, but are the very foundation of them."[27] The same writer continues, "Events in the environment are not the psychic (mental) causes of an affect, but rather the bodily reactions which are going on in us. These are ordered by the vegetative system. The vegetative system is thus decisive in determining the way in which psychically apprehended events of the outer and inner world will be experienced." From such a perspective the vegetative nervous system clearly occupies a crucial mediating position between outer and inner, between body and psyche, between conscious and unconscious.

FREUD'S "PROJECT"

While both Freud and Jung eventually broke decisively with a nerve- and brain-oriented psychology, the metaphorical structures of such an approach became embedded within their respective metapsychologies. At times both thinkers seemed unwilling to fully relinquish the literal, physical tangibility of the nervous system and with it the hope that one day their psychological ideas could be grounded in the empirical "truth" of biological science. As we shall see, it was particularly the vegetative nervous system which became incorporated into their psychologies. When the theories attempted to describe the deepest regions of the unconscious, they began to merge psychic processes with the physical or bodily dimension. The result was a conceptually grey, twilight zone, neither matter nor psyche, where notions of instinct, libido, and psychic energy ruled.

In his *Project for a Scientific Psychology* of 1895, as outlined in his correspondence with Fliess, Freud created an imaginal brain/nerve structure in which neurons were conceived as the building blocks or basic units of the nervous system. The anatomical doctrine of the neuron had only recently been accepted by neuro-anatomists, and the idea that a transfer of excitation could occur at the junctions between neurons was exactly what Freud was looking for. Basically, neurons were imagined as discrete units that always tried to discharge any excess energy, thereby maintaining an inertia in the system. The ego was imagined to be an organization of neurons that could control incoming "nervous excitation." Following on from Fechner, Freud "postulated the existence of nervous energy on the model of physical energy."[28]

It has been said that this project was "the outcome and legacy of a century of brain mythology." It found its way into both of Freud's seminal works of 1900: *The Interpretation of Dreams* and *Three Essays on the Theory of Sexuality.*[29] A hypothesis of the process of sexual excitation and discharge, from a neuro-physiological perspective, can be found even earlier, in his first paper on anxiety neurosis (1895). While he soon abandoned this approach, many of the terms crucial for Freud's subsequent psychoanalytic theory had their origins in this "project": mental energy, sums of excitation, cathexis, quantity, quality, intensity, and so on.[30] "Systems of neurons were replaced by *psychical* systems or agencies; a hypothetical 'cathexis' of psychical energy took the place of the physical 'quantity'; the principle of inertia became the basis of the pleasure . . . principle."[31]

The polarity of charge/discharge runs through all of Freud's work and culminates in his ideas on pleasure/unpleasure, particularly as formulated in *Thanatos*, or the death instinct. The state of absolute quiescense to which the death instinct aimed was originally called "neuronic inertia" in Freud's *Project.*[32] Time and again we can detect echoes of this nerve/brain mythologizing in Freud's work on *Thanatos.*[33] In some way too, there is a distant murmur here of the ancient ambivalence toward the vegetable soul. As we saw in the last chapter, the sensible and vegetable souls grounded the rational soul, profoundly modifying and reducing its scope for independent action, its transcendent yearnings for spirit and abstraction, its hopes of immortality. While nourishing and energizing this "higher" soul, the vegetable soul kept it in constant contact with death, with immobility and loss of will.

REICH: VEGETOTHERAPY AND ORGONE

In his classic work *The Function of the Orgasm* Wilhelm Reich wrote:

> Freud had made no mention of the vegetative nervous system in connection with his theory of anxiety . . . [and] he rejected the connection between anxiety and the vasovegetative system. I never understood why. It became increasingly clear that the overburdening of the vasovegetative system with undischarged sexual energy is the fundamental mechanism of anxiety.[34]

Reich was a psycho-metaphysician of the vegetative nervous system. In his work, nerve/brain mythologizing reached one of its fullest flowerings. He had a vegetable faith, a belief that, by dissolving the rigidities or "armoring" that a repressive culture imposed on the body via the so-called "higher" faculties of mind, there could occur a liberation of vegetative energy. All ills—from cancer to schizophrenia, from war to environmental pollution—could be understood by means of this repression of vegetative energy, these "disturbances of vegetative life."[35] For Reich, all ideas could be traced back to vegetative impulses;[36] all psychic disturbances had a vegetative-biological core.[37]

In his pursuit of the "deepest layers" of the psyche, Reich came to the vegetative nervous system. Although it may appear that his notion of this system was acutely literal and materialist, nevertheless in it we can see Reich's refusal to relinquish the substantiality and materiality of the psyche. These were precisely the qualities in Fechner's vision of vegetable life that appealed to William James. Dynamic psychology's root metaphor, the metaphor of its roots, is depth. Freud, Jung, and those that followed have, each in his or her own way, attempted to ground their psychologies in this fantasy of depth. At the same time they have sought to connect psychopathology with the body and with the worlds of Nature and culture. The question has always been, how to *imagine* depth? While all of the depth psychologies have some reference to the nervous system, only Reich embraced it fully, particularly its most ancient and "deepest" aspect, the vegetative: "the Freudian 'unconscious' is actually tangible in the form of vegetative impulses. . . ."[38]

We can read Reich's work as a vegetative mythologizing. For example, he imagined schizophrenia to be the result of "body sensations, . . . vegetative currents" being experienced only abstractly, as ideas and concepts.[39] Reich's vegetotherapy attempted to liberate the "bound-up vegetative energies" and thus restore to the patient his or her "vegetative motility."[40] The eighteenth-century disavowal of the vegetable soul returned with a vengeance in Reich's supreme faith, and almost naive confidence, in the goodness and rightness of this repressed vegetative energy. "God," he proclaimed, "is the mystical idea of the vegetative harmony of the self with Nature."[41] He wrote of the "perception of one's vegetative wholeness" as being "the natural and the only safe basis for a strong self-confidence. . . ."[42] Such a state brings a "feeling of wholeness . . . the feeling of an immediate contact with the world"; there will then be a return of "depth and earnestness"; people will remember a time when "they felt one with nature, with everything around them. . . ."[43] All these rich experiences are lost to "emotionally blocked and vegetatively rigid individuals."[44]

In addition to "depth" and "metaphorical substantiality," the various dynamic psychologies also value motility, a psychic flexibility and mobility. Jung, for example, was critical of a rigid persona or attitude toward the world. He also wrote that the only "problem" from a psychological point of view was getting stuck.[45] Reich expressed this psychic fixity in terms of "body armor": a damming of vegetative energies, a perverse conditioning of vegetative behavior deep within the body musculature. Almost directly echoing the ancient location of the vegetable soul, Reich placed the "vegetative center" in the lower regions. He imagined a hierarchy of descent running down the body, through the stomach and abdomen into the deepest vegetative center at the pelvis. This pathology of fixity and rigidity can also be found in the formulations of early researchers into the nervous system. For example, Nicholas Robinson in his 1729 treatise on "the Spleen, Vapours and Hypochondriack Melancholy" attributed the cause of all nervous and mental disease to the degree of elasticity of one's nerves.[46]

Reich directly followed Freud's, and Fechner's, ideas on the principles of pleasure and unpleasure, correlating them respectively with the parasympathetic and sympathetic aspects of the vegetative nervous system.[47] The ambivalence of the vegetable soul, its vigorous animation of life and its pull into a morbidity of the depths, finds its exact parallel in Reich's vision of these two aspects. Vegetative life takes one both out into the wider world and also deep back into oneself. Significantly, Reich described the former in terms of "pleasure and joy" and the latter in terms of "sorrow and pain."[48]

With his later "discovery" of "orgone energy," Reich completed his project of reuniting psyche, body, and the world. While fully conversant with Bergson's notion of an *élan vital*, Reich was dissatisfied with its insubstantiality and generalized vagueness.[49] Rather like Mesmer with his "magnetic fluid," he wanted something that could be seen, harnessed, and measured. He wrote: "The living organism contains orgone energy in every one of its cells and keeps charging itself orgonotically from the atmosphere by the process of breathing."[50] This is an almost plant-like process, and indeed Reich continues: "The plant chlorophyl, which is related to the iron-containing protein of the animal blood, contains orgone which it takes up directly from the atmosphere and the sun radiation." The intensity and range of the "orgonotic field" that surrounds humans vary according to the individual's "vegetative motility."[51]

It should come as no surprise that Reich was a vigorous critic of modern society and was involved in pursuing radical social change. We have already seen how Mesmer's universal fluid permeating all existence served as a medium of hope. Resensitizing people by means of this fluid, or in Reich's case orgone energy, could heal the destructive divisions between individuals, between communities, and between humanity and Nature. For example, Robert Owen, the early nineteenth-century Utopian Socialist, was deeply interested in mesmerism and saw it as a way by which a millennial reform could take place.[52]

Despite his literalisms, Reich must be seen as a genuine precursor to an *Anima Mundi* psychology. His unique value lies in his attempt to formulate a substantial vision of psyche, one that was grounded and nourished in body: an imagination of body as well as a bodily imagination. A spokesman for the "lower" or vegetable soul, he tried to articulate its demands in its own language, rather than in the abstractions of the "higher" or rational soul. Unfortunately, psyche became lost within his materialistic metaphysics. The urge for scientificity smothered metaphoricity. Imaginal substantiality became confused with literal materiality. The result was a generalized materialistic abstraction without any specific relation to the things of the world.

JUNG: PSYCHOID AND EARTH

When we turn a green eye on Jung's monumental output, we encounter a serious and dedicated attempt to respect the wisdom traditions of the ancients. It is therefore not surprising to discover a psychology in which echoes of the doctrine of the tripartite soul reverberate throughout.

Like Freud, Jung was quite clear about the neuro-biological roots of modern psychology. He was also determined that a psychological understanding should not be reduced to mere biology. To reduce "psychic happenings to a kind of activity of the glands . . ." or to regard thoughts "as secretions of the brain . . ." produces "a psychology without the psyche."[53] On the other hand, Jung wrote that there was no sense in denying "the close connection of psychic happenings with the physiological structure of the brain, with the glands and the body in general."[54] Here was Jung's dilemma: how to include the body within a truly psychological psychology? "The separation of psychology from the basic assumptions of biology is purely artificial, because the human psyche lives in indissoluble union with the body."[55] It was therefore quite understandable if psychologists "should fall back on the security of the biological standpoint and to borrow freely from physiology and the theory of instinct."[56] However, psychic functioning should not be derived from the brain.[57]

What was needed was another way of looking at "body" and "mental" functioning. "Matter is just as inscrutable as mind," Jung wrote.[58] Neither a materialist nor a spiritual explanation was appropriate for the psyche. "The functional psychological disturbances, or psychoneuroses, are by nature a special field impinging neither on the psychiatric clinic nor on the domain of neurology."[59] Jung insisted that a third, or intermediate, way of perceiving reality was needed, a form of perception appropriate to the psyche. " 'Psychic' means physical *and* spiritual. . . . All attempts to explain the psychic factor in terms of more elementary physical factors were doomed to failure."[60] But such a standpoint was difficult for people in the West to comprehend because the notion of an intermediate world had been lost. "Without soul, spirit is as dead as matter. . . . Man originally regarded spirit as a volatile body, and matter as not lacking in soul."[61]

This form of psychic, or intermediary, cognition is crucial, for it enables us to view both body and mind metaphorically, as expressions of psyche, as vessels for soul. "The place or the medium of realization is neither mind nor matter, but that intermediate realm of subtle reality which can be adequately only expressed by the symbol. The symbol is neither real nor unreal. It is always both. . . ."[62] In this way, matter is granted a certain psychic faculty and the psyche a kind of materiality.[63] Jung was well aware that the attempts by neurology and psychiatry to explore, classify, and delimit the area of neuroses had compelled the discovery of the psyche. But this was a discovery that was not welcomed by modern science.[64] Jung believed that even the work of Freud and Adler was based too much in nineteenth-century science, in the need for facts, to fully accept the reality of fictional and imaginative processes.[65]

But how should this fictionalizing of the body, of matter, be envisaged? Jung was sceptical of the value of such vague terms as *energy* or *élan vital*. Not only did they confuse spirit and nature, they also lost contact with materiality; they spiritualized matter.[66] It is therefore understandable that in his earlier work Jung returned to his roots in neuro-biology in order to find images with which to express this material imagination. He coined the adjective *psychoid* to refer to "quasi-psychic" phenomena, such as "reflex-processes."[67] "Just as, in its lower reaches, the psyche loses itself in the organic-material substrate, so in its upper reaches it resolves itself into a 'spiritual' form about which we know as little as we do about the functional basis of instinct."[68]

To go deep, to descend into the deepest levels of the unconscious, was symbolized by Jung in terms of an increasing engagement with the body; indeed, at times he found it difficult to sustain the metaphorical nature of his body-mythologizing and it seemed as if he was proposing a split between psyche and body with the former grounded in the latter. For example, he insisted that "neuroses are to be influenced or cured by approaching them not from the proximal end, i.e., from the functioning of the glands, but from the distal end, i.e., from the psyche, just as if the psyche were itself a substance."[69] As late as 1948 he wrote of "the general human precondition, the inherited and inborn biological structure which is the instinctual basis of every human being."[70] Indeed, after his prolonged studies into alchemy, Jung insisted that psyche was a substance, not literally but metaphorically. He was determined to "do away with the awkward hypothesis of psychophysical parallelism."[71]

He wrote that the deeper levels, "the dark regions" of the psyche, "are quite inaccessible to consciousness. Thus our conscious reason can never destroy the roots of nervous symptoms; for this emotional processes are needed, which even have the power to influence the sympathetic nervous system."[72] The vegetative nervous system is used here both as a symbol of absolute psychic depth and as an indicator of the power of depth psychology to reach such dark, mysterious, and fundamental regions.

> The collective unconscious is . . . the mighty deposit of ancestral experience accumulated over millions of years, the echo of prehistoric hap-

penings. . . . [It] is, in the last analysis, a deposit of world-processes embedded in the structure of the brain and sympathetic nervous system. . . .[73]

This neuro-biological model therefore gave Jung a crucial metaphorical basis for ideas such as archetypes and the collective unconscious. In the early years, this quasi-medical and evolution-oriented anatomizing prevented Jung's somewhat spiritually inclined psychology from losing all contact with the body. Subsequently, alchemy not only gave him access to the same intensity of bodily, or material, imagination but also reconnected him with the *Anima Mundi*, the soul of the world. When he wrote that "The soul . . . is only partly confined to the body," he was merely reiterating alchemically his neuro-biological comment: "The psychoid process is not the unconscious as such, for this has a far greater extension."[74] But he never completely abandoned the neuro-biological model, and, as we shall see, it remains a powerful metaphor of fundamental, almost unreachable depth in analytical and archetypal psychology.

These depths fascinated Jung, and he was convinced that they were the home of a certain type of consciousness. Even while using the biological model, Jung saw evidence of "'meaningful' or 'intelligent' behaviour of the lower organisms, which are without a brain."[75] Quite clearly, such intelligence was totally different from that associated with the cerebral cortex, but for Jung it provided an anatomical basis for his belief in the profound intelligence of dreams and the unconscious. He mused over "whether dreams . . . are produced not so much by the activity of the sleeping cortex, as by the unsleeping sympathetic system, and are therefore of a transcerebral nature."[76] Neurology gave Jung an invaluable metaphor for a deep, if somewhat alien, intelligence and also, despite his insistence on the primacy of fiction, lent some scientific and material credibility to his theories. "Thus we are driven to the conclusion that a nervous substrate like the sympathetic system, which is absolutely different from the cerebrospinal system in point of origin and function, can evidently produce thoughts and perceptions just as easily as the latter."[77] The fact that the autonomic, or vegetative, aspect was not only structurally the deepest, but also the most ancient part of the nervous system, merely confirmed its metaphorical power for Jung.

While the neuro-biological model continued to linger throughout Jung's work, it quickly reached the end of its usefulness for him. He began to turn instead to the prescientific ideas of alchemy. Neuro-biology was itself a product of the rational soul, and while it provided a view of the deeper intelligence, this was from afar, from above, abstracted. Jung wanted to understand these deeper and perhaps more fundamental psychic processes from within their own frame of reference, on their own terms. For this project, the strange and often bizarre symbolism of myth and alchemy was invaluable.

> Plant-like growth . . . represents an entirely different psychological experience from that which we are used to, for we ordinarily think of our psychology in terms of warm- blooded animals, not plants. Yet it is a strange fact that spiritual development is symbolized by plant-life. It is the impersonal life of man, the life beyond his own psychology. And that kind of life has to follow other laws . . . quite unlike those arising from the mentality of the personal, warm-blooded life.[78]

Not only was Jung convinced that the so-called unconscious was in fact a "multiple consciousness," he was adamant that each of these autonomous "multiple luminosities" had its own logic.[79] For Jung these multiple consciousnesses represented a fundamental quality of nature. They were the "forms or sparks of the world-soul. . . . The seed-ideas of Nature. . . ."[80] On the other hand, this idea of a multiple consciousness paralleled traditional ideas about a plurality of souls within the individual: "Primitives assume the existence of several souls. . . . I am therefore inclined to think that autonomous complexes are among the normal phenomena of life and that they make up the structure of the unconscious psyche."[81] In a sense, as Jung went deeper into the unconscious, he found evidence of alien but fundamental intelligences, as well as of an interconnectedness between the human psyche and Nature. The unifying image was that of the World Soul: "The world-soul is a natural force which is responsible for all the phenomena of life and the psyche."[82] The *Anima Mundi* pervades the whole of Nature, expressing itself throughout the animal, vegetable, and mineral kingdoms.[83] "The extension of God as the *anima media natura* into every individual creature means that there is a divine spark, the scintilla, indwelling even in dead matter, in utter darkness."[84]

For Jung the vegetable level was, after the mineral world, the deepest realm of the unconscious. But it was both where the roots of the self were to be found and also where a profound, fundamental life-energy originated. He repeatedly referred to the "*spiritus vegetativus*" as a Mercurial principle of animation to be found in vegetative reality. He also related the "blessed greenness" of vegetative life with the Holy Spirit.[85]

Bridging the mineral and animal kingdoms, the plant world expresses the profound mystery of the emergence of life from inert matter: "Plants get their nourishment immediately from the elements. . . . So the primary form of life is plant life. . . ."[86] Jung wrote of "the miracle of the living plant rooted in the inanimate earth. The alchemists described their four elements as *radices*, corresponding to the Empedoclean *rhizomata*. . . ."[87] Such a mystery also found expression in the alchemists' imaginative animation of matter: "Suffice to say that the adept saw branches and twigs in the retort, where his tree grew and blossomed. He was advised to contemplate its growth, that is, to reinforce it with active imagination."[88] This was of course no ordinary "tree" but the "philosophical tree."[89] This process has its parallel in Eastern yoga or tantra where consciousness is imagined as originating in the lowest chakra: "that would be in *muladhara*, which is the darkness where things begin. There the green shoot or bud is Shiva."[90]

While identifying with these lower levels of consciousness was "invariably accompanied by a heightened sense of life," Jung was also aware of the danger and ambivalence associated with the vegetative level. Mercurius as *spiritus vegetativus* was unreliable, devious, unbounded, a trickster. At this dark level, the tension between spirit and matter is the most extreme; there is no moral distinction between good and evil; the consequences of two thousand years of contempt for matter and the body by the Christian West lie waiting to be released in a devastating return of the repressed.[91] In traditional cultures, these deeply complex vegetative principles and powers were acknowledged and celebrated as vegetation deities, as ancestral souls, as nature spirits. Such imaginative vessels have long been forgotten in the West.

But although the vegetative level is found in the depths of the unconscious, it is paradoxically the most widespread metaphor for spiritual growth:

> animals live on plants, we are parasites, we are a kind of lice on the forests of the earth. The life of man and the life of plants is a sort of symbiosis. . . . Our whole system adapts to the system of the partner—in other words, the life of the plant is in us as well as our own—and in us it becomes the symbol for a non-biological quality, for what we call spiritual. The unfolding of the spirit is based upon an analogy with plant life.[92]

We have already noticed his correlation of vegetative greenness with the Holy Ghost. In addition, Jung pointed to the parallels between the immobility and quiet rootedness of vegetable life and the injunctions toward a calm abiding found in Eastern yoga and meditation.[93]

Clearly, in his revaluation of vegetative life Jung was not advocating a simplistic return to "Nature." Quite the reverse. Fostering vegetative life was a work contrary to the apparent naturalness of things; it was an *opus contra naturam* dedicated to a spiritualizing and ensouling of life. In this regard the dwellers of the vegetable kingdom function as manifestations of anima, as guides not to a more "natural" life but to an imaginal one.

For Jung, therefore, the vegetable soul embodied an intense verticality: upward toward the spirit and downward into the material darkness—both aspiration and rootedness. This tension finds its fullest expression in his two "vegetable" essays: "The Philosophical Tree" and "Mind and Earth."[94] In the first work Jung emphasized the upward movement: the "analogy between the natural growth of the psyche and that of a plant."[95] In alchemy the tree represented "the growth of the arcane substance and its transformation into the philosophical gold (or whatever the name of the goal may be)."[96] Of course, the transformation process was and is fraught with paradoxes and contradictions; so it must also be firmly rooted. Nevertheless, when imagined as a tree or "wonder-working plant," it is primarily revealed as a "process of growth."[97] But in his other essay, Jung explores a very different terrain: the predominant orientation is downward, into the roots.

It may perhaps surprise many who associate Jung with lofty spiritual flights to learn that, by all accounts, he was an extraordinarily earthy man. There are numerous anecdotes: Marie-Louise von Franz mentions how when he was required to vote Jung consulted his gardener at Bollingen about controversial political issues;[98] Barbara Hannah recounted the time during the war when Jung plowed up some of his ground to plant potatoes;[99] Ruth Bailey remembered when she outraged Jung by using tomatoes that had been bought rather than taken from his garden.[100] Jung himself praised small gardens and said each person "should have his own plot of land so that the instincts can come to life again." He directly blamed modern disease on the rootless and gardenless existence of so much city life.[101]

This rootlessness was a concern to which Jung constantly returned. When recounting his frightening but pathbreaking active imaginings of 1913–1915, Jung expressed his fear: "Nietzsche had lost the ground under his feet because he possessed nothing more than the inner world of his thoughts. . . . He was uprooted and hovered above the earth, and therefore he succumbed to exaggeration and unreality. For me, such irreality was the quintessence of horror. . . ."[102] When reflecting on the importance of mythology in human psychology, Jung wrote:

> a man who thinks he can live without myth, or outside it, . . . is like one uprooted, having no true link with the past, or with the ancestral life which continues within him, or yet with contemporary human society. . . . The psyche is not of today; its ancestry goes back many millions of years. Individual consciousness is only the flower and the fruit of a season, sprung from the perennial rhizome beneath the earth. . . .

He suggested one should take "the existence of the rhizome" into consideration: "For the root matter is the mother of all things."[103]

Jung continually contrasted, unfavorably, modern Western life with that experienced by the earth-related traditional cultures, particularly those of Africa and Australia.[104] "Certain Australian primitives assert that one cannot conquer foreign soil, because in it there dwell strange ancestor-spirits who reincarnate themselves in the new-born."[105] Jung took the relationship with the earth very seriously: "The mystery of earth is no joke and no paradox!"; "The soil of every country holds some such mystery."[106] For Jung, the "earth" and "history" were profoundly connected: "Alienation from the unconscious and from its historical conditions spells rootlessness. . . . That is the danger that lies in wait . . . for every individual who . . . loses touch with the dark, maternal, earthy ground of his being."[107]

Jung even suggested that his own Swiss roots were somewhat shallow, going back only five hundred years on his mother's side![108] Indeed, most of European culture was a fairly recent arrival: "It was only a short while ago that the Anglo-Saxons immigrated from northern Germany to their new homeland . . . and it is much the same with practically every nation in Europe."[109] Matters of earth were clearly slow and ancient to Jung, who saw a profound correspondence between the cultural veneer sitting atop an unfathomable ground and the thinness of consciousness resting precariously on the primordial depths of the unconscious. One simply had to be held firm and nourished by one's psychological roots—whether biological, historical, cultural, ancestral, or earth-related. In his essay on "The Soul and Death," Jung warned: "Restlessness begets meaninglessness, and the lack of meaning in life is a soul-sickness." Creative imagination was closely bound up with the "tap-root" of instinct. Without a living connection to these deep roots, one was left only with a "sapless, almost sad, dusty point of view." Such was the perspective on the world inherited from "late" Christianity.[110]

Deeply concerned about the way that modern Western culture had stripped Nature of soulful animation, Jung lamented that the "seemingly universal and metaphysical scope of the mind has . . . been narrowed down to the small circle of individual consciousness," that we have lost "a world that pulsed with our blood and breathed with our breath."[111] Jung argued that modern city-dwellers have lost contact both with their own instincts and with the reality of the natural world. How different was the reality of the individual in traditional cultures, who dwells "in his land and at the same time in the land of his unconscious. Everywhere his unconscious jumps out at him, alive and real. . . . A whole world of feeling is closed to us and is replaced by a pale aestheticism."[112] But all is not entirely lost, for such associations and feelings still live on in the unconscious.

When Jung writes "The whole opus is depicted as the sowing and nurturing of the tree in a well-tended garden," he is in fact referring to the labor of the alchemists huddled over their alembic. He continues: "The soil consists of purified Mercurius; Saturn, Jupiter, Mars, and Venus form the trunk (or trunks) of the tree, and the sun and moon supply their seeds."[113] But he might just as easily have been referring to the study of dreams or the practice of active imagination, or he could have been giving advice on the importance of actually gardening—vegetable gardening as a way of soul-making. From his earliest work on the development of sexuality and libido in childhood to his most mature work on alchemy, Jung continually reached toward metaphors drawn from the vegetable kingdom, not just as convenient, abstract analogies, but in an attempt to unite the body and psyche of the individual with that of the wider world. Above all, he used these metaphors to develop a form of perception that was appropriate for psychological understanding, that did justice to the complex multiplicity of the psyche, that expressed its substantiality and its paradoxical depths.

NEUMANN: PSYCHIC EVOLUTION

In *Symbols of Transformation*, Jung developed the first major statement of his own unique psychological approach. Deeply symbolic, it is a profound study in the archetype of "the

Hero" and decisively marked Jung's split with Freud.[114] Following directly from this seminal study, Erich Neumann integrated a rich diversity of biological, mythological, and cultural metaphors into an impressively coherent psychological system.[115] A devoted evolutionist, Neumann assigned the vegetative level to the earliest stages of the "development" of consciousness. It is associated both with the *Uroboros* (the earliest state of unity: unconscious and undifferentiated) and with the archetype of the Great Mother. Neumann's is an uncompromisingly heroic-oriented psychology, and he imagines the ego struggling first to emerge from the uroboric womb and then to separate itself from the realm of the Mother. Individual consciousness is imagined to pass through the same archetypal stages that characterized the history of human consciousness as a whole.

For Neumann, the "uroboric principle is . . . associated with the predominance of earth and vegetation symbolism"; it corresponds to "the stage when ego consciousness is undeveloped and still embedded in nature and the world."[116] Jung's paradoxical metaphor, of conscious life beginning in the depths of the vegetative level, is concretized by Neumann into a *historical event* in the life both of culture and of the individual child in the modern world.

Neumann is a mythological materialist and grounds the "development" of consciousness in neuro-biological anatomy:

> The nervous system, particularly the cerebrospinal system whose final exponent is consciousness, is an organic product of the unconscious, designed to hold the balance between the outer world and the inner. The inner world ranges in extent from physical reactions and their modifications to the most intricate psychic reactions. . . . All these inner tendencies must be recognized by the conscious system and the ego, balanced and adjusted to the external world.[117]

Plurality has been swept to one side; the autonomous intelligence and wisdom of the alien "soul sparks" are subordinated to ego-development.

Neumann proposes a uni-directional ego-development through a literal hierarchy of stages:

As the ego's activity and the intensity of its libido increase, so the symbolism varies. At first, plant symbols are the most prominent, with their passivity and earthiness. . . . The predominance of vegetation symbolism means the physiological predominance of the vegetative (sympathetic) nervous system; it also denotes, psychologically, the predominance of those processes of growth which go forward without the assistance of the ego.[118]

Neumann overlooks that for Jung the symbolism of vegetative life indicated an *opus contra naturam*, a work against the natural order of things. By virtue of its apparently alien character as compared to that of the ego-world, vegetative symbolism tended to indicate spiritual and imaginative—not literal, naturalistic—growth. But Neumann is firmly committed to his schema of a hierarchical, orderly development: "As the activity of ego consciousness increases, the vegetation symbolism is followed by the animal phase. . . ."[119] The fragile, paradoxical balance in Jung's work vanishes; gone too is his constant call to a metaphorical perception grounded neither in mind nor matter.

All the functions of the vegetable soul as outlined by Burton are located at the very bottom of the evolutionary ladder: "eating, digesting and assimilating the world."[120] Neumann calls this nexus the "alimentary uroboros" and busily places a considerable amount of "primitive psychology and mythology" within its domain.[121] Not only is Neumann's psychology heroic, it is also ethnocentric and species-centric. Failing to assess either traditional cultures or vegetative life on their own terms, it instead equates them as early, lower stages in a fantasy of idealized, linear development. Vegetative life is placed firmly and unequivocally within the realm of the Great Mother. Neumann passes all of his rich vegetable material singlemindedly through this one archetypal hoop. Not surprisingly, he views all vegetation deities as subject to the "sovereignty of the Earth Mother."[122] "[T]he vegetation deities, are not fertility deities only; as something sprung up from the earth, they are the vegetation itself."[123]

Perhaps the most significant aspect of his work is the full and evocative attention that he gives to the dark ambivalence of the vegetative realm, the richness with which he details the ego's fears of being devoured and extinguished within the vegetable soul—its place both as the "nutrient earth, the cornucopia of the fruitful womb . . . mankind's instinctive experience of the world's depth and beauty" and the "black, abysmal side of life and the human psyche . . . death and destruction, danger and distress, hunger and nakedness. . . ."[124]

Neumann's approach is not unique within depth psychology; indeed, as we have seen, it traces its genesis to one of Jung's most formative studies. Echoes of this approach can be heard, for example, in Marie-Louise von Franz's study of the puer aeternus, where images of vegetation are always taken as symbols of the Mother and any upward movement read as a defensive attempt to escape Her realm. On the other hand, any transformation into vegetative life is invariably read as a sign of psychological regression. Similarly, in Gerard Adler's work *The Living Symbol*, the sympathetic nervous system is associated with the spider's web and viewed as a shadow mandala.[125] Such negative evaluations of the vegetable realm are difficult to shift.

When Jung wrote *Symbols of Transformation*, he was involved in a struggle to emancipate himself from "the constricting atmosphere of Freudian Psychology."[126] The attention that he gave here to the archetypal Hero is therefore understandable, but he was *not* doing what Freud did with the myth of Oedipus: he was not claiming the archetype of the Hero as *the* myth of consciousness. The Hero is just one, albeit important and pervasive, root metaphor for psyche. To view psyche exclusively through the window of the Hero always relegates the vegetable soul to a "lower," "earlier," "primitive," "inferior," or "undifferentiated" level. At best vegetative life, along with creatures from the animal kingdom, will assist the Hero in his/her remorselessly uni-directional quest. At worst it signifies a distraction, a hindrance, a regressive entanglement. From this perspective too, vegetative life will always be identified almost exclusively with the archetype of the "Great" Mother. To revalue the vegetable soul imaginatively means relativizing the all too dominant role of the Hero, not just explicitly in depth psychology, but also implicitly in much psychology and psychotherapy, in spirituality, as well as in science.

GRINNELL: VEGETABLE FAITH

A less evolutionary reading of Jung's ideas can be found in Robert Grinnell's work, especially his *Alchemy in a Modern Woman*.[127] While we still find references to "psychoid levels" and "neurobiological processes," these are within a framework that is archeological rather than evolutionary, transformational rather than developmental, and pluralistic rather than hierarchical. Above all, Grinnell never compromises the integrity and autonomy of the vegetable soul. He writes of "the transcendental mystery and paradox of the sympathetic and para-sympathetic psychoid processes."[128] For Grinnell, these lie in the uttermost depths of humanity's psycho-anatomical archeology, deeper than even the "animal souls of Pithecanthropos and the hominoids . . . or the 'psyche' of the cold-blooded saurians. . . ."[129] It is at such an abysmal level that any effective "cure" must begin.

This imaginal archeology of psychoid levels describes humanity's direct involvement with the *Anima Mundi*, which in itself follows a similar structure, pervading all Nature, extending itself through the mineral, vegetable, and animal kingdoms. Each of these "kingdoms" has its own form of "intelligence." Staying rigorously with his biological metaphorizing, Grinnell describes the alien vegetable and mineral intelligences in terms of "a sort of immanent 'photosensitivity' traceable even in the minutiae of neurobiological life"; a "deep reflective capacity, this 'photosensitivity' and 'innate luminosity' in the depths of the soul"; a "bioluminescence."[130]

Like the alchemists of old, Grinnell works along a fine line between mythologizing and materializing. Where can we actually locate his psychoid archeology? Is it simply metaphor, or is he referring to the literal body? At times it seems as if even Grinnell is unsure, and he holds out hope that the physical and biological sciences will contribute to the discovery of new manifestations of psychic energy.[131] But this is an attendant risk when trying not to lose the substantiality and materiality of psyche, when trying to express something that is neither mind nor matter but both. Nevertheless, at times Grinnell scarcely avoids a simplistic psychophysical parallelism. What redeems his approach is its intense blending of divergent perspectives and its close attention to the phenomenology of images.

Grinnell combines the symbology of alchemy, astrology, and mythology with the "fiction" of neuro-biology. This permits us to understand that the "dream gives us a subjective picture of how the psyche views activities going on at a psychoid level of the organism. It correlates the subjective factor active in neurobiological processes with the images of psychic experience."[132] This understanding is otherwise inaccessible to the abstractions of the rational mind. But we can gain access to these psychoid depths through dream and hence assist the vegetative healing process.[133] However, this process is fraught with risks and fears. At this level, as the archetype recedes "into totally unrelatable forms of life," we are approaching a realm of psychic death, "at least as far as human experience is concerned"; yet "in this transpersonal and even transpsychological sphere we find the deepest, most unchanging, and most creative vitality of the archetype."[134]

At this point we must rely on "psychological faith." Grinnell suggests that, unlike religious faith, this is not a belief in something but a confidence in the process that permits, sustains, and vitalizes our experience of belief. Psychological faith is the gift of the anima which keeps us intimately connected to both the psychic depths and to the image-making process itself. As such, psychological faith is not just the prerogative of the ego or the rational soul; rather, it can be found at every level in the psychic-psychoid body. We can therefore have recourse to a vegetable and animal faith, one that both sustains our "inner" life and intimately links us to the wider world of animate nature. Edward F. Edinger, in his well-known study *Ego and Archetype*, similarly views the supportive, healing aspect of the vegetable nervous system, commenting that it is "a reservoir which can take up destructive excesses of energy that may accumulate in the conscious personality."[135]

This vegetable faith is one of the most profound conclusions to be reached by depth psychology. It is a fitting culmination to centuries of investigation and reflection on vegetative life. As we shall see, it has far-reaching implications for the healing both of the individual and the world, the anima and the *Anima Mundi*.

CHAPTER THREE
Archetypal Psychology and the Vegetable Soul

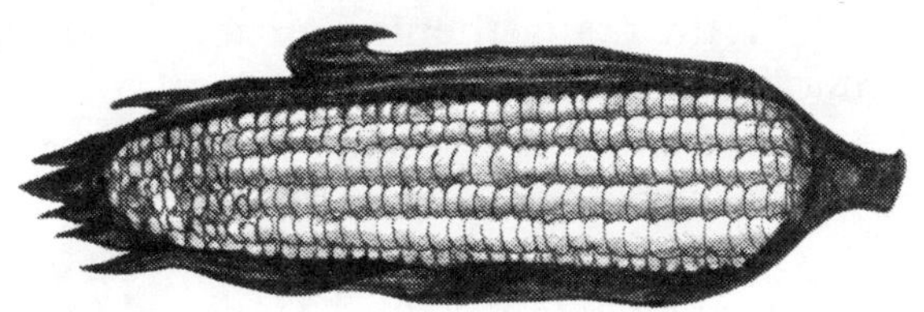

JAMES HILLMAN: A POETIC POLYTHEISM

While they bear an unmistakably "Jungian" stamp, the psychological ideas of James Hillman are not simply post-Jungian but owe a direct allegiance to those of the Renaissance. Hillman calls this approach "Archetypal Psychology" to distinguish it from both Freud's psychoanalysis and Jung's Analytical Psychology.[1] Of course, Hillman acknowledges his debt to Jung, as well as to Henri Corbin and Gaston Bachelard, but only insofar as these thinkers are modern exponents of an ancient Western way of imagination or, as he calls it, "soul-making."

However, there are still traces of the nineteenth century's neuro-biological roots in Archetypal Psychology. So, Hillman writes: "In a man's dreams the anima is often the image for neuro-vegetative symptoms and emotional lability; that is, she represents the semisomatic events which are not yet psychic experiences, which have not yet undergone enough psychization."[2] Elsewhere he writes: "The vegetative, nature-like anima figure seems . . . to be intimately connected with the vegetative involuntary nervous system, its moods and fluctuations and reactions, its inaccessibility to direct control by the will, by the voluntary nervous system."[3] We also find traces of the negative value given to the vegetable level: Daphne's transformation into a laurel tree, when she is chased by Apollo, is read as the psyche being driven "into vegetative regression."[4] Finally, in a similar way, he writes somewhat critically of "the nymphic imagination, an anima style of consciousness that hovered in nubile not-yetness and horror of sexuality, in fainting, in the neurasthenic retreats into the vegetative nervous system of . . . misty Victorian England. . . ."[5] Although these are isolated references from Hillman's extensive and highly sophisticated work, they are worthy of mention simply to underscore the persistence of nineteenth-century neuro-biological attitudes. But that point having been established, with Hillman we move into a very different world from that of "scientific" psychology.

Hillman insists upon the metaphorical basis of psychic life and on the *reality* of "imaginal" perception.[6] He makes no exception for neuro-biology: "The movements of the libido are mythical events in which we participate. . ."; "Studies, experiments, research results . . . have no bearing on soul-making except to provide materials for fantasy. . . ."[7] For Hillman, the body is "a place of fantasy" that includes, but also far exceeds, the "flesh." He writes of the "enigmatic relationship of flesh to body. . . . Our contemporary symptoms force us to enter the flesh in a new way, through the psyche, inwardly, symbolically." He celebrates the "happy reappearance of the ancient religious doctrine of the 'subtle body' and the 'animal spirits.' "[8] We must approach the body metaphorically, in a way that is similar to that adopted toward the dream: "Both provide ways of developing the inner connection and expanding psychic reality."[9] In one of his most recent works he playfully refers to the "symbiotic connection between complex and vegetative nervous system—or, in my reading, between insect and plant. . . ."[10] Neuro-biology is for Hillman simply a powerful fiction. However, in some ways, like most scientific terminology, it is too powerful and, in the modern reader, tends to evoke literal belief. For this reason, and perhaps also because of their closeness to Renaissance psychologizing, Hillman prefers to use the imaginal languages of myth and alchemy.

Alchemical language is itself substantial: "its thing-words, image-words, craft-words" portray concrete materials and processes.[11] Alchemical language "re-materializes our concepts giving them body, sense, and weight. . . . Its beauty lies just in its materialized language which at the same time we can never take literally."[12] Hillman insists that psychology must begin by deliteralizing its own tools, seeing through its own language and concepts so as to become aware of its own fictions. As a radical pluralist, determined to sustain the autonomy of all imaginal voices, he calls for a variety of perspectives in order to do justice to the richness of the psyche: "no single perspective can embrace psychological life, and norms are the delusions that parts prescribe to one another. . . . [P]athology for one part may be normal from another perspective within the same individual."[13] He particularly insists that the archetype of the Hero cannot continue to function as the dominant motif for psychology without doing considerable injustice, if not harm, to psyche.

Hillman claims that there is something fundamentally wrong with psychology's notion of consciousness.

> What we have been calling "consciousness" all these years is really the Apollonic mode as hardened by the hero into a "strong ego". . . . Thus therapeutic psychology has an inherent contradiction: its method is Apollonic, its substance Dionysian. It attempts to analyze the collectivity, the downwardness, the moisture of libidinal fantasies, the child, the theatricality, the vegetative and animal levels . . . of the Dionysian by means of the distance, cognition, and objective clarity of the other structure.[14]

Such an approach, continues Hillman, always moves from the outer to the inner and from below to above. It will therefore always hold vegetative life in relatively low esteem.

Hillman's insistence that psychological perception is akin to entering the underworld—to experiencing a descent into dark, downward regions without any question of transforming them, redeeming them, or even of returning to the dayworld—is crucial. Psychology's standpoint needs to come down to the animal and vegetable levels. By bringing "our superior posture to the level of the creature, kneeling to it, condescension, we begin to see as they do; a transposed eye."[15] There is an intimate connection between the underworld, death, and the vegetable soul. Like the dream, soulful perception "takes us downward, and the mood that corresponds with this movement is the slow, saddening, introspective feeling of depression."[16] Once psychology's viewpoint has been depressed, therapy no longer involves translating the imaginal reality of these "lower" realms into the abstractions of ego-language. Instead, the ego is seen through from the perspective of these lower worlds and metaphorized.

Hillman has also been instrumental in bringing the idea of the *Anima Mundi* to the forefront of psychology's concerns and at the same time revisioning it: "let us imagine the *Anima Mundi* as that particular soul-spark, that seminal image, which offers itself through each thing in its visible form. . . . The world comes with shapes, colors, atmospheres, textures—a display of self-presenting forms. All things show faces, . . . things speak, . . . announce themselves, bear witness to their presence: 'Look, here we are.'"[17] The *Anima Mundi* perspective insists that the world is ensouled and animated. It seeks a reconnection with the variety of possible imaginative styles presented by the world: How do things call us? It involves a shift of the center of gravity of imaginative reflection away from individual, experiential subjectivity and into the ensouled world of things. Attention is given to the aesthetics of images whether in dreams or in the world—their specificity and interconnectedness.

Hillman is proposing an imaginal-ecological psyche, rather than, say, a developmental or evolutionary one. He suggests that psychological perception should return to the Renaissance ideal and shift itself from the head to the heart, not in terms of literal body feelings or subjective sentimentality, but as the organ of an aesthetic apprehension of beauty. *Beauty* here refers back to the Neo-Platonic idea of simple manifestation, the "colors in the face of things, the radiance of the Gods shining in the material world, visibility, presentation."[18]

Hillman has given special emphasis to the animal kingdom, to the place both of animals in human dream and fantasy and of the animal in our way of regarding psyche and the world.[19] He writes that the animal "reveals itself to the observing senses as a behavioral, aesthetic phenomenon . . . and not only as a philosophical, symbolic, textual one."[20] An awareness of form is particularly crucial in the case of the vegetable kingdom. The poet Francis Ponge writes: "Fauna move . . . [but] flora unfold to the eye." Plants do not wander around. Without voices they can only draw attention by means of their postures.[21] These "gest-ures" are integral to a vegetable way of working with psyche, to a vegetable epistrophé.[22] Hillman suggests that the education of psychologists should include a close attention to the sensual, behavioral, ecological reality of things: a psychology of extraversion.

Vegetables express an aesthetic tension: cactuses with their combination of spikes and soft, watery centers; carrots with their soft green plumes above ground and their hard, red bodies below; artichokes, the edible thistles, the aristocrats of the Renaissance kitchen, with their exquisite combination of flavor and elegance, pointedness and fleshiness, of increasing delight by anticipation as one moves toward the center.[23] An aesthetics of soul-work means staying close to the vegetable images: their form, structure, seeds, skin, flesh, color, environment.

We are drawn to recognize the soul of the world primarily through ecological breakdown, our fears about the dangers that lurk in things—the food we eat, the air we breathe, and so on. Our soul-sicknesses are caused by the loss of connection with an animated world. Our symptoms can therefore be read as an attempt by psyche to cure this dis-ease: "The symptom reattaches us to the tropisms of the cosmic parade. The sympathetic and parasympathetic nervous systems reflect our sympathy with all things, the presence in the body of its concord with an ecological cosmos."[24] The sheer abundance and interweaving of psyche are reflected in the ecological interconnections not just between various plants or animals but also between plants *and* animals.

Hillman, for example, points to the constant relationship between insects and the plant world, in dreams as well as in Nature. There is a sympathy between them: they often look alike; they need each other, perhaps even enjoy each other.[25]

Clearly for Hillman, not only do the mineral, vegetable, and animal "souls" have their own unique perspectives, but also there are myriad different perspectives contained within any one realm. For example, even the

> bug modes of being in the world—despite the rigidity of insect behaviors . . . —are infinitely differentiated. Six hundred and forty thousand species of insects, each with habits, forms, patterns, displays; each a slightly different ecological affirmation. This vast variety allows us therapists to view the complexity of symptom formation . . . requiring from us the attentiveness of the entomologist.[26]

The plant/insect world has an astonishing complexity that defies simplistic forms of symbolic interpretation and reduction. It insists upon a close attention to the phenomenology of the image: "In a single tomato plant 24,688 aphids have been counted, and an acre of soil . . . may bear in it from one to 65 million insects."[27] The "anarchy" that could result from this diversity "can only be resolved in terms of a deeper perspective that takes full account of the ceaseless interconnections and fantasies going on among the persons of the psyche."[28] For Hillman, this deeper sense of order is provided by the "polytheistic perspective described in myths."

One of the main problems with this return to the "vegetal" world (whether to the neuro-biological body, or to the alimentary system, or in terms of the need for psychological roots, or as an ecological awareness of the vegetable kingdom) has been its evocation of a naturalistic fallacy. Words such as *earth, soil, growth, natural* are easily taken literally. Hillman points out that there are at least sixty connotations of the word *Nature.*[29] Reflection, metaphor, and psyche can quickly become lost within a dense vegetable-moralizing. Determined to sustain a poetic perspective, Hillman is always on the alert for any reduction. For example, he writes that "Foodstuffs evoke concrete, naturalistic associations. . . ." We need to see through to the soul-food, to the organs of the soul-body; we need to put to one side our dayworld associations. Just because spinach is supposed to be healthy in the dayworld doesn't mean it is necessarily so in the underworld. Food images could simply relate to the need that psyche has to be fed.[30] Food and feeding do not automatically indicate the realm of the mother and child. Similarly, "growth" doesn't necessarily signify the Great Mother and her growing child; cancer, the national debt, and spiritual awareness can all experience growth. But the Great Mother, writes Hillman,

> prefers a slippery intertwined holism to distinctions among parts. She it is, as vegetation Goddess, who nourishes an idea of psyche among a welter of confusing similars—organism, life, *élan vital, bios, zoe,* the feminine, nature—as well as keeping tangled and buried the subtle differences between growth, increase, differentiation, development, evolution, progress, individuation, change, transformation, metamorphosis, and the like.[31]

In one paper he calls for an appreciation of natural beauty *without* Nature: "we cannot take nature just 'naturally,' unconsciously. . . . To be natural has come to mean to be simple, un-selfconscious, without art. . . . This as well implies that nature is objectively pure, without subjective artifice, genuine, and therefore the one remaining place where truth, beauty, and goodness abide."[32] "Nature" then becomes a utopian symbol for a straightforward reality somehow outside of psyche, with all its labyrinthine, shadowy complexities, its infuriating paradoxes, and its constant relativizing. This onesided, neo-Rousseauian optimism had dire consequences even for Rousseau, whom Voltaire described as one of the unhappiest people alive "because he was one of the most evil." The shadowy paradox of Nature, excluded from his conscious mind, manifested instead in his paranoia, his disturbing dreams, and body symptoms.[33]

For Hillman, imaginal reflection, discrimination, and order come from a constant mirroring of events, experiences, and images in the complexities of traditional mythology. Earth, for example, is not just "earth" but has been mythically portrayed in many guises: Demeter (horizontal, green, fertile soil); Ge (the "physical and psychic ground of an individual or community, its 'place on earth' "); Chthon ("the depths, the dead's world").[34]

Words such as *earth* and *ground* need to be deliteralized and remythologized. "We may thus gain earth," writes Hillman,

> not only by working the earth of Demeter, the agricultural fantasy of returning to the soil as diggers, being natural. We may become earthy also through Ge, working on one's fate. . . . There is [also] a third way of making matter, and this is through *chthon*, working into the cold dead depths of the psyche, the underworld of night and dreams and ghosts, and the incurable changeless essence of character imaged in our chthonic complexes. This is the deep home ground, the House of Hades.[35]

Even death needs to be psychologically reimagined, especially when it is associated with metaphors drawn from the "natural" world. For example, suicide has been called unnatural:

> On the face of it, those who attempt suicide in order to find a vegetative stillness before the completion of their round are cutting life unnaturally short. But this is how it looks from the outside. We do not know what complexities set off senescence and death in plants and we know less about a "natural cycle" or span of years in man.[36]

Each of Hillman's moves—dethroning Heroic consciousness, upholding the validity of a radically pluralistic psyche, insisting upon the fundamental fiction of a sensual, imaginal language—is crucial to a deeper recognition of the vegetable soul. But perhaps his most important contribution has been his revisioning of the ancient image of a World Soul, the *Anima Mundi*.

GASTON BACHELARD: PLACE AND VEGETABLE REVERIE

"One enters the world by admiring it," writes Gaston Bachelard.[37] As we have seen, archetypal psychology emphasizes both the aesthetic particularities of the world and the mirror of myth in which to reflect them. Although mythology offers us a profoundly soulful means of reflecting on vegetative life, we must also attend to the display of the world, what Hillman has called "a fantasy on show. . . ."[38] For Bachelard, reverie and repose, plus a care for words and appearances, are the most appropriate ways to enter the vegetative imagination. Acutely sensitive to the subtleties of the material imagination, Bachelard writes: "an image is a plant which needs earth and sky, substance and form." Being rooted or rootless, digesting images, ripening, stemming, grafting, pruning are all vegetable metaphors. Perhaps we can see in the tap-root, the deepest root of all, the child who one was—the connection with deep ancestral nourishment. For Bachelard, the concept of grafting is essential: "It is the graft which can truly provide the material imagination with an exuberance of forms, which can transmit the richness and density of matter to formal imagination. . . . Art is grafted nature."[39]

The plurality of the vegetable soul finds expression in our use of language. As another writer has mused: "Boredom, writer's block, footnotes and deadlines" all draw us downward; "Scholarship is always drawn to death. It takes morbid delight in unearthing the rotting fragments of culture."[40] Footnotes drag us away from a merely horizontal and linear reading of the text to "suggest the dimension of depth" and to recast "the essay [as] . . . a dialogue of the dead."[41] The word *boredom* is related to *bor* (OE), to "auger," to *foro* (L), "to bore, pierce," and to *farao* (Gr), "to plow." "Scholars may pierce with their insight, sift through data, dig up new material, and break new ground. But they are at the same time bored and boring: moles, bookworms, . . . in a rut, and plowed under."[42].

The immobility of boredom can deepen into the immobility of reverie; restlessness can transmute itself into repose. "Vegetable permanence," exclaims Bachelard, "what an *anima* truth, what a symbol for a soul's repose in a world worthy of dreams. . . !"[43] The idea of repose invokes the fundamental importance of place in soul-work. "Soul inhabits space in getting placed," writes Edward S. Casey.[44] Basic to the vegetable soul, habits and habitations locate us in places; they allow us to "dwell poetically on earth."[45] Poetic dwelling can occur physically, in terms of geographical locations or within our own bodies, or it can occur within our psychological processes or within our use of language. But in every case it is metaphorical, involving a descent into the materiality of images, an intimate encounter with the vegetable soul.

Bachelard eloquently captures the force and presence of vegetative life within the material imagination: "In the depths of matter there grows an obscure vegetation; black flowers bloom in matter's darkness."[46] When the alchemists stared into matter and its transformations, they repeatedly saw miraculous plants, like Dorn's metallic tree, whose trunk and branches had the substance of a strange liquid, "not after the manner of water, nor oil, nor of clay, nor of slime, but is not to be thought of otherwise than as the wood born of earth, which is not earth although growing from it."[47] Similarly, the vegetables and plants we have been considering in this book are imaginal; their substance and forms are not literal but metaphorical. They are paradoxically both of the earth and yet not of it. As perhaps no other aspect of psychological reality, the vegetable soul demands an alchemical vision, demands that we endure paradox, that we have "at least some inkling of the scope of paradoxical truth."[48]

But in his deep admiration for the vegetable soul, Bachelard becomes seduced into the simplicity of a green sentimentality. "Vegetable reverie," he writes, "is the slowest, most tranquil, most restful of all reveries." He celebrates "the tranquil oneirism of the vegetable world" and proclaims: "There are no contradictions in vegetable life."[49] We hear an echo of Reich's vegetable optimism and faith in Bachelard's green reverie: "The life of the vegetable world, if it is a part of us, produces the peace that comes from slow movement, its own great, peaceful rhythm." There is also the lingering desire to feel in a state of deep union with the "natural" world: "an enthusiastic participation in the vegetable world will allow us to imagine the different seasons as though they were primitive vegetable forces." Even the day itself can seem to become "a part of vegetable activity."

With Bachelard's beautiful reveries on "vegetablism" we have reached the limit of a particular kind of rapport with the vegetable soul. Subsequent chapters reveal a far richer complexity of vegetable imaginings, although there are few that come close to his sense of a profound green confidence and intimacy.

THE VEGETABLE SOUL AND DEEP ECOLOGY

The vegetable soul occupies a crucial place within an imaginal Deep Ecology. The alchemical preparation of the vegetable stone, the *lapis vegetabilis,* was not only a quest for a medicinal elixir or a search for a spiritual truth; it also expressed the very ground, the essence, of a *vegetable faith.* Limited neither to individual psychology nor to the vegetable kingdom, this faith extends throughout the full breadth and depth of "Nature." It provides the world with a particular earthing in soul: rooted, placed, nourished, digestive, reproductive.

The vegetable kingdom is so vast that not all of its members have yet been classified. Estimates put the total number of species at around eight hundred thousand. Although I have concentrated on the more "everyday" vegetables, the plant world also contains its equivalents of lions and tigers, serpents and peacocks. The two vast areas of medicinal and magical plants have scarcely been touched in this study.

But we should remind ourselves of the immense power and range of the vegetable world, and hence of the vegetable soul. Red-bean, mescal bean, peyote cactus, sacred morning glories, mushrooms, tobacco, nutmeg, cannabis, the sacred vine of souls, ergot growing on grasses, and opium are just a few of the plants that have long occupied esteemed places in traditional cultures as ways of connecting with the "other world." These plants have been drunk, smoked, snuffed, licked, eaten, sucked, and even injected rectally as enemas for thousands of years. Used for soul or spirit journeys, many of these plants, like peyote or morning glory seeds, have been revered directly as deities and as objects of worship, used to "validate and reify the culture, not to afford some temporary means of escape from it."[50] The very power of these plants is revealed in the destructive shadows that they cast once removed from their specific sacred and psychological contexts.

Although generally arrogantly dismissive of the sacredness of the vegetable soul, Western culture is racked by the negative effects of the misuse of plants: tobacco, sugar, chocolate, coffee, alcohol, heroin, petrol, even plastic, to name but a few. Torn from their complex mythological roots, such plants and plant derivatives have wrought their revenge on a culture that has relocated them within a fast-living, rootless, consumer-oriented world. For example, secular smoking of commercial tobacco for pleasure was totally unknown in the pre-Columbian Americas despite tobacco's rivaling maize in its distribution and being used for a greater variety of sacred purposes than any other plant in the New World.[51]

We need not focus on the tragic despoliation of the rainforests, deserts, wetlands, or other sensitive and rapidly disappearing eco-systems in order to draw attention to our neglect and disdain of the vegetable soul. For example, in Australia in 1989 the majority of houses being bought were by people who already owned one. These second properties were inevitably seen as secure ways of saving and of cashing in on escalating real estate prices. The result, of course, was a desperate housing shortage among the young and the low-income groups. In the past people hoped one day to buy their own homes; now people buy houses for investment. In a country with one of the most ancient and viable of earth-related cultures, the Aboriginal, such a rootless attitude toward dwelling is cruelly highlighted.[52]

Similar situations are repeated throughout the Western world. No amount of jogging, aerobics, health diets, civic beautifications, or public information campaigns about drug misuse, eating disorders, pollution control, or energy wastage will compensate for the sickness that lies in the heart of the vegetable soul. We have to relearn how to once again dwell; how to be imaginally grounded in a green faith; how to find repose within our bodies, habitations, habits; how to respect the imaginal complexity, divinity, and power of vegetal life. We have to regain a psychological reflection that perceives the world through a vegetable eye, to retune our imaginations to the bewildering sensual presence and subtle interweavings of the vegetable kingdom within the whole of imaginal ecology.

CHAPTER FOUR

Myth and Vegetative Deities

Given the central place of mythology—particularly that of classical Greece—in a polytheistic psychology, it is important to reflect on some of the deities that are most specifically associated with "vegetative" life. However, it is also crucial to remember that all of the Greek Gods and Goddesses have some relationship with the vegetative realm, in much the same way that each has an associated animal aspect. There are, for example, the domestic "nature" of Hestia (the family meal, vegetable preserving), the civic "nature" of Athena (municipal gardens, tree-lined piazza), the voluptuous beauty of Aphrodite's "nature" (the sensual appearance of things). Hillman also reminds us that "Nature" has not inevitably been personified by a female deity: "oceans and rivers belong to Okeanos and Poseidon; . . . a lord of vegetation and zoetic life, and of childhood too, is Dionysus; and . . . even the earth itself can have, as in Egypt . . . a masculine personification."[1] We have seen how Hermes-Mercurius was imagined as the *spiritus vegetativus*, a twilight trickster that inhabits border regions of all kinds. Even Saturn expresses a "mechanistic rational" facet of the *Anima Mundi*.[2]

DEMETER, PERSEPHONE, AND HEKATE

Traditionally associated with agriculture, the seasons, and the horizontal green world of vegetation's growth, Demeter is in many ways the "archetypal" archetype of the good Earth Mother: fertile, bounteous, caring. Both Jung and Neumann have written extensive commentaries on her and especially on the sacred mysteries celebrated at Eleusis, which culminated in the revelation to the initiate of a single mown head of corn. Above all, she is associated with grain and with the mysteries of life and death, growth and transformation. For Jung and for many other scholars of the Eleusinian mysteries, the principal symbolism was that of resurrection and rebirth. From out of the mown corn comes new life, the cycle is endless, and death is a mere temporary necessity; the tragedy of Persephone's abduction, rape, and residence for one third of the year in the underworld is mitigated by the certainty of the resurrection. The Christian parallels are blatant.[3]

However, there is something too formulaic about this continual emphasis on rebirth, as if one goes down only to come up. Also, we are less concerned with the question of what the Eleusinian mysteries meant as a religion in ancient times than with what they mean psychologically now.

Karl Kerényi questions Demeter's role as the Goddess of cultivation-in-general and insists instead on her relationship to the revelation of the single head of cut grain.[4] She is the Goddess of a vegetative revelation at whose heart is a terrible paradox: the unity of dayworld and underworld; life and death; Demeter, Persephone, and Hekate. The mowing of the grain, its corruption in the earth, and its subsequent reemergence parallel Persephone's fate. Demeter and Hekate are the two polarities of dayworld and underworld. We also have to consider the role of Gaia, the even greater and immeasurably older earth mother who grew the flower that precipitated the rape. As Patricia Berry points out, "for the Homeric Greeks the psyche was found *only* in Hades. The underworld—not life—was the place of psyche. . . . Gaia, who supports all physical life, was at the same time an accomplice to Hades. For her the underworld is also part of nature."[5]

Demeter experiences her daughter's time in the underworld as a loss. From her perspective, therefore, Persephone's reappearance most certainly expresses the miracle of resurrection. But it is equally true that from Hades' perspective this "resurrection" is in fact a loss. Persephone's descent transforms a simple, naturalistic perspective into a psychological one. Demeter would keep her daughter naive, unaware of psyche. She wishes to protect Persephone from the experience of pain, grief, and paradox so necessary to psychological understanding. Hillman writes:

> The Persephone experience occurs to us each in sudden depressions, when we feel ourselves caught in hatefulness, cold, numbed, and drawn downward out of life by a force we cannot see, against which we would flee. . . . We feel invaded from below, assaulted, and we think of death.[6]

The presence of Hekate in the trinity—indeed the division of the year into three—confirms that we have left behind any naturalistic, seasonal vegetative cycle and instead have entered a mythological realm.[7] Persephone and Hekate bring an experience of depth to Demeter's horizontal world.

If Demeter experiences the mytheme as a profound loss followed by a reunion, then Persephone experiences it first as a rape, subsequently as a crowning enrichment—Queen of the underworld. She lives a double life as both dark queen and innocent daughter. From the vast perspective of Gaia, the most ancient, patient, and earthy mother, the whole mytheme is neither tragic nor dramatic.[8] Hekate, she with whom the Greeks associated "sniffing dogs and bitchery, dark moons, ghosts, garbage and poisons," calmly witnessed the entire drama. As Hillman writes: "Part of us is not dragged down but always lives there, as Hekate is partly an underworld Goddess. From this vantage point we may observe our own catastrophes with a dark wisdom that expects little else."[9]

Grain is not only a symbol of rebirth nor even of fertility and growth. The full richness of its symbolism is not contained within the archetype of Demeter. There is a complex relationship between "grain" and Persephone, Hekate, and Gaia, as well as Demeter. As Berry points out, to imagine, for example, Persephone

> as plant life would seem to require a metaphorical observation of the plant itself, to ascertain those underworld qualities inherent in it *throughout* its stages of development. Mere organic death at the end is a too-literalistic reduction of underworld qualities, which can be said to be present within all life, not just in its running down.[10]

Nor can grain or the world of vegetation be imaginally encompassed solely by female deities. Poseidon, for example, was known as "nurturer of plants."[11] Similarly, the seventeenth-century mystic Thomas Traherne remembered the grain fields of his childhood in terms of a union with God the Father.[12]

Contrary to much contemporary holistic health rhetoric, or to a simplistically Christianized emphasis on resurrection, or else to New Age dogma about reincarnation, grain has an ancient association, not with health or life, but with death. The trinity of Demeter–Persephone–Hekate beautifully encapsulates the tensions and paradoxes of the vegetable soul as manifested in the mystery of grain. To isolate the Demeter-rebirth aspect does the vegetable soul a grave injustice. It does not even express the fullness of Demeter: her grief, her lack of understanding, her rage, and her suffering, which—it should be remembered—are not removed by Persephone's return but only confined to part of the year.

Dreams of corn or corn fields can often be related to the death fantasies of European folk-culture. In many areas it was the custom to dedicate the last ears of grain to the Corn-Wolf or Corn-Aunt, the Rye-Wolf or Rye-Aunt, which Edgar Herzog suggests could be a manifestation of Frau Holle, the Death-demon.[13] Grain, including its fermentation as beer, was also associated with the burial rituals of Osiris. The vegetable soul is profoundly connected, not only with spiritual immortality, but also with bodily mortality. The latter is no less a mystery, paradox, and fundamental aspect of our existence than is the former. "The decay and pain around us is not the wasting and grief of a mere residual world in which we chanced to occur; it is the decay and pain of us, the fact of our substance."[14] To deny death a certain permanence, finality, and materiality—in the name of a spiritual rebirth—severs our connection with the "autonomy of Nature. The natural breakdown of Nature, the need of nature to relax into itself, even to collapse into itself. . . ."[15]

The fate of the grain was not just a convenient metaphor on which to hang spiritual truths, nor was it a spiritual way of explaining vegetation-cycles, a kind of agricultural spirituality. In pre-modern culture there was a constant echoing between myth and nature, the one enriching the mystery of the other.[16] In this way, there was a possibility of individual soul and World Soul being deepened and reunited.

APHRODITE

The fascination of depth psychology for the Great Mother (and to no other archetype did Jung assign the adjective *Great*) has confined the God Adonis to her circle as her son-lover. His early death and resurrection are almost uniformly seen as extensions of the Great Mother Demeter's fertility and mystery rituals.[17] Adonis is casually grouped together with other "son-lover" Gods such as Attis and Osiris, as well as with Christ. However, it has been forcefully argued that Adonis is more truly associated with Aphrodite in a relationship that stands almost in opposition to that being proposed with Demeter. From this perspective Adonis has little to do with fertility or general cycles of vegetation. His early death is less a sacrifice to the Great Mother of a failed hero (one who never succeeded in breaking free from her embrace) than a symbol of passionate intensity, its fragility and short-lived nature.[18] Part of the vegetable soul burns with a brief, virile, beautiful intensity; it is at one and the same time strong yet fragile, assertive yet transient. The lettuce, traditionally linked to Adonis, expresses so well the shadow side of such passion: "sexual impotence and a lack of vital force."[19]

Aphrodite is "the lure, the nudity of things as they show

themselves to the sensuous imagination."[20] She is the sheer beauty of appearance, the display and manifestation of the world. She is "the color in the face of things, the radiance of the Gods shining in the material world, visibility, presentation." Aphrodite was commonly imagined in alchemy as a sensual manifestation of the *Anima Mundi*. It was said that when she first stepped upon the ground the earth burst into bloom. At her side are Eros and Himeros, love and longing. Sacred gardens were dedicated to her, as were spring blossoms, especially fragrant roses. Rapture and attraction, whether in the vegetable or animal kingdoms, are her gifts. When we stand in the temple of Aphrodite, we gaze out at a world of "ensnaring, heart-winning splendor in which all things and the whole world stand before the eye of love, the rapture of propinquity and fusion into oneness. . . ."[21]

While Adonis dies, the victim of irresistible seduction, the tale of Eros and Psyche offers us another way of engaging with the overpowering, voluptuous seduction of Aphroditic nature. Psyche's painful struggles bring an imaginal depth to Aphrodite, a sense of the beauty of the underworld. Without Psyche, Aphrodite's compulsions are both irresistible and lacking in psychological understanding.[22]

ARTEMIS

As the virgin who loves the solitude of undomesticated Nature, Artemis is both the guiding deity of contemporary wilderness protection and the expression of the feminine that is complete within itself. "Artemis is the ever-distant," writes W. F. Otto.

> She loves the solitude of woods and mountains. . . . He who is devoted to her plucks garlands for her "from a virgin meadow, where no shepherd presumes to pasture his flock, nor has iron ever come there. . . . Purity waters it like a garden." Her whole quality is unfettered being, raised above all bonds.[23]

One returns to the realm of Artemis to replenish a soul that has wearied of modern life. She is the healing power of untouched Nature: sublime but also harsh and seemingly cruel at times. Hers is not a comfortable nor comforting world. It is one that constantly eludes the reach of those that seek it, always just slipping away in front of comprehension and full experience. Artemis comes closest to expressing the sublime yet terrible divinity of ecology:

> Here is a teeming concourse of elements, flora and fauna, life unnumbered which sprouts, blooms, spreads its scent, bubbles, hops, leaps, flutters, soars, and sings; an infinity of sympathy and discord, pairing and struggle, rest and feverish movement, and yet all is related, interwoven. . . .[24]

As Adonis is to Aphrodite, so Actaion is to Artemis. Both youths die young: Adonis of a dreadful wound in his thigh caused by a wild boar, Actaion torn to pieces by his own hunting hounds after stumbling upon Artemis bathing naked and being transformed by her into a stag. Actaion's fate is not punishment but reveals the "terrible death-dealing side of pure nature . . . that is wild, dangerous and unpredictable. One does not wander too far into the untamed wilderness of nature or of the soul without risk."[25] Artemis also expresses the verticality, the lofty idealism, often associated with wilderness. We can therefore understand the attraction she holds for many who seek spiritual solace in her pristine realm but who lack a certain earthy warmth, a dark grounding. (Pothos, the yearning of the puer, was associated with the upward striving of plant life, the vitality of the sap.) Actaion's fate describes the initiation of naive innocence into Artemis's realm. She "has the power to 'uncivilize', to return things to their earlier forms. In the dark, deep interior where Artemis rules, one cannot trust impulses and instincts which in a more cultivated world serve their master."[26]

DIONYSUS AND VEGETABLE MADNESS

Apart from the Great Mother, the other archetype which has traditionally been associated with vegetative life is Dionysus. Since his earliest manifestation in Crete, Dionysus has been identified as "the divine force of living nature *(zoe)* and the taming of that nature."[27] Hillman suggests that *zoe* is not just "the force that drives the green blood of nature, the *élan vital* of vegetative life, but also . . . the interiority of that force, personified as Dionysus. . . . His 'dismemberment' is the fragments of consciousness strewn through all of life, through every erogenous zone and plexus of our physical bodies."[28] Imagined as Dionysus, this "universal libido" is bisexual, both masculine and feminine, active and passive, creative and destructive. It brings together life and death. When we view the body through this window, "we may recall those early images of Dionysus, sombre, still, long-robed, unheroic, soft: a figure of vegetation and the vegetative reactions of the psyche."[29]

Through Dionysus we can reexperience the body poetically, as an extraordinarily rich source for metaphor. His dismemberment "severs the only natural connections, the habitual ways we have 'grown up' and 'grown together'. It disconnects the body's habits at the animal-vegetable level, releasing a subtler appreciation of the members and organs as *psychic representations*."[30]

Otto argues against simplistic interpretations, so popular in the last century, of Dionysus's madness as a "romantic empathy with the fate which befell the year's vegetation."[31] Dionysus really has little to do with any vegetation cycle. He is rather associated with the primal idea that any new birth is a reemergence of the ancestors from out of the darkness of death. "Generation after generation must constantly rediscover," writes Otto, "that the most uninhibited growth and fertility are shrouded in the exhalations of death. This is not to be taken as a warning or an admonition, but it symbolizes the most profound never-ending nature of desire."[32]

It is only from the perspective of death that we can begin to comprehend the meaning of a Dionysian intoxication on the fermented fruits of the earth, the revelry, the somber madness. When we enter the vegetable soul through Dionysus, we are initiated into the vitality of death, not growth, vegetation cycles, or resurrection.[33] "All intoxication arises from the depths of life which have become fathomless because of death. From these depths comes music—Dionysiac music—which transforms the world in which life had become a habit and a certainty, and death a threatening evil."[34]

Each God has her or his favorite plant: the laurel for Apollo, corn for Demeter, lettuce for Adonis. For Dionysus it is the vine, and also ivy. In these two plants we see two sides to the God. The vine "intoxicated with light is a child of warmth and gives birth to the fiery stream which sets body and soul aglow when it is drunk. The ivy, on the other hand, seemed to be cool in nature . . . it was used to decorate graves." The demonization of ivy in the Victorian Gothic fantasy can be associated with that era's refusal of Dionysian consciousness. As a signifier of the "Gothic" and as a Dionysian shadow, ivy lingered on in the films of the inter-war years.[35] In ancient Greece Dionysus was also associated with trees: fig, pine, myrtle. The sacred staff, the *thyrsus* of his followers, was made from the wood of the ivy. With the power to release vital energy, moisture, and growth from seemingly inanimate things, it liberated the pent-up animation of the world. Through Dionysus we are led to a vital rootedness in the earth—dark, wild, and disturbing—but without it we are left with what Jung has called a "sapless" existence: dry, sad, dusty.[36]

What is this madness that Dionysus brings? While his nature is not confined to the vegetable level, it nevertheless has a definite affinity for this green realm. When Dionysus was unwittingly "captured" by some Etruscan pirates and taken to sea, their ship suddenly sprouted vines, a luxuriant growth of ivy entwined itself around the mast, wreaths appeared on all the rowlocks. When the three daughters of King Minyas arrogantly refused Dionysus's call to leave their domestic life and to go celebrate in the mountains, ivy and vines suddenly grew all over their weaving-chairs.

The God appeared as terrifying animals, and the women in their fear and madness cast lots to decide whose child should be offered as a sacrifice. After tearing one of the children to pieces, they roamed over the mountains wreathed in ivy, bindweed, and laurel.[37]

In rejecting a simplistic notion of Dionysus as a vegetation deity, we must be careful not to ignore his deep association with vegetation and vegetative life. Although not connected with annual cycles, Dionysus expresses the primeval miracle of endless, self-sustaining procreation: "He who begets something which is alive must dive down into the primeval depths in which the forces of life dwell. And when he rises to the surface, there is a gleam of madness in his eyes because in those depths death lives cheek by jowl with life. The primal mystery is itself mad."[38]

This vegetate madness springs directly from the word *vegere*, meaning to animate, invigorate, arouse. In his lucid style Otto writes:

> The primeval world has stepped into the foreground, the depths of reality have been opened, the elemental forms of everything that is creative, everything that is destructive, have arisen, bringing with them infinite rapture and infinite terror. . . . The form in which the truth appears is the frenzied, all-engulfing torrent of life. . . . Rocks split open . . . everything that has been locked up is released. The alien and the hostile unite in miraculous harmony. Age-old laws have suddenly lost their power.[39]

We are vividly reminded of the swift engulfment of whole cities by the jungle at Angkor Wat or in Central America. The Italian explorer Fosco Maraini encountered this vegetable madness deep in Himalayan valleys:

> The valleys . . . were hot and wet, full of a voracious, imperious or cunning, aggressive or insinuating vitality. . . . Night is even more alive than day. . . . You seem to be surrounded by strange secretions; you feel the touch of strange breath upon you; invisible desires and terrors entwine themselves into the dense tissue of branches, leaves and soil . . ., death

is decomposition, a minor, unimportant phase in the cycle of living; it is the state which permanently gives nourishment to the vortex of new lives.[40]

Here are the simultaneous roar and deafening silence of Nature, the violent urgency of vegetable life, the raging compulsion of vegetative creation, the pandemonium of chaos and order, the ecstasy of heaven and earth united.

Dionysus had numerous vegetable surnames: "the tree-god," or "he in the tree," or names such as Phleon, Phleus, or Phloios, that connected him with vegetable "luxuriance and growth."[41] Above all he was connected with the life-giving moisture, "the element in which the primal mysteries of all life dwell."[42] This element includes not only the waters of the earth but also the juices of fruits, the sap of plants, and all bodily juices and moistures.

To refuse the call of Dionysus, to scorn his divinity (whether due to its excess, its madness, or his "effeminate" weakness that could not even protect the God himself from madness, dismemberment, and death), or to attempt to voyeuristically view his sacred rituals with detached aloofness brings only madness and destruction. Pentheus, the disbeliever, tried to watch the mysteries from a position high in a tree, but was discovered and torn to pieces by his own mother and her sisters.[43]

PAN

The other great male divinity of Nature in classical Greece was the goat-god Pan. The specific quality of "Nature" inhabited by Pan was "uncultivated wilderness": "dells, grottos, water, woods and wilds."[44] This landscape was both physical and psychic. "This Pan nature is no longer an idyllic display for the eye, something to walk through or long back to for sweetness. Nature as Pan is hot and close, his hairy animal smell, his erection. . . . To grasp Pan as nature we must first be grasped by nature, both 'out there'

. . . and 'in here.' "[45] The fabled death of Pan signaled the end to this way of experiencing Nature. We no longer hear Nature call us, no longer acknowledge the God creatively, insistently, compulsively, bodily. Instead we experience Pan in nightmares, rape fantasies, panic attacks. "With Pan dead, so too was Echo: we could no longer capture consciousness through reflecting within our instincts. . . . Stones became only stones—trees, trees."[46] The Gods vanished from the sensual presence of Nature and reappeared as psycho-physical "symptoms."

The *Anima Mundi* as signified by Pan has much in common with the substance and materiality of Reich's orgone vision.[47] Through Pan we once again connect with the fullness of our instinctual kinship with all forms of life. Pan joins 'in here' with 'out there'; he "keeps these reflections from falling into disconnected halves where they become the dilemma of a nature without soul and a soul without nature, objective matter out there and subjective mental processes in here."[48] Our psycho-physical symptoms, such as panic, are attempts to heal this split. Not only do they force a reconnection between fantasy and body, soul and instinct, the subjective and objective worlds, in here and out there, but they also remind us that from the perspective of Pan such a dichotomy is alien—an insult.

> This reality cannot be borne home in abstract concepts. Nature's metaphor is concrete and shaped. It must be felt, sensed, visioned in the actual, very real experience of hair and hooves. We must be paralyzed and suffocated by this reality . . . through the nightmare the reality of the natural God is revealed.[49]

The denigration of Pan as Christianity's shadow, its Devil, and the subsequent ambivalence toward him are indicators of each era's fantasy of body, instinct, sex.

APOLLO

At first it may seem that the realm of Apollo, perhaps the most "spiritual" of all the deities, stands almost in direct opposition to everything we know about "Nature" or "vegetable" life. But, if all the Gods have a vegetative aspect, where and what is Apollo's? In some ways, given the dominance of an idealized Apollonic fantasy in our culture—its physical sciences, laws, morality, medicine, religions, and psychologies—it could be argued that an understanding of Apollo's relationship to the "natural" world is the most important of all. If there is no way out of a myth, only ways deeper into it, then we must delve into Apollo's difficult relationship to vegetable life.

Like Dionysus and Pentheus, or Aphrodite and Adonis, or Artemis and Actaion, Apollo is linked to a number of minor figures who suffer a tragic fate through their relationship with him. Hyakinthos, who resembled Adonis, was much loved by Apollo. But he was accidentally killed by Apollo's discus. From the blood of the victim sprang the hyacinth, a wild flower with dark blue blossoms. Another boy, named Kyparissos or Cypress, unintentionally killed a stag that was sacred to Apollo and Artemis. As he loved the creature, Kyparissos was inconsolable. All that Apollo could do was to offer to transform his friend into a sorrowing tree, the evergreen cypress. There was also Apollo's sexual union with the nymph Dryope, daughter of Dryops, the "Oak-Man." She used to play with the Hamadryades, the oak-nymphs.[50] But perhaps the best known of Apollo's liaisons was with Daphne. Resisting his passionate advances, she fled until it seemed her capture was inevitable. At that moment she begged Mother Earth to save her and was transformed into a laurel, which from that time became Apollo's favorite tree whose branches he wore as wreaths.[51]

The Apollonic perspective finds its "ground," its connection to the earth and vegetative realm, in these stories, however tentative and unsatisfactory they may seem. Accidental death, unsuccessful rape, mistaken murder, and deceptive seduction scarcely seem "divine" ways of manifesting vegetative life. But we are in the realm of myth, not literal reality. Hillman, in a somewhat Dionysian mood, interprets the Daphne story negatively: "Apollo pursuing Daphne, is self-defeating because it hyperactivates the male, driving the psyche into vegetative regression, Daphne into a laurel tree."[52] But we cannot assume Apollo has done something wrong. Artemis is not to be judged for her treatment of Actaion, nor Dionysus for the fate of Pentheus, nor Aphrodite for the tragic death of Adonis. Like the rape of Persephone, these events *must* be: they belong to the deities. Apollo has to chase Daphne, who has to flee and be changed into a tree; Hyakinthos has to be killed and his blood produce the hyacinth, and so on.

We need to look more closely at Daphne's tale, for it could hold the secret to Apollo's elusive vegetative nature. Such an understanding is of some urgency given that the unrecognized shadow of the Apollonic ideal has had dreadful consequences for all vegetative life, whether in "Nature" out there or in the individual's mind and body.[53]

Daphne was a daughter of the river-god Ladon and of Earth. She was therefore intimately a creature of Nature; indeed, she was "a wild virgin like Artemis, who herself, as Daphnaia or Daphnia, had her own sacred laurel-trees."[54] Daphne was not the only Artemis-like female for whom Apollo experienced an intense desire. There was also Kyrene: "She was a virgin huntress, a figure resembling Artemis. . . . It was told that Artemis gave her two hunting dogs."[55] Apollo carried her off, and she bore him a son, Aristaios, "a Zeus, a holy, undefiled Apollon, . . . the best god of all . . . [a] second Apollon. . . ."[56] The desire that Apollo experienced so intensely was therefore a form of brother–sister incest, albeit displaced. It is the Artemisian aspect of "Nature" that Apollo longs for, longs to embrace, possess. Both Apollo and his sister Artemis are unapproachable, distant, pure. Both act from afar. Both "disappear" for long periods: Artemis to her solitudes and wilderness, deeper into pristine Nature; Apollo for part of the year to the fabulous, secret, and distant land of the Hypoboreans. Apollo is drawn to *pristine* Nature, which, despite his blood connection to it, must by its very definition retreat from him. Although so intimately close, the purity and sublimity of this brother and sister are in fact poles apart.

This incestuous desire and attraction are also mirrored in Apollo's relation to Hyakinthos and Kyparissos. Kerényi writes: "In all these tales the beautiful boys are doubles of Apollon himself."[57] Apollo can only desire the most sublime and pure, which is of course himself or those most like him. The destructive aspect of such enclosed love is all too obvious in the stories, but in each case a vegetative transformation occurs. Also, despite the sorrow, violence, and melancholy that accompanies it, each of these transformations leaves Apollo spiritually satisfied. So, he loves and praises the tree into which Daphne has changed, raising it to the crown of his head as a wreath in remembrance of her, his sister substitute. It would seem that Apollonic consciousness (perhaps imagined as the scientific spirit) searches for, is bewitched by, and desires to possess the intimate soul of pristine, pure, untamed Nature.

The subsequent transformation is not a vegetable regression but a statement of pure spirituality, albeit in a form that is untouchable by Apollo. The spiritual is not alien to vegetative life; indeed Jung, when discussing a dream of a woman's metamorphosis into a tree, wrote: "the life of the plant is in us . . . and in us it becomes the symbol for a non-biological quality, for what we call spiritual." Not only is the tree firmly rooted, but also its growth, like that of the spirit, "is steadily upward."[58] Through the laurel, the Apollonic spirit touches the ground. The laurel, along with the cypress and hyacinth, is the all too tentative, but no less sublime, earth-end of the aloof Apollonic spirit.

Under the attention of Apollonic consciousness, pristine Nature, in the form of Daphne, is forced to go deeper into herself and must call on the more ancient Earth Mother for assistance. Like Persephone's, this relationship to the Earth Mother reveals hitherto unseen psychological depths. Apollo finally gazes in awe and reverence at the purest expression of untamed Nature—the tree itself. He departs satisfied with the transformation, for he has witnessed the supreme manifestation of his "sister's" epiphany, her enigma, her hallowed purity, her sublime spirituality. Here we are in the presence of the Nature mystics, including the scientifically inclined Goethe and Swedenborg.

Apollo is present when Saturnian concerns with symmetry or with geometrical patterns in Nature, such as crystals, leaf forms, or atomic structure, become the springboard for lofty spiritual revelations. For example, Jung displays this Saturnian–Apollonic conjunction when he observes that a tree in cross-section forms a mandala or image of psychic wholeness.[59] Maraini shows a reverence for Apollonic nature in the ice-fields of the Himalayas: "Up here we are in a realm of ice and clarity, of ultimate and primordial purity . . . night is nothing but light and space. . . . Time and matter seem to no longer exist. Hence death immediately suggests eternity. . . . Up here night has the solemn, crystalline dignity of the great truths. . . ."[60] Maraini significantly contrasts this vision with the tumultuous, Dionysian expression of Nature in the steaming valley below.

Nor can we exclude the contributions that the findings of botany, biology, physics, chemistry, and other Apollonic sciences have made to the spiritual appreciation of Nature. Insight into the sublime geometric laws and patterns of vegetative life has been a direct result of the Apollonic vision. But the imaginal substance, the soulful materiality, of the living form eludes the Apollonic perspective, and hence Nature remains forever virginal. I am reminded of a man, a scientist, who devoted his life to finding the "secret" of Nature. He suddenly became caught up in environmentalism, particularly the preservation of wilderness regions. He pursued this aim relentlessly, and part of him longed to step out of his "intellectual," "objective" shell and directly touch the wilderness in all its sensual materiality. Although this encounter eluded him, he nevertheless had what could be described as a number of mystical experiences. But gradually he slipped into abstraction; the wilderness, like the laurel, became only a revered but indirect symbol, rather than a sensual reality to be appreciated directly. The "thing" itself became lost.[61]

A poem by Abraham Cowley (1618–1667), "Ode Upon Dr.

Harvey," dedicated to the discoverer of the circulation of the blood, sums up both the desire and the vain arrogance of Apollonic consciousness:

> Coy Nature (which remain'd, though aged grown,
> A beauteous virgin still, enjoy'd by none,
>   Nor seen unveil'd by any one),
> When Harvey's violent passion she did see,
>   Began to tremble and to flee,
> Took sanctuary, like Daphne, in a tree. . . .
>   She spoke, but ere she was aware,
>   Harvey was with her there. . . .[62]

Despite its pretentious claims, Apollonic consciousness can only respectfully approach, neither enter nor embrace, the Artemisian aspect of Nature. Nevertheless, Apollonic consciousness can reveal its own kind of sublimity in Nature. Following his edict to "know thyself," Apollo reveals Nature in a process of "knowing" itself, disclosing its spirituality to itself. However, the Apollonic approach to the untouched purity of material Nature always seems painful and violent, wounding both to the God (or his likenesses) and to Artemisian Nature. Apollo's connection to vegetative life is full of sorrow and melancholic tragedy, as well as triumph and spirit. "Spiritual" and "Natural" are the polarities that evoke fantasies of somehow being outside of psyche, of escaping its complex paradoxes, its shadowy corners, its bottomless relativizing. Both polarities seem to offer hope of attaining to something absolute, a tangible truth. Perhaps only this apparent wound to pristine Nature can earth the Apollonic spirit and force some kind of psychological reflection.

We cannot leave Apollo without commenting upon the reverse of the displaced brother–sister relationship. Aristaios—the second, "undefiled" Apollo, the son of Apollo and Kyrene (an Artemis figure)—in turn had a son, Actaion. It was this same Actaion who, after stumbling across Artemis bathing naked, was transformed by her into a stag and torn to pieces by his own hounds. Actaion, a secondary Apollo figure, intrudes upon pristine Nature. But unlike the case of Apollo and Daphne, it is the

Apollonic figure, rather than the Artemisian one, that must undergo suffering, transformation, and initiation. In each case, the Artemis–Apollo polarity is sustained as both Artemisian consciousness (Daphne) and Apollonic consciousness (Actaion) are in turn forced to manifest in the most pure and fundamental expression of their natures.

We should also note in passing that Actaion's aunt was Semele, the mother of Dionysus, which illustrates the interweaving of all of the Gods and Goddesses and shows how false it is to isolate any one of them, labeling this one a "Nature" God and that one not. Each of the deities is an invitation to a deep appreciation of the plurality of the vegetable soul. We can see each deity as an aspect of vegetabling.

CHAPTER FIVE
Vegetables in Dreams

FROM THE RATIONAL TO THE VEGETABLE SOUL

Cabbage-heads

A thirty-year-old woman dreams:

I am in prison, feeling hopeless. Long dark corridors stretch out like underground tunnels. Then it becomes a P.O.W. camp. The soldiers are listless and depressed. There are lots of browns, greens, and greys, especially in their uniforms. I suddenly notice that their heads are all cabbages. It becomes a field of cabbages.

A standard cabbage interpretation would indicate boredom or a fear of just vegetating and so on. But perhaps it wasn't the dreamer who was imprisoned, who was the victim of war, but the cabbages and the other vegetable imaginings. In many ways this dream marked my initiation into a consciousness of the vegetable soul. I only just resisted the seduction of well-trod interpretative routes, scarcely hearing the muffled cry of the humble(d) cabbage entrapped within the prison of psychological orthodoxy, scarcely able to acknowledge the wisdom of the vegetable.

This dream is about roots, about immobility, loss of will—about the slow downwardness of the vegetable soul. The dream gives back to the head its cabbage, the stillness of an earthy reverie. Ares and the hero are grounded. Surface conflict is replaced by immobility, with which comes awareness of an underworld. Individuality seems lost in the uniform(ity). Then the cabbage is revealed. Like the ancient mysteries at Eleusis, the darkest moment, the presence of psychic and physical death, summons vegetative divinity, raising it to the crown.

I can remember some years ago, during a challenging but personally difficult time, staying in a small country cottage that was surrounded by rolling fields of cabbages. Stepping outside during the warm summer nights, I experienced the immense blanket of stars above, while all around the pungent, compulsive smell of a thousand breathing cabbages pulled my imagination downward into the earth. Ponge writes of plants at night exhaling carbon dioxide like an endless sigh of contentment, like a continuous bass note in music.[1]

A man in his early thirties dreams:

> I am cooking a head in a large cauldron of soup with vegetables. I'm looking down into it. Other people look and turn away in disgust. I continue to stir, then get nauseated and have to throw it out.

Here is vegetable alchemy at work, an elixation of the rational soul: seething, cooking, boiling. After abandoning a professional career and following a lengthy "drop-out" period of self-examination and spiritual questing, the dreamer wanted to get "a-head," to reengage with the world, albeit in a more meaningful way than before. Such a "reentry" is always a difficult time of transformation. In the dream he is *cooking a-head:* moving forward slowly, in a vegetable, digestive way; looking downward and into the process, not upward and out. The only movement is circular, a stirring. Other characters gather and look. The dreamer is drawn into their view, feels their nausea, thereby loses the vegetable ground, and abandons the opus. He can't *stomach* the *sight.* The head abruptly abandons its place in the cauldron-stomach. The vegetable-head, the vegetable-view, is thrown out in disgust.

It's not easy for the "higher" faculties, or souls, to come down and admit their interdependence with the vegetable level—that our plans and ideals intimately coexist with intestinal tracts, gastric juices, and nervous disorders, whether literal or metaphorical. Where such visceral matters cannot be successfully made pleasant or sanitized, society has pushed them disdainfully downward and outward to the half-hidden periphery of its "civilized" world.

Another dreamer finds himself inside a police headquarters listening, along with some underworld leaders, to a naive but overconfident police chief describing his methods. It seems that the main problem he has is one of "hiding police on the beat." The gangsters call such police "carrots." Instead of the wolf disguised as a sheep, here we have the senex disguised as a carrot or vice-versa. Is this the carrot-lure of acclaim and promotion dangling before the eyes? Or is it the upright citizen or the phallic carrot penetrating the earth with its bright redness? Perhaps it is the mercurial carrot pointing the way downward? But the disguise is to no avail. The leaders of the underworld are privy to the plans and schemes of law and order; they can see through them.

View from the Backyard

A young woman dreams she is waiting in a back garden to see a video of her spiritual guru. She is leaning against the fence and wonders how she will be able to see from where she is standing. "Then a blond curly-haired man, with blond beard and pearly teeth, turned to me and said that he thought this a strange city because they allowed intellectually disabled people to mix with others." The dreamer vehemently disagrees.

Vegetables are traditionally consigned to the backyard. The intellectually disabled, often dismissed as human vegetables, are pushed, fearfully, disdainfully, to the back wards, perhaps not so much literally anymore, but certainly in terms of psychological recognition and financial support.[2] It is indeed difficult to see the guru from these backyards of our psyches. When the dreamer tries to peer over the fence, across the well-defined boundary, an Apollonic caricature appears. This too white shadow figure of a too pure spirituality is summoned by the dreamer's attempt to see the spirit from the backyard and hence to connect, perhaps to confuse, these two realms.[3] The white-shadow is disturbed by the soulful promiscuity of the place; he wants to preserve a spiritual/psychological apartheid. Faced by a clear image of her spiritual shadow, the dreamer reasserts the validity of all the imaginal characters.

A thirty-year-old male professional dreams of the working-class area of the city where his parents live. In fact, for many years he has been living far away from his parents, although a short time before having the dream he had made a lengthy trip to see them. In the dream the general area where his parents live is portrayed as "ruined, broken-down":

> Some areas have been cleared and are like allotments. We own quite a few. They are roughly planted with vegetables. My parents are very proud of these plots. It's what they have acquired over the years, the family land, although I'm not sure if it's officially theirs. Anyway, what a terrible place to have it—still the same old environment and they aren't really growing anything. Same old pretentious but sad place.

The dreamer returns to his wounded and rejected roots. But they have already begun to be digested, "broken-down," in his psyche. Despite his absence, the vegetable soul continues its work in the depths. Although he is scornful, some of these regions have been cleared and transformed into allotments. Vegetables are growing. For better or worse, this is his family land, his ancestral earth. We have already referred to Jung's favorable comments on allotments. These crucial places in the urban backyard are where the working-class city-dweller can once again touch the earth. This is not an out-front act of instant suburban beautification but takes place slowly, in the odd corners, generally out of sight.

Four years later the same man, after a particularly difficult but also rewarding period, again dreams of his parents:

I am dying. A cold tomb-like grey is all-pervading. No one seems to care. I am alone and ignored even though in a crowded public baths. Then I'm with my parents. They seem indifferent. I am in the backyard. It is night and very dark. My father gives me a torch. It is very feeble and barely of any use to find my way.

The return to his ancestral roots is experienced as a dying. But at this dark night of the soul a poignant encounter takes place in the back garden, a transmission of wisdom, of light, from father to son. It seems feeble and scarcely of any use, but it's all he has and perhaps all his father can give.

A young woman dreams of her family home as it was when she was an adolescent and the parents were going through an unexpected and traumatic divorce. At the time of the dream the woman was living overseas, trying to start a new life in another country:

I am in the backyard. I feel very sad at how rundown everything is and remember how we used to play here as children. Then I notice some vegetables—carrots and turnips—hanging in rows as if tied onto a washing-line.

Later in the dream she goes to a large tub that has been left outside and is full of murky water:

I look closely into the tub and, rather nervously, I roll up my sleeve and put my arm into the tub. To my surprise I start pulling on a string to which are tied, one after another, a number of aubergines (eggplants).

Although the family breakdown had been acknowledged on one level, this was extremely superficial. The deep wound within each family member remained unworked and scarcely articulated. The result was psychological uncertainty, insecurity, restlessness. There seemed to be an unbridgeable rupture through each person's memory, a chasm between "before" and "after." Little was said. The whole question remained alive but unresolved, held—like the backyard vegetables—high above the ground, in a state of suspension. The restless young woman was acutely aware of the dilemma. For years she had wearily and protectively held a crucial part of herself back from a full involvement and commitment to her circumstances. But now she had reached a critical time and, rolling up her sleeves, was bravely trying to get on with the task of finding a "place," both metaphorically and geographically. Aubergines were not a part of her childhood and represented a completely new taste, one that she had discovered herself. Here was a new "line" of approach to the question of her roots, to the wound in her vegetable soulfulness, one that seemed to hold a fuller, richer, more mysterious and enticingly darker promise than before.

In the dream the root vegetables are strung-out, suspended clear of their "home" in the earth. Yet the painful memories do find a place to express themselves—in the backyard. Here she can find her "roots," although they, like her, are in exile.

Vegetables draw us into the backyards of the psyche, close to the compost, the washing-line, the gossip over the fence, the intimate other side of the family facade out-front. Backyards are close to the kitchen, "the alchemical stomach of the house where the *pepsis* (digestion) goes on, turning the raw into the cooked."[4] Here we find the melancholy wisdom of the back porch; the young child's playground; wistful, nervous longings; family gatherings; family rows.

Coming Down

Encountering the Vegetable World

There are many ways of being brought down to "earth." We can be thrown, lured, seduced, or just suffer a fall. Frequently coming down requires a strong blast:

Somewhere deep in the South American jungle is a large hotel resort. There are many European types in formal evening wear promenading around a raised quadrangle. On three sides are the hotel rooms, while on the fourth is a low wall. It is twilight and a woman exclaims, pointing over the low wall. I look and see a fearsome sight. A tornado is approaching fast from the jungle. Everyone panics and tries to get indoors. I realize I can't make it, and seeing a manhole I lift the cover and climb down the stairs into the darkness. Safe from the tornado, but what's down there? What about the rats?

As if tempting fate, the dreamer promenades in the middle of the jungle, lifted clear of the earth, in formal evening wear. The creatures of the dark are not amused and certainly not impressed by this over-cultured attempt to claim and civilize the vegetal night. From the untamed vegetative depths, on the back of a terrible storm, through the "low," unprotected side of the psyche comes Pan or Dionysus. The dreamer is forced to descend rapidly, fearful of the creatures that live down there.

Vegetable and animal kingdoms are intertwined, inseparable. Individual plants harbor bugs that incessantly creep and gnaw their way into our lives; beneath our kitchens and our food cupboards, around our garbage, in our sewerage live rats, mice, cockroaches; in the grass there are snakes; in the jungle, tigers; and in the forest, wolves. We are food to these creatures, and in this age of ecological degradation they are usually very hungry. "Not only do bugs invade your realm," writes Hillman, "they also live off your property and share your body, thriving on your vegetative roots. . . ."[5]

Detour on Habitats

We could, of course, discuss the other myriad vegetative dream-contexts in which we may find ourselves: forests and woods (places of refuge and retreat, of profit and destruction, as well as of fear); plantations and orchards; swamps, bogs, and marshes; meadows, cornfields, botanical gardens, flower gardens; moorland, heath, and tundra. The list goes on and can take us far from our prime concern in this chapter: to stay as close as possible to the humble vegetable in its most mundane aspect. Also, many of these other vegetative contexts will occur, and be considered, when we look at folktales and other literature.

But they are vital to a consideration of the contemporary ecological circumstances, as one unique habitat after another comes under threat and vanishes, taking with it myriad fauna and flora. How can we suppose that the psyche, supported for generations by its daily contact with such places, will not be aware of and mourn their elimination from the *Anima Mundi*? Ancient woods, old grasslands, bogs, heaths, and commons are also part of our ecological heritage, repositories of ancestral habits, crucial doorways into *memoria*.[6] Historical ecology takes its place alongside archeology as a vital metaphorical field for imaginal psychology. In a like manner we should not be so quick to discard our unwanted habits/habitats, to replace them with something that is more efficient, cleaner, supposedly better for us. These annoying habits ground us, pull us back and down. They are our home and the place where our complexes flourish.[7]

Enough has surely been suggested to banish forever that curse of naive interpretation: the reduction of any mass of vegetation, any expansive patch of earth, into a general symbol of the "unconscious" or of the "natural," all imaginal discrimination lost, plurality homogenized (usually under the groaning form of the "Great Mother," burdened as she is with anything that is vaguely green, dark, earthy, fertile, growing, or vegetal).

Checking the Roots

A man in his late twenties dreams he is at a gathering of people in a farming countryside:

The place has a strange familiarity about it. As we talk I notice some vegetables growing amid some weeds and grass. I reach down and pull up a bunch of celery. The celery is planted in a neat, single line. I remember planting it about five years ago. I also remember buying this land then, when I was going through a psychological crisis. I say to myself that this line of celery *is* the existential question. Next to it is a shorter, parallel row of celeriac, which I say is the *answer* to the previous question. I am enthusiastic, but I wonder if this land and its little cottage are still mine. Although the property is not very large, I feel a nostalgic attraction when I remember buying it just as I was coming out of my depression all those years ago. Do I still own it, or have I lost it through neglect?

After years of neglect, misuse, forgetfulness comes the crucial question: are the roots still available to me? Are they still mine? We may well have found them, have reconnected, but what is their condition?

Just as the dreamer was beginning to emerge from a depression, he attempted to establish roots, saw the need for a piece of land, some imaginal ground and a place to dwell, no matter how small. In this imaginal soil he planted the seeds of both the question and answer to a profound dilemma. This is vegetative spirituality: the answer lies in the soil. Literal depression is replaced by vegetative consciousness—an awareness and care of the vegetable soul. Although this moment was lost, the seeds continued to grow of their own accord, unheeded, neglected.

Here is an imaginal tangibility to which the dreamer can return, the psyche revealing the active basis for our vegetable faith. It is the celery that first catches his eye: upright, cool, crisp, a fresh green, vaguely medicinal, still showing above the obscuring weeds. Next he sees the celeriac: the same taste as celery, but a bulbous root, belonging below the ground, its skin convoluted, often dirt-encrusted and difficult to clean or to peel. An unfashionable vegetable when compared with celery, at least for the dreamer's Anglo-Saxon culture. Question and answer belong to the same family, have the same taste, are vegetable-kin. The one reaches upward while the other points down; the one is tall, clean, and straight, the other fat, dirty, and lumpy. Neither seems much affected by the dreamer's quick, nervous enthusiasm. Their seasons and moods are steadier, quieter, perhaps even serene.

In a dream a man in his mid-thirties is with his ex-wife:

We are exploring the overgrown ruins of an old country house of ours. It is all very green and damp. Initially I have a slight fear of snakes. It feels like an archeological investigation.

Time and again we find ourselves returning to the abandoned ruins of earlier social relationships, only to find them overgrown, weeds inhabiting the cracks between the stones. Like the sight of a miniature Angkor Wat, the vegetable kingdom returns, reasserts itself, becomes visible through the places we have abandoned, the loci of our failures and wounds. With the return of the vegetable world come other creatures; the ground feels unsafe, uncertain, tricky, alien, dangerous. But a new life is emerging: green, damp, sinuous.

Regaining Body

A man in his early thirties dreams:

There is the body of a rather heavy man in the fridge. He is frozen solid so he must have been in the freezer along with the packets of frozen vegetables. I want him removed. There is something repulsive and gross about it. A green plastic garbage bag is left.

The dreamer is deeply involved in spiritual and psychological questioning. The body has been put into cold storage, into deep freeze. Along with the packets of homogenized, mass-produced vegetables, the body is kept under plastic wraps. Both the plastic and the freezing contain fantasies of immortality, indestructibility, incorruptibility. But the spirit has become too extreme, revealing its shadow side: the body/vegetables are in suspended animation, removed from their seasonal rhythms. This lofty, icy, spiritual vision often finds something disturbingly gross about the vegetable soul. Earthy, clumsy, slow, immobile, basic, intestinal, digestive, seemingly dull-witted, the vegetable soul can evoke and confirm all the prejudices that the spirit, in its quest for transcendence, has about materiality and body.

A Gross Detour

Gross exists in contrast with *refined*. The civilizing process has been the determined quest for refinement and the relentless banishment of grossness. Education, alchemy, art, and psychotherapy have been in the vanguard of this relentless transformation of the gross to the refined.

But nowhere has this process been more explicit than in the realm of food: its production, cooking, and consumption. The slow and painful quest by the aspiring social classes for ever more refined table manners and bodily habits has pushed so-called grossness to the "lower" end of the social spectrum or else has kept it hidden: all that is coarse, scurrilous, rank, indecent, thick. The result in matters of cuisine is well-known: fine white sugar, fine white flour, white rice, and so on—the elevation of aptly called haute cuisine above unrefined food.

The consequences of the remorseless pursuit of refinement at the expense of grossness has become apparent in recent years: a suffering and morbidity of the body—various intestinal cancers, diseases of the heart and other major organs, obesity, gum disease, hyper-activity—not to mention the array of social, even global and colonial, problems associated with fast, instant foods. As food and manners become more "purified" and "refined," the individual body, the body politic, and the body of the world (the eco-body) become more gross and dis-eased. Grossness now has to be deliberately reintroduced: unrefined grains and sugar and high-fiber diets.

But "grossness" is still not truly accepted; it's still refused its place. Safely packaged and contained within the refinements of "health" and "diets," grossness is subsumed under "whole food," "whole grain." Bodily/imaginal grossness is packaged and contained within therapy sessions, refined and explained within "regression" therapy and fantasies of purification. Coarseness has become refined through the fashionable use of natural fibers. In its raw state, grossness is tolerated, perhaps even admired at a distance, in comedians, children, animals, "primitives," the intellectually handicapped (developmentally delayed), and in various psycho-pathological disturbances. In the dream the garbage bag, although plastic, is green. Does this point to the vegetable origins of plastic (refined from decaying plant to oil to infinite malleability)? Is the image of green plastic a well-measured irony? Does it indicate an awakening of vegetable-body within the plastic-coated psyche?

A thirty-year-old woman dreams she is with a male friend. They are both somewhat "hippy" and "alternative" in their lifestyles. They are talking in an empty room in a brand new, rather flashy, pink-decorated, and pretentious hotel. She had previously bought some perfume which, though cheap, appealed to her. As she leans toward her companion, a "very large tube" drops to the floor from under his sarong. "A thick green liquid" leaks out from it. He is undisturbed, but she quickly points out that "the liquid was running all over the carpet." He nonchalantly apologizes and says it's just his colostomy.

Upwardly aspiring, materialistically assertive yuppiedom and laid-back, spiritually inclined hippydom meet in a bizarre but archetypally not unexpected conjunction.[8] In its own way each style is out of touch with body; each simply uses materiality for its own "ideals," shunning its dark melancholy, its coarse earthiness. The vegetable-body reasserts its presence in a particularly gross way, quickly bringing the vision downward, staining the pastel pinks with thick green, digestive liquid. Perhaps the sap is returning?

An intellectually inclined man dreams:

> I am invisible. How can I get back to the body from a disembodied voice? I remember something to do with the earth. The nitrogen deficiency? I get a fluid made up. I can't take it orally, but I can rub it on.

Only intimate contact with the imaginal earth makes us visible. Without it we are disenfranchised exiles, part of the great invisible, homeless population of the planet: refugees, street kids, vagrants, émigrés. We can have a body or a place but no voice, or a voice but no body. Perhaps as hopeful wanderers we can take delight in the freedom such invisibility brings, but this is short-lived unless we can find our imaginal ground: an earth that sustains and nourishes us, that gives us a place. "To be human," writes Edward Relph in his classic study of placelessness, "is to have and know your place."[9] We have to em-body our voice, give it its ground. But perhaps this earth lacks nutrients? The cure cannot be taken orally—i.e., through disembodied speech—but must be rubbed on, in a bodily way, like ointment, or body paint, or dirt.

Feeling the Earth

It is twilight, on the border between town and country. Everywhere is muted grey and green. I am with a group of thin, grey, muted people going to a ritual in a depression in the ground. I realize I have been marked for death, as have all these people. One part of the mournful ritual consists in symbolically pouring earth on ourselves. I panic and try to leave, but a sort of spherical force-field prevents me. It is inevitable and indeed has already begun.

The dreamer, a man in his thirties, is in the final stages of what has been an intensely painful personal crisis. Paradoxically, as one part of him emerges at last into the dayworld, the underworld permanently claims a part for itself. Like Persephone, the dreamer must acknowledge this claim. As in many traditional mourning rituals, participants immerse themselves in the earth, pouring it over themselves in an act of humility and of empathy with the corpse as it returns to its home. "The vegetable soul in man . . . returns to its origin, there to blend and be lost, not to survive there autonomously."[10]

An enthusiastic young man deeply involved in alternative, "Eastern" spirituality dreams:

I am carrying water in the desert when I meet a monster-ape. He pours out the water. Then he picks up a handful of black peat-bog and says: "This is from Mother Nature. Drink/take this."

"Carrying water" and "deserts" are almost spiritual clichés, particularly in the ascetic puer regions of "East–West" religiosity with its inspiration from Sufism, Buddhism, and Christian desert mysticism. A more earthy representative of the psyche throws away the clichés and offers black peat-bog instead.

Such earthy, slightly scornful wisdom can also come from other directions. A man in his late twenties, involved in sixties-style radical social and personal politics, dreams he is being followed through the city by a trampish-looking old man. The dreamer goes to a friend's place but then escapes through the backyard, over the back wall and into the countryside. Then he is with his radical friends in a shack in a wood on the side of a hill:

> I looked out and saw the old man digging with his hands into the earth. He seemed to have found something he had buried. Then he moved to the other side of the shack and dug again. Then to our surprise and outrage he comes in! We all ignore him and continue with our discussion about imperialism and the politics of food. He seems serene, so I go up to him and yell sarcastically: "Are you quite comfortable? Is there anything we can do for you?" He says he agrees with our discussions but thinks we also need the existing system. I argue with him.

Here we have the conjunction and struggle between the grey and the green: age and youth, senex and puer, stability and change. The trampish old man, serene, with his hands searching in the earth; the angry, inspired youth with his ideals up in the hills.

Some years ago, after living for many years in Australia, I had a dream about a return to my origins. This was just one of many such dreams over the years that attempted a reconciliation between the "place" of Australia (my adult home) and the "place" of England (the home of my childhood).

> With another, I return after a long journey and a long absence to our "home" territory. (It's like an Aboriginal attitude to the land.) We had both been in the city and had become "sophisticated." The place is a green English field with many trees and hedges. I remember that at one end of the field is the ruin of a stone platform as in an amphitheater. It is overgrown. We get off a bus, climb a fence, and there it is. We let out a primitive yell of recognition and joy. Suddenly, from out of the bushes come, very slowly, these naked, grey/brown primitive people. They are our family tribe coming out, as if from the earth, to greet us.

Getting off the bus, leaving the road, going over the fence. We have paused from the usual journeyings along the well-defined routes of our lives and have put to one side the restless mobility of modern life. Then we remember our ancestors and sift our way through the ruins of the past. When we find a place to dwell, our ancestors arise from the vegetal depths, from the earth, to greet us. In their founding myth, the ancient Athenians claimed that their ancestors were not settlers but arose directly, growing from the very soil itself. In this way they banished the specter of not belonging—that at bottom we are all placeless. Such fears haunt us as we desperately scan convergences, searching for that depth at which place and archetype coincide.

Of course, one's "origins" are both unfathomably deep and inestimably complex. Too often we prefer to simplify them into naive genealogies, into the stereotypes of racial and nationalistic absurdities, embracing a sentimentalized past, a nostalgia for a more basic life replete with verisimilitudes. Nevertheless, there is a radical, archetypal necessity for the fiction of being in connection with one's roots. The dilemma of the exile, émigré, or emigrant is only a more explicit variant of that facing anyone who has suffered displacement, an abrupt dislocation of past, place, and ancestral purpose. This, as Jung stressed time and again, is the common predicament of modern, Western individuals. From this fracture comes the terrible existential pain of placelessness. But, as so many religions and myths testify, this same experience activates the imaginal imperative for psychological depth, indeed initiates the very call to become psychological.[11] In what way do we belong, or, rather, who in our personality belongs to which places, and which archetypal powers lay their claims upon us? In what imaginal earth shall we find our origins?

Vegetable Water

A dream:

A tribe of "primitive" people living in the desert have a largish lake as a water supply. They change their social behavior to a more "cultivated" and "sophisticated" one. It uses up more water. Will the supply last? It seems as if it's being drained too quickly.

It is naive to believe that we can both "reconnect" with our roots and at the same time continue to live as before. Freud's dominant metaphor was that of the engineer "draining" the marshlands around Rome or reclaiming the Zuider Zee.[12] Ours must now be that of the deep ecologist, listening to the unique habitats, appreciating their richness and their limitations, and estimating precisely what changes they can sustain without suffering irremediable damage.

A thirty-five-year-old man dreams he is among some wooded mountains. A new hotel under construction is nearly completed. It looks to be an unattractive and trendy building:

> It overlooks a very deep crater which is usually full of water. However it is now nearly empty. The construction has used most of it, but it was expected that the hotel would be supplied by it. I ponder the possibility of damming some river but reject it (not that I'm being asked) on aesthetic and ecological grounds. As I look down into the crater I see a huge, magnificent tree that has been chopped down.

Why do we want to "develop" psychologically? Above all, who wants to? These are fundamental questions. Is it ecologically and aesthetically sustainable, let alone morally justifiable? Much of the rhetoric of contemporary psychotherapy dovetails perfectly with that of development: industrial, building, economic. The psyche, with its myriad habitats, fauna and flora—not to mention dispossessed characters and oppressed cultures—is simply viewed as a "free," ever available resource. The view is too narrow, too simple, too arrogant, and, basically, unsustainable.

In a long involved dream, a man becomes aware of a dangerous build-up of salinity in the water. It has been caused by a malfunction in a highly sophisticated submarine used for the underwater inspection of ships' hulls:

> I stand with a farmer on top of a hill. His plants won't grow. He blames the trees which are around but some way off. I protest so as to protect the trees. Someone asks if the surrounding countryside will be brown and dead soon. I say yes, although it is hard to believe because everywhere looks so green. The farmer moves quickly to try to do something about the salt. He goes to his pumping room, which has black slime and mud everywhere. What will he do? By pumping perhaps he can adjust the balance? Will he flush using fresh water?

Vegetable water is not only "natural" but also includes drainage, supply, and irrigation.[13] Despite the appalling record of modern "literal" farmers in environmental matters, they are, like the foresters with their equally bad record, still a vital metaphorical image of vegetable wisdom.[14] This dangerously high salt content is the result of a onesided over-development—too much senex sophistication.[15] If anyone will correct the salinity, it must be the senex/farmer.

While the dreamer bemoans the view, the farmer points the way and sets to work in the depths, in the pumping room, amid black slime and mud. Perhaps he is right; perhaps the trees do have something to do with it. Perhaps the dreamer is too intent on protecting their vertical, spiritually satisfying growth, replete as this is with metaphors of Self and upward aspiration.[16] Perhaps, like the conifer plantations of the northern Scottish moorlands and peat-bogs, those trees are inappropriate and ultimately destructive for that particular environment.[17]

Reclaiming the Bogs

Habitats, like fauna and flora, are subject to the particular aesthetic currently in vogue. If you are furry and big-eyed then you are lucky, but too bad if you are black, small, and crusty. The same applies in the vegetable world. Tall, majestic trees evoke more conservation sympathy than scraggly weeds. The fashion for "natural" aesthetics is of course the result of complex processes, from archaic myth to capitalist economics, from Protestant use-value to heroic associations. Among the least favored environments are bogs. Interpretation invariably follows the cultural prejudice: bogged-down, stuck in a bleak, black, and useless wasteland, threatened with being sucked down, devoured by its ooze. In the meantime the slightest evidence of a tree proclaims "growth," "potential," "aspiration," and so on. But trees/growth can frequently be entirely inappropriate and harmful for the circumstances.

The bogs of Britain are being afforested with conifers, which are destroying them. Most of the conifers being planted in Scotland are for purposes of tax relief. The problem, of course, is that bogs are not high on the rating of public appeal. They do not easily fit into prevailing environmental aesthetics, despite their unparalleled uniqueness. In this regard they join other "unfashionable" habitats, such as the mulga forests of Australia, whose stumpy, twisted monotony scarcely endears them to the heroic mind for whom straightness and verticality have more appeal. Alas, not only are bogs replete with ancient mythic prejudices while conifers are integral to all that is noble and heroic, but also the latter are more profitable. In contemporary Western culture this is a powerful combination.

Created by the actions of Sphagnum mosses, bogs are constantly growing, extraordinarily complex eco-systems supporting many unique species of creature and plant. They have also proved to be remarkable repositories of ancestral remains, preserving Mesolithic harpoons, Viking ships, and foundations for Bronze Age dwellings, embalming the bodies of victims of ritual sacrifice, and even yielding up evidence that apples were among the earliest of domesticated fruits.

Bogs "breathe." They expand and contract continually depending upon how charged they are with water. Some of the Sphagnum moss plants are ancient. They have been growing and branching in the same spot for hundreds, perhaps even thousands of years. Since 1850, over eighty percent of British bogs have been destroyed—"reclaimed" by drainage for agriculture or forestry. In Ireland the situation is even worse. Virtually all the great raised bogland of central Ireland has been fed into its peat-fueled power stations. The aptly named International Mire Conservation Group have pronounced the peat-bogs of Scotland one of the world's unique eco-systems and have put out urgent calls for their preservation.

Rejuvenating the Earth

A dream is situated in a future time when the Earth has lost many natural qualities:

A "giant man" standing on the Earth catches meteors and hurls them onto the planet so as to rejuvenate the crops. I then skim over beautiful, tranquil purple or lilac fields of crops.

The vegetable world needs the connection with the heavens, depending upon this archetypal relationship in order to rejuvenate. This is an *opus contra naturam*, an "unnatural" work that deliteralizes the vegetal world, thus allowing the play of insight and imagination. From this conjunction "new" crops arise, an imaginal vegetation emerges, as in the alchemist's retort. This process carries, of course, the ever present danger of an over-idealization, an over-spiritualization.

A young woman dreams she is standing with her analyst on the back porch of a rather basic country shack. It is night:

> We were watching the lightning hit the earth in big puffs of fire, and as it hit, a circle of fire would start on the earth. It was fascinating to watch. I'd never seen anything like it before. My analyst was explaining to me what was happening.

After a slightly erotic interlude, she looks again at the fires and sees

> two black figures dancing/darting through the flames. As I watched they changed from human forms to black panthers. I was fascinated. The next moment I found myself in the house fighting with my mother. She told me off for eating all the broccoli and asked if my analyst had eaten yet. I didn't think so and imagined by the way she was carrying on that there was no food left for him.

The dreamer is "fascinated," awe-inspired, by the spectacular transformations that are occurring in front of her. The Earth itself comes alive as it is fired and charged by energy from the heavens. Her own body starts to become eroticized. But she is simply feeding herself and has apparently forgotten that the process itself must be fed, cared for, nourished. Her mother aspect, about which she is extremely ambivalent, comes to remind her and is forcefully resented. Two fundamental parts of her wrestle: a brash, assertive, down-to-earth, working-class mother (with a raunchy sense of humor) and an introverted, introspective young woman, seriously involved in alternative spirituality and the occult. The argument about the broccoli ("it's good for you") reasserts the crucial role of vegetableness in her life: nourishment, support, a sense of place, a care for the environment and for the processes she is involved in.

Saving the Seeds

A forty-year-old man dreams:

I come across a strange plant. It has very large red-brown leaves. A voice tells me it is wild rhubarb. I crouch down very low to inspect the roots where there is a small, black-leather pouch like an old-style money-pouch or rosary-bag. I look inside to find black, dried seeds from the plant.

The plant lures the dreamer downward, to the roots, to the seeds. This is a truly vegetable way of propagation: through the attraction of insects, birds, and animals. The dreamer eventually saves, and carries away to plant, a single seed. The plant lures the dreamer downward to the roots through ancestral fantasies (it is associated with the ancient Celts in the dream), through sex, prayer, ritual, wealth—the scrotum-like pouch filled with blackened seeds preserved through *calcinatio*.

With its temptingly large, green, but poisonous leaves and its strangely purple-colored, astringent-tasting medicinal stem, rhubarb is an underworld plant. In Iranian mythology it was related to the semen of the God Ohrmazd, and from it emerged the first human couple. From China to Europe it has long been credited with a powerful capacity to break down the painful rigidities of constipation. It has a privileged place in absurdist, anti-establishment humor. In the dream, a stern mother figure, who seems to be the gardener, abruptly awakens the dreamer from his reverie, scattering the seed-pods as she brusquely sweeps up around the plant. He is lucky to get and keep a single seed. But it is enough.

A recently married woman is searching for a place to live. It is difficult. The couple has very little money; house prices are extravagantly high; neither she nor her husband has regular work. They are in a strange place, far from friends and family. She dreams that she and her husband are with an attractive young woman and are looking at some plans. The buildings are all very grey, dull, and clinical. Her husband and the young woman seem to be attracted to each other. The dreamer goes off on her own to a plain, basic cafe, where she peels and eats a juicy orange. She spits the seeds into her palm, enjoying the juice. She becomes angry at her husband's behavior and tells him so.

After the romantic build-up to the marriage, the task of finding a house—in which perhaps to start a family—is taking its toll. She seems to have lost her eros and is fearful and angry. The orange brings relief, especially the juice, and it moistens the aridity of planning and decision-making. This process of withdrawal, isolation, reflection, and nourishment ends with the separation of the seeds. Here they are, in the palm of her hand. What is she going to do with them? She confronts the situation and through outrage returns eros to a central place in her relationship.

Sensing the Sap

A man dreams that a group of humans have established themselves in slightly alien surroundings. The people, too, have a degree of "genetic engineering about them," something a bit "plastic":

> A man and a woman ride out to investigate a tree on a hill. They cut it with a large knife to inspect it. Sap pours out, and the beautiful dark woman stands under it as if it were a shower. The man also feels the spray on his face. Then their faces begin to wrinkle and deform. White fungus begins to grow on their faces. They warn the others that the trees contain some property which affects their biology. Apparently a nearby power station is disturbing the trees. What can they do? They can't cut the trees down because doing so would release the spores.

Many people now experience themselves, if not in exile, then as being slightly out of place, slightly artificial, estranged from Nature and from their bodies. Dangerous disturbances seem to be "in the air," acting on us at a distance, through the atmosphere.

These disturbances originate in those very institutions and processes that provide contemporary civilization with its energy and definition.

Many people long for a return to Nature and romantically yearn to bathe in its untouched purity, to anoint themselves in its moistness. But a return to the sap brings the unexpected. Instead of refreshment comes deformation, a wrinkling of the man's and woman's smooth, well-cultivated faces. A white fungus begins to grow on them. This decay wasn't the transformation or growth that was anticipated. Their safe circumstances have been irrevocably changed. Danger lies all around. Nature itself threatens their biology. Are they *too* estranged from the sap? Are they willing to undergo a transformation that brings the underworld growth of decay, rot, fungus? Do they have any choice?

A young woman dreams that she and her friend are preparing for their baptism. They are crushing into a container lots of tomatoes, many of which are getting very ripe and squashy. She remarks how they could turn them into pulp and bottle it. After discussing the technical details of bottling, she jokes with her friend that they could always be baptized with tomato pulp instead of water.

As in the previous dream, here is a vegetable baptism, an initiation into the moisture of the vegetable soul through its sap or pulp. Bottling or preserving fruits and vegetables without sacrificing their moisture is an activity of Hestia's. The dreamer was going through a crucial time in her life when she was withdrawing from a career and trying to establish a "place" that would support her writing. The cool redness of the bottled tomatoes related to her desire to preserve a voluptuous inner resource that she had steadily accumulated over the years.[18] Indeed, it was through her confidence in this interior richness that her decision had come about, a decision that had slightly bemused some of her colleagues. She was certain that the moment was *ripe* for such a move, perhaps even just a little concerned that if she delayed any longer it would become over-ripe.

The Vegetable Wilderness

A man in his mid-thirties dreams he is with a young woman living in a cabin, far from any towns. The country is covered with forests and rocks:

I notice a small lioness near the house. We have a table outside with lots of bits and pieces, including a sack of potatoes and other food, utensils, etc. The young woman is hesitant, but I insist on taking everything into the house so we can take cover if necessary. The lioness isn't threatening, but we pass things into the home. I keep the "cat" off with rolled-up plans or maps. Then the "beast" appears in some rocks behind the house. It is black and white, large, baboon-like, highly intelligent, and ruthless. We stand no chance. Even if we can keep it out, we'll run out of food. I am in despair and fantasize about being ripped apart. We carry on halfheartedly to do what we can.

The dreamer finds himself, puer-like, in a shack in the wilderness. All his kitchen things, like his enthusiasms, are spread outside, vulnerable and exposed. But at the first sign of "danger," he hides behind his senex plans and, overriding his feminine "anima" companion, retreats inside, dragging his sack of potatoes, other food, and kitchen implements with him. But the lioness wasn't threatening, merely announcing her presence. Like some representative of the *genius loci*, a manifestation of Artemis or Dionysus, the cat is calling the dreamer's attention to the soul of the wilderness. His refusal summons a darker, more formidable presence, shattering his fantasies of domestic life in the midst of the wilderness. The vegetative power that has been apparently tamed and contained in sacks of potatoes and kitchen implements is released and confronts him. Now *he* becomes food; he and his fantasies are under threat of being ripped apart, devoured, digested.

"Like a sack of potatoes" is frequently a term of scorn, suggesting mere lumpy bulk, a shapeless inertia, at best a dull but reliable means of sustenance. Such a vegetal insult may be overlooked, perhaps even redeemed, within the domain of Hestia, but domestication is intolerable to Artemis or Dionysus. As the poet Takahashi reminds us: "Inside of one potato/There are rivers and mountains."[19] How formidable must be a whole sack!

A man in his late twenties, living far from his home country, dreams an attractive woman friend shows him some "rough" land on a steep hill outside a city:

It is wooded, with long, unruly grasses. It has no center to it, is scruffy and unattractive to me. I doubt I will be able to grow anything here.

Later he dreams of his homeland, with rich wheat fields and a sense of pastoral abundance.

The dreamer is led outside the city and shown land that lacks coherence and beauty for him. The vegetation is unruly. Doubting its capacity to yield any crops, he retreats into idyllic fantasies of "home." But the place is already growing plants and crops, albeit not what he wants or expects. To the city eye, grass and trees can exist as a vegetal Musak, a mere background, a fill-in that one comes to expect in the country. It just *is*; no one has to plant it. But grass, for example, isn't merely a suburban decoration that somehow extends itself into the country, establishing a pleasant, unbroken continuity between city lawns, parks, and golf courses, and country fields and moorland. Of course it is that, but it is also one of the most important crops grown by farmers. Through its extraordinary variety it imparts green character to places, giving them their uniqueness, binding the soil, regenerating it. The wild places of psyche or the planet are not dead or lifeless. We have to learn to listen to their intense particularity without imposing our own fantasies of "growth" or value upon them.

Totemic Vegetables

In a dream a young mother is organizing a birthday party. All the food is set up outside. It begins to rain, and chaos ensues as she brings the table indoors and attempts to reorganize things.

Cousins arrive unexpectedly, bringing luxury food as gifts—champagne and chocolate. These just add to the clutter and chaos. Meanwhile,

> some children have arrived and are standing at the table eating out in the rain. The most predominant "morsel" being lettuce, whose greenness acts as a decorative cover to the table.

The dreamer then goes to a delicatessen to buy more elaborate food for the party. How serenely lettuce-like is this lettuce, as it quietly gathers the children with its edible pale greenness, a delicate center to the general confusion and the widening search for more extravagant food.

Lettuce has a long pedigree, reaching back to the Middle Kingdom of ancient Egypt. It cools and moistens martial heat. Sacred to Adonis in its fragility, its totemic potency is often overlooked. Of course, the amplifications could be extended to the association made by the ancients between the milky sap of the lettuce and mother's milk, as well as with semen. But the simple aesthetics of the image speak eloquently.

Vegetables are *social* in the fullest sense of the word: cultural, political, religious, ancestral.[20] They gather cultural hopes and fears; they provide a coherence for a group's memories and aspirations. They give expression to a desire for stability and tradition as well as providing symbols of change: potatoes or rice? wheat or maize? cabbages or kohlrabi? The Puritans looking askance at the heretical potato and the Edwardian English nervously perusing the Aphroditic tomato, 1960s hippies and health freaks radiantly chewing through mounds of brown rice, aspiring young trendies of the '70s clustering in celebration around the exotic avocado—each of these groups gathers up a thread of the culture's imagining. From pumpkin pie to Yorkshire pudding, sauerkraut to oatcakes, vegetables bring an imaginal coherence to cultures that goes far beyond merely mundane or secular habits. With their stories, rituals, and images, they are truly totemic—sacred, deeply imaginal. As we gather vegetables and other plants/crops, they simultaneously gather us.

An Australian woman in her mid-thirties dreams she is

younger and traveling in America with a group of young people. She is a little bit disturbed but also reassures herself: "an odd collection, lads that were pretty rough and streetwise but good-natured, joking." They arrive at a "casual, homely style restaurant." On a large table in a big room are "potatoes baked in their jackets." She comments favorably: the dish "instantly eases the stomach pangs" while they are waiting for the other food to arrive.

Then the other dishes started coming: a bowl of thickly cut cucumber with the skin still on—no frills. It looked very fresh, wholesome food. There were great big wooden bowls. Then came bean-sprouts and some mayonnaise in a jar and other salads.

She remembers that she has some leftover salad and tofu (bean curd) from lunch and adds them to the general meal.

And then I thought about nutrition, whether the food had the right balance of protein, and realized the bean-sprouts would balance the other salads and liked the fact that this group didn't seem to go much for meat.

In slightly alien and disturbing surroundings, the woman, who is into an alternative lifestyle and Eastern spirituality, invokes her totemic foods and gathers her known world comfortingly around her. In her daily life she is about to give up her career and embark upon a major change. Although she is outwardly confident and self-sufficient, there are unsettled, uncertain murmurings in the depths. Her dayworld concerns about balance, nutrition, economy are echoed in the dream. The bean-sprouts provide the meal and circumstances with their coherence: they have a lightness, almost to the point of lacking substance; they express a tentative vegetableness that is almost etherealized, dematerialized. Any earthiness in the dream comes from the "large table," the "great big wooden bowls," from the way the vegetables are cut and presented: thick, with their skins, "no frills." Here is the tension: a basic, down-to-earth, matter-of-fact exterior that provides a vessel for the finely tuned spirituality, but which also functions as a bluff, a protection for uncertainty and vulnerability. Bean-sprouts and great wooden bowl complement each other. Around this bowl are gathered both the dreamer's vertical aspirations and her horizontal concerns.

The Gardener

A man in his mid-thirties, who is just emerging from a particularly painful period in his personal life, dreams he has inherited a very large "stately" mansion:

It is old and dark, with endless rooms and corners. I wander through it, looking into different rooms, etc. It is too big for just me, and I'll have to invite others to live here. But then will it be out of my control? I puzzle about this. Then I meet the gardener.

The "new" imaginal spaces that we may come to inhabit as a result of our wounds and vulnerability are a part of our inheritance: we belong there. But these imaginal homes are not vacant dwellings waiting for us as landlords to fill them. They already have their occupants: characters who have been living in these places and caring for them while our attention was firmly engaged up on the surface. In this case the gardener comes to meet the dreamer:

He is a rather dour man in his 40s. I am the new young owner, but he has been working here for years. The gardens are large and encircled by tall, grey walls. Parts are planted with vegetables and others are overrun. I want it tidied up and the vegetables moved. But I realize that at least he is keeping it going and that I should not be over-concerned or over-organizing, etc.

The dour gardener is the psyche's vegetable worker. The fresh young aesthete is offended by the seeming mess and confusion of the vegetable garden. On second thought, realizing that he knows little about such matters and has no time for them, he reluctantly acknowledges that at least the gardener is keeping things going on a vegetative level. Unlike many people who try to "take charge" of their vegetative processes, to clean up their act, get themselves organized—through diet, aerobics, body therapies, home beautifications, civic planning, wilderness experience weekends, and so on—the dreamer is prepared to make contact with, and then defer to, the practical wisdom of the gardener, to let the psyche's deep vegetable worker remain in control of that realm.

Unlike the sentimentalized gardener of Victorian romanticism and its modern derivatives on greeting cards, in country and garden journals or magazine columns, in advertisements for wholesome food or healthy lifestyles, gardeners in dreams are rarely mellow, languidly philosophical characters. They either seem to be doing nothing or are more frequently busy, gruff, and impatient with the dreamer's preoccupations. Like the woman gardener in the rhubarb dream who brusquely sweeps away the old seed pods, these characters are attuned to the intentionality of the vegetables, not to that of the dayworld. The busy disorder and earthy patience of the vegetable garden doesn't usually conform to the quick aspirations of the dreamer.

Claustrophobia and Vegetable Depths

A young man who has been living away from home for many years has a dream:

> I am at my drab, claustrophobic childhood home with my old parents. They seem to be rejuvenated and are moving out. Dad says they are going to the country, a farming area. He is cooking a large pot of pease-pudding (dried peas), which is swelling out of the pan. They are in good spirits but I am desolate. I notice my meditation things but don't want to be left alone in that house.

The return to one's roots is often painful, claustrophobic. In this encounter, the dreamer's parents—in a sense the imaginal guardians of his roots—are rejuvenated by his presence and are moving out, leaving the place to him. Now that his father is relieved of the burden of the son's imaginal absence, his pot "runneth over" with the substantial, earthy-tasting, moist, old-fashioned nourishment of pease-pudding. Aesthetically unappealing to the young man, recalling only the drab tastelessness of his childhood, this mash of dried peas is the essence of his family roots. This is what his "father" has been preparing: a vegetable transformation, an alchemy. This is the source of ancestral nourishment, but the dreamer finds it difficult to accept and fears the lack of vision, cramped confinement, and immobility symbolized by that place.

A man in his mid-thirties dreams he is an archeologist exploring some ancient, almost tribal tombs, amidst dense jungle or forest. They are overgrown with tangled, dark green vegetation. The first chamber is known, but he discovers

> another, deeper chamber through a small, narrow opening in the floor. It is an important discovery. I don't feel *too* claustrophobic as I examine the site. The people of that time lived directly over the tombs. They liked to be on top of them, to have them under their feet. At least then they knew where the spirits were. All around in the "jungle" were huge concrete structures, now abandoned, that were evidence of earlier failures to develop/exploit this part of the world. Also, news had got out about the new find, and already people were arriving to exploit the tourist potential of the place.

The vegetable soul consistently emerges as a metaphor of depth. "Deeper" even than the known archeology of the psyche, the vegetable soul takes us into a region of primordial, ancestral continuity. Our search for roots leads us into deathly regions of stillness, immobility, containment. Yet even before these dark, downward regions have been contacted, acknowledged, and digested, dayworld consciousness is rushing to "develop" them. All around, the primordial vegetable world is littered with the abandoned junk of previous attempts at exploitation—massive, concrete, literal—whether this is understood on an "inner" individual level, as the ego of the dreamer (under the influence of the puer? hero? Great Mother? senex?) wanting quick results from his vegetal descent (personal growth, meaning, acclaim), or on an "outer" cultural level (economic growth at the expense of either the vegetable kingdom or the vegetal world of ancestral *memoria*).

Vegetable Wisdom and Humor

A man entering middle age dreams of a return to his problematical childhood home from which he had fled. Despite a heavy backpack, he skips lightly in the sun down the drab inner city street. He is warmly greeted by his old parents who have full, open, somewhat simple grins on their rounded, countrified faces.

> Over the road, directly opposite, some of the terraced houses have been displaced, and instead there is a small field with a single, very straight row of giant cabbages—dark green, solid, grounded.

In this idealized return to ancestral roots, sunny, jolly home and dark, earthy cabbages face each other. Not opposing each other, they rather mirror two sides of cabbageness: solidity, orderliness, and an almost regal presence complement a rounded, simple amiability, which in its own way is no less grounded. Not so much cabbages and kings, as cabbages *are* kings, and the fool as well.

A man in his late twenties dreams:

> I am feeding my guru Lebanese brown beans. He eats them voraciously with a wild look on his face. Although I appreciate good food and join in the eating, I feel apprehensive. He can change from humor to disdain so suddenly.

In calling for a return of imagination to the world, imaginal psychology has emphasized a natural wisdom of things themselves. To respect animals in dreams as theophanies of the Gods, to attend to their aesthetics, has liberated them from reductive, devalued, and stereotyped interpretations. Yet it seems so much easier to bow to the divine presence of certain animals (the roar of a lion, the peacock's display) or to listen with respectful seriousness to the vast, oceanic promptings of the "unconscious in general" than to grant wisdom to the cabbage, the bean, and humble vegetables. Indeed, the very thought provokes a smile, a quiet humor. The cabbage as theophany? It sounds slightly ridiculous.

This amusement is an essential aspect of a vegetable

wisdom. A particular type of digestive humor is fundamental to the vegetable soul. The "jest" of vegetables is part of their way of working imaginally. Cabbage, rhubarb, pumpkin, and bean—each marks an outer limit of a divine vegetable humor. The image of the cabbage as a theophany perhaps evokes a chuckle, proffers an amiable, slightly foolish form of absurdity. Rhubarb, whether ingested physically or through a goonish kind of madness, has a surreal, nonsensical acidity that breaks up the rigidity of extreme imaginal constipation. Pumpkin humor, through the pranks and wiles of Halloween, is akin to black comedy. Beans can be quite wild and, as in the above dream, generate a nervous uncertainty. They have their own scurrilous, windy way of provoking laughter/wisdom.

Each of these forms of vegetable humor acts as an imaginal loosener. Each views the world from a basic, earthy rootedness. Reflected in this complex green light of vegetable consciousness, the pretentious claims of so-called higher consciousness are undermined, broken down, thrown back on themselves. Sanitized manners are defenseless against the flatulent joviality of the bean; staid religion is vulnerable to the underworld challenges, pranks, and antics of the pumpkin; heady speculation has no answer to the amiable foolery of the cabbage; senex dignity and density fall apart under the insistent promptings of rhubarb.

SOME CONCLUSIONS

If I have avoided, or just lightly brushed, more familiar vegetative themes—flowers and flower gardens, fruits, trees—this was to allow some of the other aspects of the vegetable kingdom to express themselves. For example, under the masterly influence of authors from Jung to Mircea Eliade, trees have been captured by the archetype of spirit; gardens, particularly rose gardens, have suffered a similar fate, albeit a more feminine variant.[21] "Trees of life," "Axis Mundi," "the Self" as a process of growth, "Ego–Self axis"—these interpretive concepts, so authoritatively substantiated by copious mythological, folkloric, religious, and psychopathological material, have come to obscure the complex phenomenology and ecology of the tree itself. A plurality of possible imaginative arboreal moves shrinks in the face of this overwhelming consensus. So often we cannot see the trees for the concepts. Both tree and flower garden would benefit from a more ecological eye: perhaps a bug-eyed view of the rose, a fungused approach to the tree.

Vegetables in dreams are rarely dramatic. Indeed their presence is commonly announced by a certain stillness, a poise that is easily overlooked. But this is certainly not a place of inaction but one of vegetable-ing, vegetables at work within the dream, in their own dark, downward, digestive way. The vegetable marks the place where some elemental rawness surfaces and confronts the dreamer, something both intimate and yet remote. One can well understand how the vegetable has regularly been metaphorically equated with the autonomic nervous system, that most intimate aspect of the dreamer's own body which is simultaneously furthest removed from his or her control.

Perhaps we could also say that the vegetable marks the point where the dream breathes—the place where a unique transformation occurs, a green alchemy where carbon dioxide is exchanged for oxygen. The dream thrives on what is poison to the dayworld. To enter the dream through the vegetable is to descend into a world whose atmosphere is inimical to human or animal life. When we enter the dream at this point, the dream itself becomes vegetable.

This place where the dream breathes is not usually a fulcrum or a hiatus; it is not a place of rest or of inaction. It marks a point of repose: darkly active, constantly transmuting, incessantly gathering and harvesting the world that surrounds it, drawing the dreamer into its habitat. In dreams *we* are food for the vegetable; our dayworld views are drawn into and nourish *its* unfathomable depths.

CHAPTER SIX
Vegetables in Folktales

"Jack and the Beanstalk," "Cinderella," "Hansel and Gretel," "Peerifool," "The Princess and the Pea"—the presence of vegetables in many of Europe's best known folktales is frequently overlooked. Indeed, when we look at collections of such tales with a green eye, vegetables begin to sprout everywhere. True, this appearance is not always dramatic or necessarily central to the story; but as we have seen in previous chapters, this is the way vegetables frequently exert their presence: in the odd corners, from beneath, from out back, quietly, insistently.

VESSELS FOR FANTASY

This lowly position in the story also results from the cultural devaluation of vegetables. Consider one of the most famous of European vegetable folktales, "The Pumpkin at the Ball"—more commonly called "Cinderella." Usually the poor young woman is thought to be the lowest and most oppressed character, the social outcast. But what about the pumpkin! All the glitter and show are carried by and within the pumpkin. The literal immobility of this generous vegetable contains within it an imaginative mobility symbolized by the coach and by a dream of upward aspiration. But at the depth of midnight, the pumpkin will insist on bringing us back to our vegetable senses. A creature of the night, the pumpkin belongs with Halloween, witches, and broomsticks, with the return of souls from the land of the dead, with rats, lizards, and mice. Originally in Europe turnips were used as lanterns. Now we find hollowed-out pumpkins with a candle inside. In these cases the light is within the vegetable, looking out from inside the pumpkin or turnip—vegetable consciousness.[1]

Like the pumpkin, the bean in Jack's famous tale surely contains within it the stalk, the staircase to the giant's realm and the gold. Both pumpkin and bean contain an upward aspiration and a downward rootedness, the promise both of success and of a fall. Both vegetables for a limited time also provide the means for the mobilization of deepest longings. Placing the vegetable at the center of such tales provides them with a totally revised coherence.[2]

Sometimes this imaginal containment is even more explicit. For example, in the story of "Handsome Andras" from Hungary, the hero finds himself, Hercules-like, having to clean out an endlessly dirty stable. It is an impossible task, but aid comes at the moment of despair. Not only does one of the horses reassure Andras that by morning the work will be completed, but also he is given a "copper nut" from the horse's left ear: "Crack the nut open and you'll find in it a fine silver sword and garments woven of gold."[3] In his quest to escape poverty by marrying a fairy princess, Andras has need of several such gifts from the intelligent horse: "Put your hand under my tail and there you will find a bean with a hole in it. Crack it open and inside you will find garments sparkling like diamonds and a sword to match"; "you'll find a golden hazel nut in my right ear. Take the golden garments and sword out of it."

In an Italian folktale from Calabria, "The Handmade King," a standoffish princess creates her husband from flour and sugar. But he is captured by a jealous queen, and the princess sets out to find him. In this quest she receives assistance from three brothers, old men with long beards, all hermits, who give her a chestnut, a walnut, and a hazelnut. When the chestnut is broken open, out of it "came a golden loom, with a maiden seated at it and weaving pure gold"; from the walnut "came a golden tambour and a maiden embroidering with pure gold"; when the hazelnut is cracked open, "out came a little golden basket and a maiden sewing with pure gold." With these riches she achieves her goal and gains back her husband.

We could say that the princess, narcissistically in love with her own creation, refusing to embrace her unknown masculine aspect, has to suffer such a loss if there is to be any psychological deepening. Her creation is captured and claimed by her shadow mother (her real mother is dead), and, given the ineffectualness of the King, her father, she must seek help from the old wise men who live deep in the dangerous forest. Their gifts return her to the vegetal core, the kernel, of her aspirations, of her pride and world-denying insularity. Here, in a nutshell, are contained images of her royal wealth and maidenly virginity, both of which she must give up to her shadow for the return of the consort, her soul.[4]

But perhaps one of the richest and most audacious of these tales is "Dealer in Peas and Beans," also from Italy.[5] One day when a desperately poor man from Palermo feels hunger "gnawing at his stomach," he finds a single bean lying on the ground. He sits down and contemplates it, pouring all of his aspirations into this tiny, humble vegetable:

> What a fine bean! I'll plant it in a pot at once, and a bean plant will come up, with lots of nice pods. I'll dry the pods, then plant the beans in a basin and have many more pods. . . . Between now and the next three years, I'll lease a garden, plant the beans, and no telling how many will come up then! The fourth year I'll rent a storehouse and become an important dealer. . . .

One wonders how a single bean could possibly hold such grandiose schemes. It seems laughably absurd, pathetically tragic. But Don Giovanni Misiranti has had his vegetable faith restored, his vegetal powers awakened, and he sets off confidently down the road.

Supported by his impossible vision, Don Giovanni instantly acts the part of a wealthy dealer in peas and beans. He borrows a set of clothes from a friend, negotiates to rent a whole row of stores from a prosperous family, gains the hand of their daughter in marriage plus a considerable dowry, extravagantly spends most of it, and then gets married in fine wedding clothes, "with the bean in the pocket of the vest." Naturally, his in-laws want to see his rich estates. Don Giovanni appeals to the bean to bring him luck and sets out on horseback just ahead of his bride and her mother who follow in a carriage across the countryside. He claims vast fields as his and bribes the farmers to confirm this when questioned by the women. Obviously he can't keep this up all day, and eventually he arrives at a place "where there was nothing more to see." Resigning himself to his fate, Don Giovanni resolves to wait for his wife and mother-in-law to catch up. At that moment he sees an enormous palace "with a young lady in green standing at the window." She calls him inside and promptly tells him the sumptuous place is his. "It is a present from me," she says. "I am the bean you picked up and kept in your pocket. Now I shall take my leave."

The simple bean is to the peasant what the beloved's handkerchief is to the chivalrous knight: both inspire great thoughts and impossible deeds; both are anima-tokens, images that awaken and inspire the soul. Talismans of the knightly quest find ready acceptance within psychology's heroically and spiritually inclined paradigm, but the more earth-bound, worldly, materialistic aspirations of the "peasant" are scarcely considered, let alone acknowledged to be of a similar worth. The hero in our inner pantheon has received too much acclaim; now it is the peasant's turn. Now the urgent question is less one of uniting with an imagined transcendent God than of recognizing the soulfulness that is contained within the most humble bean. The quest is less upward than downward, to regain connection with the imaginal ground and materiality of things. As Bachelard bemoans: "The soul . . . suffers from a deficiency of material imagination."[6]

A VEGETABLE ASPIRATION

What is this special combination of aspiration and rootedness that we find so perfectly expressed in these vegetable tales? Unlike the dreams discussed in the previous chapter, which give spontaneous voice to the psyche of late twentieth-century, well-educated, urban Westerners, the folktales arise from an ancient, rurally oriented milieu of economic and political hardship. In this regard there are two, seemingly opposed, traditions for approaching the meanings contained within folklore. On the one hand are the dynamic psychologies, and on the other are the cultural and sociological/anthropological perspectives.

From the standpoint of the former, whether Freudian or Jungian, folktales express fundamental, deep, timeless psychological processes occurring within the individual. In this respect they differ but little from the dream or from any other symbolic material. Of course, the psychologies differ: for psychoanalysis, the aspirations are in the nature of a hidden "sexual" wish-fulfillment, whereas for depth psychology such aspirations express the healing and helping capacity of the psyche in its "natural" drive toward wholeness and individuation.[7] The "ground" expressed within these tales is either taken to be the primary processes of the unconscious or the archetypal structure of the collective unconscious. For Freudians, folktales merely reiterate, endlessly, the permutations of the Oedipal myth. For Jungians, they are akin to cryptograms that demand endless amplification in the light of the quest for individuation.

Sociological/anthropological and cultural approaches to the folktale fall into two main divisions. First are those which suggest a formal and internal approach to the stories, emphasizing their structural grammar and suggesting a direct correspondence between the logic of the tale and that of the culture: its kinship relations, trading patterns, etc.[8] For this approach, images of aspiration are merely signifiers of grammatical relationship, while any idea of grounding merely refers to a deep structure of inexorable semiotic laws. There are also approaches that try to situate folktales within their specific historical and cultural milieus. For example, most European folktales of the type to which I refer in this chapter are products of a pre-industrial oppressed peasantry, and it has been suggested that they express the radical imaginative utopianism of this group in an era just prior to their political capacity to enact their frustrations and desires.[9] From such a perspective, it is precisely these aspirations for social and imaginative mobility that are contained within the vegetable images discussed, while they are grounded in the daily ritual of hunger and work.[10]

But both perspectives suggest that these folktales help to draw us deeper into the complex soul of the world. In these tales, the vegetables function as archetypes which, as Bachelard reminds us, "are reserves of enthusiasm which help us believe in the world. . . . Each archetype is an opening on the world, an invitation to the world."[11]

VEGETABLE REDEMPTION

The "Tale of the Blue Light" (from *Grimm's*) contains many of the motifs that are basic to vegetable folktales.[12] At the end of a war, a soldier who has served his King faithfully for many years is forced to retire from a military life because of the numerous wounds he has sustained. The King dismisses him without thanks or reward. Worried about how he will earn a living, the ex-soldier leaves the city; and as evening approaches he enters a forest. In the darkness he encounters a witch, and in return for shelter he digs her garden. The next day he chops wood and on the third is lowered into an old dry well to retrieve her light, which burns blue and never goes out. As he is hauled to the surface in a basket, the witch reaches down to take the blue light; but, wisely not trusting her, he insists on having his feet firmly on the ground before handing it over. She goes into a rage and lets him fall to the bottom.

As he sits on the soft ground, he takes out his pipe for a

consoling smoke. Death seems unavoidable. But as he lights the tobacco at the blue light, a small black dwarf appears asking for instructions. Naturally, the soldier wants to escape from the well. This the dwarf achieves by leading him through an underground passage, past the witch's secret hoard of treasures to which he helps himself. Next he has the witch taken into custody, where she is tried and hanged. Finally he decides to extract vengeance on the ungrateful King. This he achieves by having the dwarf bring the King's daughter to him in her sleep, setting her menial household tasks and then having her returned to the palace before dawn.

When the princess awakes, this episode seems like some disturbing dream. The King advises her to fill her pocket full of peas and make a small hole in it. Then if she really were carried through the streets that night, a clear trail would be left. The little dwarf overhears this and scatters peas throughout the city so that when he carries her to her menial tasks it is not possible to pick up any trail. Again in the morning, she awakes exhausted and with memories of a bad dream. Next the King advises her to leave her shoe behind in the place to which she is taken, and his men will soon locate it. Despite the little dwarf's warnings, the soldier insists that the abduction go ahead as usual that night. Sure enough, the next day a city-wide search discovers the shoe, and the soldier is thrown into prison to await execution. But he manages to have the blue light smuggled to him and, when granted his final request of a smoke, summons the dwarf to beat the King and his officials. The King, terrified, gives the soldier his whole kingdom and also his daughter to marry.

The heroic, militantly assertive aspect of the psyche, when wounded and vulnerable, finds itself dismissed by the ruling consciousness. Retreating deep into the vegetative unconscious, the wounded and rejected hero finds dangerous support from a dark, malicious aspect of the feminine from which he has for so long been estranged. Yet, she forces him, as her gardener, to descend into the earth and almost consigns him to it forever. Only his wit and good fortune save him. The small dwarf is like some elemental personification of earth and fire; the blue of the light is a reflective consciousness that must accompany one in any descent.

Below ground are found riches, while above a just vengeance is sought. The split-off hero is most dangerous when wounded and rejected, especially after a successful descent into the underworld. He exacts revenge from the King's feminine while she is in deep sleep. Desperately the senex attempts to protect this doubly vulnerable aspect, to follow the trace of this aggressive interference to its source. He wisely reaches for the vegetable as being the only way to mark the trail into this region. The peas fail only because of their overabundance. As the ruling patriarchal consciousness is forced to descend, to direct attention into the depths of the dream world, the streets are filled with peas. Eventually the King loses everything, and the wronged soldier gains all.

This is not a pretty tale. There is no talk of love or of a happy ending. The feminine hovers in the background, either evil or pliable, a crucial, albeit secondary aspect to the masculine struggle between senex and hero. Yet for this very reason, the presence of vegetative metaphoricity (garden, well, peas) is all the more remarkable, a testament to the profound ubiquity of the vegetable soul. In fact we can see these elements at work in a number of folktales.

In another tale from the Grimm collection, "The Turnip," two brothers, one rich and one poor, have been soldiers.[13] To escape from poverty, the poor one then turns to farming, planting turnips. One turnip grows to an enormous size, and the poor brother, out of wisdom, gives it to the King as a present. The King is delighted by the gift and, impressed by the poor man's humility, rewards him with many gifts of gold and land so that he becomes immensely wealthy. The rich brother is jealous of what has been obtained from a single turnip and tries to win the King's favor by giving him gold and horses. While the rich brother expects much wealth in return (after all, look what the gift of a single turnip has brought), the King presents him instead with the wonderful enormous turnip. Outraged, the rich brother attempts to have his brother murdered. Luckily, the would-be assassins are interrupted, and some quick thinking saves the day.

Like the previous tale and the dream of the cabbage P.O.W.s in chapter five, we have here the powerful theme of a "wounded" soldier forced to embrace his vegetable soul. In this last story, the ruling consciousness has wisdom enough to recognize and value the humility and generosity of the soldier's vegetative transformation. Spirit and earth are united.

This association of the vegetable with an initial experience of humiliation, vulnerability, and woundedness that is subsequently transformed into both wealth and an earthy wisdom can also be seen in "Cinderella."[14] Through these split-off, lost, or rejected aspects the senex is reunited with the vegetable soul; as the former becomes increasingly "earthed," the vegetable world becomes more valued. This is surely one of the dilemmas facing the Western civilizations today: how to deal with its dominant militaristic, heroic fantasies in an age when the repressed social and environmental voices are demanding to be heard.

BENEATH THE VEGETABLE

In "The Blue Light," the protagonist reaches wealth and wisdom through his gardening, as does the poor brother in "The Turnip." This revelation from "beneath" the vegetable is a common motif. In the Italian folktale "The Three Chicory Gatherers," this theme is even more explicit.[15] A poor mother has three daughters whom she takes to gather chicory when in season. One day Teresa, the eldest, lags behind the others because she has noticed a huge chicory plant. After considerable hard work she uproots it. So much earth still clings to the roots that a big hole is left, at whose bottom is a trapdoor. The girl goes down the hole and opens the trapdoor, only to find a dragon in an underground room licking his lips at the thought of human flesh. The dragon yields to her pleas and gives her a task instead: to keep house and to eat a human hand while he goes out hunting. Unable to bring herself to eat human flesh, the girl hides the hand in the lavatory and lies to the dragon when he returns. "Where are you?" asks the dragon. "In the lavatory!" replies the hand. The dragon cuts off Teresa's head and throws her into a room filled with the bodies of previous victims. The same fate awaits the next sister Concetta, who, when searching for Teresa, uproots the same chicory plant and fails the same gruesome test, this time with a human arm. The youngest sister, Mariuzza, sets out to look for her sisters, repeats the whole procedure, but outwits the dragon by grinding the piece of human flesh, a foot, into powder, putting it into a stocking, and hiding it under her clothes on her stomach. When asked by the dragon where it is, the foot replies, "On Mariuzza's stomach!" Overjoyed, the dragon trusts her, but she gets him drunk, finds out his secrets, and kills him. She brings not only Teresa and Concetta back to life but also all of the other victims, including many kings, princes, counts, and knights who vie with each other to marry the three sisters.

Chicory is the basis of this family's livelihood. It is the vegetable core, the root complex, the humble crop around whose gathering their whole life is built. Yet it is also a symbol of their poverty, sustaining them but with no possibility of development. Fate gives the sisters an opportunity to deal with this dilemma in a single action: to embrace the whole vegetable complex and uproot it. While they succeed after much effort in accomplishing this, their action leaves a gaping hole in the earth, in their basic way of life, in their imaginal ground. Curious, or perhaps elated, each sister descends into this new space, into the arms of the dragon, that ancient guardian and bearer of earth energy. But keeping house at these deep, vegetative regions means encountering a non-human world, one that strikes at the heart of fundamental, "human" moral questions. As Jung wrote, in these vegetative regions "life has to follow other laws . . . quite unlike those arising from the mentality of the personal, warm-blooded life."[16] Only the trickster sister with the Hermetic eye survives and reaps the reward. Only she can enter that alien realm and engage it without becoming lost in it. Solving the riddle of eating/not eating human flesh reminds us of the dream in chapter five of a head being boiled in a cauldron of soup. It is almost a reptilian sacrament: to be at one, in a digestive way, with the body. Not to literally devour human flesh, but imaginally. As in so many folktales, there is a fragment of a profound vegetable alchemy at work here.[17]

I have known many people who have been locked into a cycle of minimal sustenance at a vegetative level, usually through oppressive social, familial, and historical circumstances. Coming across the giant chicory, like the giant turnip, is like winning a vegetable lottery, surely a "peasant's" dream of getting rich quickly. But many people, when suddenly presented with the opportunity, refuse to uproot and gather this fundamental aspect of their life's rhythm, fearful of the disruption it will surely bring to their well-ordered but imaginally meager lives; or if they do, they then refuse to go deeper into the "existential" hole that results. However, this sequence of actions—the gathering, uprooting, and descent—should not be imagined heroically. In the story these decisions were taken on a vegetable level, akin to the bean deciding to germinate. The sisters were following the logic of their vegetable lives, driven by a vegetable necessity.

This otherworld digestive sacrament and the need for hermetic, trickster-like inspiration are central to the Irish tale "The Cakes of Oatmeal and Blood."[18] A flighty young man sets a task for any girl who wishes to marry him. She must go to a graveyard that night and retrieve his blackthorn stick which he left beside the fresh grave of an old woman. All but one of the girls refuse. As she fearlessly enters the graveyard, a voice from one of the graves orders her to open it. She refuses but is told she has to. Inside the coffin is a man who orders her to carry him on her back into the kitchen of one of the town's houses, where the family are all asleep. As he stirs up the fire, the man tells her to get some oatmeal for him to eat. Unable to find any milk or water, the dead man goes into the bedroom and cuts the throats of the family's two sons. Mixing the oatmeal with the blood, he urges the girl to eat it with him. This she pretends to do but really lets it drop into her apron, while bemoaning the fate of the two boys. The dead man tells her that it wouldn't have happened if they had kept fresh water or milk in the house. They didn't, so they had to take the consequences. He says that the only thing that would revive them is the mix of oatmeal and blood, but as she had joined him in eating it all there is none left. He tells her that much gold lies beneath the bushes in the family's top field. Then he orders her to return him to his grave. The next morning she awakens to the terrible news of the double murder of her neighbor's sons. At the wake she says she will bring them back to life if one of them will marry her and also if she is given the top field. The father accepts her offer, and using the oatmeal she restores the sons to life. After her marriage she tells her husband the story and digs near the bushes to find the gold.

The uncanniness experienced by the rational soul and its proximity to danger when encountering these almost unreachable "psychoid" depths in the darkness beneath the vegetable are expressed in other Italian folktales. When a poor farmer digs in the earth beneath a large mushroom, he finds two vipers which he subsequently eats by accident. This reptilian feast gives him the capacity to understand the speech of animals, although if he tells any human of this ability he will die.[19] In "The Tale of the Cats," a poor girl is sent out to pick chicory by her ill-tempered stepmother.[20] Instead, she finds a large cauliflower and after some difficulty manages to uproot it. Beneath it she finds a hole the size of a well and a ladder down which she climbs. At the bottom is a house full of cats that are busy cooking, sewing, sweeping, and so on. The girl helps them out with their work and is rewarded with beautiful clothes and jewelry. When she returns home, her jealous stepmother tells her "natural" daughter to emulate her half sister's feat. Reluctantly, for this sister is lazy and ill-mannered, she goes to the cauliflower, uproots it, climbs down the hole, but then proceeds to torment the cats. She is "rewarded" with rags and with countless worms around her fingers instead of rings. In addition, a continually growing blood sausage permanently attaches to her face, and she has to eat it constantly to prevent its smothering her. Her mother dies of shock at the sight, and this nasty half sister eventually dies of eating the sausage.

The alchemy involved when working with the imaginal powers in these remote regions—with what Grinnell has called "the deepest, most unchanging, and most creative vitality of the archetype"—is most clearly expressed in "Rosina in the Oven."[21] Rosina's mother dies in childbirth. Her father's remarriage produces another girl, Assunta, who is as plain and dark as Rosina is beautiful and fair. Despite her mother's reluctance, Assunta persuades her to set Rosina some impossible tasks and then to punish her when she fails to complete them. Rosina must tend and feed the herd of cows and also spin a pound of hemp. But the cows help her out, even when the task is increased to two pounds of hemp. Outraged, Assunta gets Rosina sent to steal some lettuce from a neighboring farmer. Instead, she comes across a turnip which, with some effort, she pulls up to reveal a toad's nest containing five toads. Rosina takes them to her bosom, exclaiming delightedly. Unfortunately, she accidentally drops one and its leg breaks. Rosina is terribly upset. But the other toads, no doubt overcome by this unusual kindness shown to them by a human, reward her by making her even more radiantly beautiful. However, the lamed toad curses her: if any ray of sunshine should touch her, she would instantly be changed into a snake and only regain her human shape if she passes through a fiery oven.

Assunta gets this terrible secret from Rosina. When the gloriously beautiful sister is inevitably summoned to the palace to marry the prince, who also knows of the curse, Assunta arranges for the carefully enclosed carriage to be opened to the sun. Rosina instantly changes into a hissing serpent and slithers off into the forest. But at the palace the assembled guests insist on being fed; so the cooks begin to fuel the fires beneath the ovens. One of them sees a snake in the bundle of brushwood he throws onto the fire. As he watches in awe, a beautiful naked woman leaps from the flames and Rosina is united with her prince.

Pure, naive human goodness is insufficient in these vegetative depths. One small slip and Rosina is cursed: she must stay in the darkness. But the quest for an alchemical union of opposites, the *coniunctio*, is not to be denied. Rosina must become part of this region, undergoing a reptilian transformation before arising triumphant and healed from the oven's flames. It is as if the shadow side, from half sister to crippled toad, constantly drives Rosina into psychological deepening.

Similarly, the urgency and desperate need to preserve the Earth's vegetable fecundity and multiplicity, from rainforest to hedgerows, should not naively simplify the complex psychological issues. Simply to proclaim an interspecies kinship with the vegetable kingdom, a joyous participation in a unified "Gaia," a celebration of our oneness with trees, moorland, or sweet-smelling herbs misses the profoundly paradoxical questions raised by the fantasy of a Deep Ecology. The vegetative tales of Dionysus, Apollo,

Artemis, Persephone, and Aphrodite tell of madness, fear, and uncertainty, as well as hope and fulfillment. For example, the jealousy in these tales, as in "Cinderella," can be traced back to Apuleius's *The Golden Ass* and authentically expresses the vegetative mysteries of Isis–Aphrodite.[22]

VEGETABLES AND DEATH

Time and again we have seen how the threat of death hovers around these encounters with vegetable depths. Vegetables are not only magical vessels filled with riches; they are also alchemical alembics where we approach psychic death. In "The Three Cottages," from Mantua, three young sisters are told by their dying mother to get their uncles to build each of them a small house.[23] One sister has hers built from rushes, another from wood, and the third, the youngest, from iron. At dusk a wolf appears and goes to the eldest sister's reed cottage, where he easily breaks in and eats the girl. The next day the wolf repeats his terrible deed at the wooden cottage.

When he comes to the iron cottage, with appeals of love he tries to trick the youngest sister to let him in. Then he insists that in the morning they should go together to collect peas from a nearby garden. However, the youngest sister gets up before dawn and goes alone to the pea-patch, picks some peas, and takes them home. She puts the peas on to cook and throws the pods out of the window. Foiled, the wolf suggests another trip to collect lupins. Again the girl agrees, and again she outwits him by going out before dawn. Finally, he suggests collecting some pumpkins together. This time he too rises early and rushes to the pumpkin patch. When the girl sees the wolf coming, she quickly hollows out a large pumpkin and squeezes inside. The wolf thinks he can smell the girl, but even though he sniffs all the pumpkins he can't find her. However, being hungry, he starts to eat them. When he arrives at the large one in which the terrified girl hides he is no longer hungry but decides to take it as a gift to lure her out of her house. Arriving at the iron cottage, he throws it through the window. The girl can't believe her luck and makes faces through the panes at the outraged wolf.

The vegetables have to be gathered; we simply have to step regularly outside of our secure, rational ego-world, our known cultural boundaries, no matter how strongly these may have been constructed. But this does not have to entail a quest into the mysterious unknown, into the boundless immensity of the wilderness: a simple trip to the vegetable gardens of our psyche will suffice to render us vulnerable. In a sense, the wolf, a creature who along with the rat epitomizes the human fear (at least in Europe) of a breakdown of civilized dwelling, drives the girl into the heart of the vegetable. The pumpkin is like a surrogate mother or like a peasant version of the initiation in the belly of the whale.[24] Not only is the senex-constructed house vulnerable to the wolf, but also it actually attracts him. The girl must be forced out of her necessary, but also falsely secure, iron house and reconnected in a deeper way with her vegetative roots. An alchemical equation is surely at work here.

In the English tale "The Green Mist," this vegetative death and initiation assume a more general, but more potent form.[25] Each year at spring, rising from the awakening earth, a green mist comes. Families stand at their doorways at dawn with offerings of salt and bread. One family has faithfully carried out these protective rituals each year, but this year in the winter their pretty young daughter has fallen sick. She can hardly stand but believes that she will be cured if she can survive to greet the spring. It seems as if the winter will never end and that the Green Mist will never come. Every day she is carried from her bed to watch for it. Finally, she feels as if she can only hang on for one more day and says she will be content just to live long enough to greet the spring, just as long in fact as a cowslip. The next day the Green Mist comes, and the girl seems to grow well, laughing in the sun. She won't allow her mother to pick any cowslips, and somehow these flowers and the girl share a mysterious beauty. Then one day a visitor picks a cowslip. The bogles, the earth-spirits, take the girl at her word, and she begins to fade and die with the plucked flower.

The proximity of death is not always just a human problem. In "King Bean," it is the vegetable itself which is under threat, its nobility and royalty which come close to death and which need the love and determination of human consciousness to be healed.[26]

In the Italian story "The Slave Mother," a tenant farmer's wife is asked by an owl whether she wishes for wealth in her youth or in old age. After some anxious deliberation she chooses old age. Some time later she is carried off by pirates as she is out gathering salad greens, particularly chicory.[27] The farmer and his sons are distraught when she doesn't return but eventually give up looking for her. Two years later, while ploughing, they discover an underground vault filled with gold. After a farewell dinner for the farmhands, they set out for a fine new life in the city of Naples, where they become educated as gentlemen. One day they all go to the slave market, but the father refuses to yield to his sons' request for a beautiful slave girl. Instead, he selects an older woman on whom he takes pity, for she looks to have had a hard life. Eventually they discover, much to their joy, that she is their long lost mother. The woman's reluctant wish has at last come true but in a way that she could never have expected.

Time and again we see that the encounter with the vegetable opens the doorway into a lengthy period of trial with the outcome by no means certain. Heroics seem of no use in these paradoxical regions. But vegetables can mark the route, showing a vegetable way both in and out of the imaginal depths. As we have seen above, in "The Blue Light," peas can suggest a way of moving into the world of dreams, although they are not always reliable. In "The Robber Bridegroom," from *Grimm's*, a young maiden has to go deep into a dark forest to meet the rich man she has been told by her father to marry.[28] Feeling a horror and distrust of this man, she fills her pockets with peas and lentils, throwing a couple of them on the ground at every step. Once at her betrothed's house, she is warned by an old woman that he is the chief of an evil band of robbers who delight in eating human flesh. This is to be her terrible fate. The young woman escapes and finds her way out of the forest, guided by the moonlit trail of the peas and beans which have sprouted and grown.

IN THE VEGETABLE GARDEN

As "The Three Cottages" showed, vegetable gardens can be dangerous places in folktales. In the Scottish story "Peerifool," a widowed Queen discovers that all the cabbages from her yard are being taken.[29] Her eldest daughter volunteers to stay up and keep watch. That night she confronts a giant who comes into the garden and cuts the cabbages. He carries her off and sets her some impossible household tasks. When some wee folk interrupt her and ask for food, she refuses. But she cannot finish the tasks, so the giant strips a length of skin from her and tosses her into the rafters. The same fate awaits the next daughter when she keeps watch over the cabbages, but the youngest, when it comes to her turn, feeds the small folk, gains their help, tricks the giant, and revives her two sisters.

The task of guarding vegetables is no less demanding in the Italian tale of "The Garden Witch."[30] Two women, desperately hungry in a time of famine, come across a cabbage patch and creep in to steal an armful. The next day they return for more and manage to sneak past a watchdog by giving it some bread. The old woman who owns the garden sees this and replaces the dog with a cat. When it meows she'll know the thieves are about. But they silence it with a small piece of meat. Next the old woman tries a rooster to guard her cabbages, but the two thieves throw it some grain. Finally, the old woman has a grave dug and lies in it, covering herself with earth until only one ear is above ground. The two women return the next day; and as they are leaving, loaded up with cabbages, one of them notices the ear. Thinking it is an unusual mushroom, the thief tries to pull it up but only succeeds in rousing the old woman who grabs her and threatens to eat her whole. Desperate, the woman, who is pregnant, promises to give the expected child to the old woman when he or she reaches sixteen. Later a baby girl is born. When she turns sixteen, the old woman comes to collect her debt, intending to fatten up and eat the maiden. Luckily, the girl is quick-witted and tricks the old woman into the oven that has been reserved for her. With the old woman's demise, the young maiden and her mother claim the cabbage patch for themselves.

Imaginal hunger drives even the law-abiding ego into the 'garden' searching for food. But the vegetable garden offers not only imaginal nourishment but also peril. The women attempt to call upon the protection of Hermes, the God of thieves. For a while their luck holds out, but eventually one of them is asked to pay the price: the child she is expecting in exchange for the cabbages (almost the witch's children) that she has already stolen and eaten. This threat of being eaten is not a maternal, or uroboric, regressive fear but a call to a vegetable sacrament—to partake of the body of psyche at the deepest level. Unlike an aerobic workout, this is akin to an attunement with the autonomic nervous system, the cellular depths.[31]

In "The Cloven Youth," from Venice, a pregnant woman craves parsley. It just so happens that next door is a garden, full of the herb, that is owned by a famous witch who always keeps the gate open so that anyone who wishes can go in and have some.[32] But the woman with the craving goes in and eats half the crop. Naturally, the witch is upset by this exploitation of her generosity and the next day catches the woman just as she is eating the very last plant. Again a terrible price is extracted: the woman promises to give the witch half of the child she is expecting.

As in the previous tale, a desperate craving drives the day-world personality deeper into the vegetative regions of the psyche. It is like the obsession that can overcome the fitness freak, the aerobic devotee, or the food faddist when, in the grip of a vegetative hunger, their desire crosses some invisible boundary and they are 'lost' to the world. This is a dangerous moment, for the vegetative regions of the psyche have a boundless abundance: "Vaster than Empires," writes Andrew Marvell.

There are many tales which relate the 'misuse' of this vegetable generosity. "The Ear of Corn," for example, describes a woman who casually uses some ears of corn to clean mud off her small daughter's dress. God, seeing that humans have insufficient respect for this plant, reduces its yield by a factor of ten. In "That's Enough to Go On With," a fat, rich, and greedy farmer falsely claims some fields of gorgeous strawberries, unaware that they are magic ones owned by the fairies and that unless you give thanks you are compelled to eat them nonstop.[33] The more he eats, the bigger grows his craving, until at length he bursts with a bang.

The boundless fecundity of the vegetal world demands we enter it with our wits about us, fully aware of its rules, its vegetable decorum. In "Sweet Porridge," a poor but good little girl goes into the forest desperate to find something to eat for herself and her mother.[34] There she meets an old woman who gives her a small pot. At the request "Cook, little pot, cook," it will cook lots of sweet porridge and only will stop when asked "Stop, little pot." The girl and her mother live well after this; but one day when the girl is out, the mother asks the pot to make some porridge and unfortunately doesn't know how to make it stop. More and more porridge is produced, filling the house, then the one next door, until the entire town is threatened. At that point the girl returns and tells the pot to stop.

Dangerous over-abundance reminds us of Dionysus. In "The King's Daughter Who Could Never Get Enough Figs," the protagonist unknowingly enlists his assistance.[35] The King declares that whoever can satisfy his daughter's capacity for figs can marry her. Three brothers digging in a field decide to make the attempt as a way of escaping from the exhausting and poor life they lead. As the eldest carries a large basket of figs to the palace, he is approached by a neighbor who asks him for a fig. The eldest brother refuses, saying he needs them all for the princess, but she just gobbles them all down and is still hungry. The next brother repeats the attempt, refuses the same request from the neighbor, and similarly fails to satisfy the princess. Finally, the youngest brother gathers up a basket of figs, sets off, and when asked by the neighbor gives him three of the precious figs. In return the young man is given a magic wand. He is told that when it strikes the ground the basket will instantly be refilled. After a couple of such refills, the princess never wants to see another fig. A royal greed exhausts itself in the face of Dionysian abundance.

Hunger, desperation, and innocence are no protection when one enters the vegetable realm in search of sustenance or improvement. There is a vegetable decorum; the realm has its own laws and logic; it is populated by psychic presences. As Hillman insists: "Dionysus may be the force that through the green fuse drives the flower, but this force is not dumb. It has internal organization."[36] No matter whether our imaginal hunger is for a greener planet or just for a greener life for ourselves—more imaginally voluptuous, nourished, rooted—it is imperative that one pay respect to the vegetable intelligences at work. Heroics, greed, naive goodness, arrogance, and understandable aspiration carry moral implications for the rational soul but not necessarily for the vegetable soul.

Although time and again in these folktales only a Hermetic quick-wittedness saves the day, sometimes one feels that such folk heroes as Jack O'Kent are too clever and that they represent peasant culture's refusal to go deeper. For example, Jack has one of his regular encounters with the Devil, walking with him through a turnip field. The turnips are still below ground and can't be seen, but Jack knows they are there. Jack bets the Devil that Jack can get more profit than he from the field when they share it. "Tops or bottoms?" asks Jack. "Tops," says the Devil, who then ends up with the worthless greens. Next year the Devil takes up the same wager but this time carefully chooses the bottom part of the crop. Jack, however, has sown wheat; so again the Devil loses.[37] In these tales we also encounter a vegetable humor, which is both ribald and slapstick but also marked by a clever wit.[38]

VEGETABLE CHILDREN

In the tales discussed above, the pledge of a human child, or part of a child, to compensate for the stolen vegetable (the witch's earth-born child) reminds us of the many stories that relate childbirth and vegetables. The image of the baby born in the cabbage patch is only the best known of these. Given the nature of 'vegetative functioning,' the generative aspect of the vegetable soul, such a relationship comes as no surprise.[39]

In a tale from Palermo, a childless queen admires a humble rosemary bush and its abundant seedlings.[40] A short time later she herself gives birth, not to a child, but to a rosemary bush. She plants it in a beautiful pot and waters it with milk three times a day. When her nephew, the King of Spain, arrives, she proudly shows him the plant, which he then steals and takes back to Spain, being sure to give it its daily milk. When the bush is planted in his garden, the youthful King plays his flute and dances around it. One day a beautiful maiden appears from the bush and dances with him. When the dancing is over, she returns into the plant. From that time on, the King frequents the garden, playing his flute and dancing with the maiden. Then, one day, he has to go to war and leaves strict instructions with his gardener to care for the precious bush, for he is very much in love with the maiden. But the King's three curious sisters find the flute and play it in the garden. When the maiden appears, they beat her until she flees back to the bush, which takes on a very wilted appearance. When the gardener sees this, he flees for his life but leaves instructions with his wife to give the bush milk. At midnight, deep in the forest, he overhears a dragon-couple discussing the rosemary bush and how it can be saved by an ointment made from the dragons' own blood and fat. Taking courage the gardener kills the dragons as they sleep, prepares the ointment, and saves the bush. When the King returns he marries the maiden, thanks the gardener, and even invites the bush-maiden's mother and father to the wedding, apologizing for having stolen the plant.

This is almost the reverse of the Greek myth in which Daphne flees from an amorous Apollo by transmuting into a tree.[41] After a period of maternal nurturing and care, an anima-inspired relationship 'draws out' the human, the rational soul, from the vegetable. But it is still fragile, still in need of vegetative care. When the King is absent and in his martial guise, the jealousy of his ignored feminine aspect drives the gardener deep into the vegetative night, where he obtains the secret dragon-substance that alone can fix the maiden in human form.

In "Pete and the Ox," from Florence, a woman cooking chickpeas refuses to give some to a hungry girl, who then curses her by hoping that all of the chickpeas become the woman's children. The fire then goes out, and one hundred little boys as tiny as chickpeas come out of the pot, crying "Mama!" Then they scatter everywhere. The terrified woman quickly gathers them all up and crushes them with a pestle. Remorseful at what she has done, she wishes that she had spared at least one of these strange children. Then a tiny voice tells her that one has indeed survived. His name is Pete, and he is most welcomed by the childless couple.[42] Here are many familiar vegetative themes: generosity, or lack of it, an over-abundance, remorse and care, then a final reconciliation.[43]

VEGETABLE REVENGE

"Donkey Cabbages" tells of a young huntsman who shows kindness toward an old, ugly woman. She then tells him how to obtain a wishing cloak and a bird's heart that, when swallowed, produces gold each morning.[44] But after he has obtained these wonderful things, the huntsman falls in love with the beautiful daughter of a bad witch. Despite her protests, the maiden is forced to help the witch steal the cloak and heart, then abandon the huntsman on a remote mountaintop. Picked up by the clouds, he is eventually softly landed in a great cabbage-garden. Being hungry he starts to eat but quickly feels very strange and changes into an ass. Still hungry, he continues to eat until at last he comes to a different kind of cabbage. After eating some of these, he resumes his human shape.

He then plans his revenge. Breaking off a piece from both types of cabbage, he returns in disguise to the home of his sweetheart and the witch. He pretends he is a king's messenger sent to gather the most delicious salad on the Earth and that he has on him the leaves of the most delicate cabbage. The greedy witch asks to try it, and the huntsman gives her, her maidservant, and the maiden some of the bad cabbage. They all quickly change into asses. He then loans them to a miller with instructions that the old donkey (the witch) is to be beaten three times daily and is to receive just one feed, the next ass is to get one beating and three meals, while the youngest (really the maiden) is to get no beatings and three feeds each day. After a couple of days, the old donkey dies; and the huntsman, feeling that revenge is satisfied, gives the other two some of the good cabbage. Upon recovering human shape, the maiden begs forgiveness and she and the huntsman are married.

Here we encounter the green of vegetable revenge. The vegetable garden is a place of trickery, of acute ambivalences. The huntsman's kindness is not enough. Too naive, he has lost his metaphorical ground; his head is in the clouds; and he is forced, almost literally, to live out his vagueness: the clouds carry him to the cabbage-garden. At the mountain summit, the axis mundi, he meets the Gods—in vegetable guise. In the garden he is painfully initiated into the ambivalence of the vegetable soul. Armed with this wisdom, his compassion tempered with an earthiness, he extracts just vengeance. Ultimately, he achieves the union he desires. Once again the tale of *The Golden Ass* hovers in the background, with its deep insights into the mysteries of Isis–Aphrodite.[45]

VEGETABLES AND PRINCESSES

Vegetables frequently figure as truth-testers, as in the case of the princess and the pea. A queen, desiring that her son should marry a true princess, places a small pea beneath a pile of twenty mattresses on which she invites a bedraggled young woman to sleep. In the morning the guest complains that the bed is lumpy and so proves herself to be a true princess.[46] However, the proof of her "royalty" surely does not only depend upon her delicate skin but also on her acute sensitivity to the vegetable.

Vegetables have specific relationships to various figures—wounded soldiers, kings, witches, children, pregnant women—but perhaps the most common is with finicky princesses.[47] What is this special connection?

In "The Mincing Princess," a king decides his daughter should marry and holds a grand party so that she can choose her groom.[48] She falls in love with the son of King Garnet, and a great feast is arranged to celebrate. However, the prince is unfamiliar with the pomegranates that are served as dessert. When he drops one of the seeds onto the floor, he bends down and picks it up, unsure whether or not it is valuable. The haughty princess sees this act, decides that the prince is of a mean nature, and so refuses to marry him. Outraged, the prince disguises himself as a gardener, gets a job in the palace gardens, and sets out to gain his revenge on the princess. By seducing her with beautiful things, he eventually makes his way into her bedroom and she becomes pregnant. In desperation she flees with him, but he withholds his true identity until she has been humbled by poor living, theft, and hard, menial work.

Scorn for the value of the vegetative soul, especially the pomegranate seed, insults Demeter/Persephone; it initiates a period of trial that brings the princess's viewpoint down to the vegetable peasant level. The princess as an archetypal figure suggests a willful puella or father's daughter—an egotistical, flirtatious, seductive feminine, who shimmers with anima fascination. But although she seems destined for "greatness," the crucial connection between the crown (royalty) and the roots (peasants) is lacking. This social order's image of harmony is not Georgic—each in his or her place. It is a shared, symbiotic experiencing—a view from the bottom levels—tempering power and status with humility and worldly understanding.

The gardener occupies a crucial place in this reconciliation. Through him the earth and its fruits are brought into intimate relation with social power and cultural values. The gardener is an intermediary figure, a go-between, and derives prestige and a certain autonomy from this ambiguous position.

In "The Gardener and the Lord and Lady," a highly successful, but humble gardener is continually unappreciated by his ignorant aristocratic employers despite producing, year after year, the most acclaimed and delicious fruits and vegetables in the country.[49] One day he brings into the parlor a large, beautiful blue flower floating in a bowl of water. The Lord and Lady exclaim over it and decide it is a rare Hindustani lotus. Everyone admires it, especially the country's princess, who is wise and good-natured. To gain favor, the Lord and Lady present the princess with the flower. But when they ask the gardener if there are any others like it, he tells them it is just the flower from an artichoke plant that he took from the vegetable garden. The aristocrats are outraged that he should have brought something from the vegetable garden into the parlor. They feel he has made them look ridiculous in the eyes of the princess, who is a keen botanist. But, when told of the flower's origins, the princess remarks that the gardener should be praised for revealing the true beauty of this humble vegetable blossom. Reluctantly, the couple praise their gardener. Later a huge storm blows down a couple of ancient, almost dead trees that have sheltered a flock of rooks and crows. The gardener is pleased: he had wanted them removed years ago so as to get rid of the birds and to make better use of the soil. But the Lord and Lady had insisted that they remain because they were part of the ancestral tradition of the place. Now that the trees are gone, the gardener sets about planting all manner of greenery. He even puts up a flagpole to which he attaches a sheaf of oats for the birds to eat at Christmas. The country's leading newspaper reproduces a picture of this and praises the revival of an old custom. Again, reluctantly, the Lord and Lady have to give credit to their gardener.

Many people today sentimentally cling to supposedly ancient ancestral practices or relics in the desperate hope that these will give them roots, a sense of continuity and belonging. But, such practices are all too often at a remove from the real concerns of the imaginal earth, disconnected from any living, rejuvenating vegetative life.

The Lord and Lady are too concerned with social status to bend their pride to respect the gardener and his wisdom. Yet his view, from the earth, brings widespread acclaim, restores the fertility of the waste ground, and perhaps moves toward a genuine ancestral reconnection. I say perhaps because there is a conservative sentimentality surrounding the image of "the gardener," one that readily lends itself to a bourgeois idealization, in much the same way as the image of "the farmer." Time and again, the gardener has been co-opted by a rather cloying and literal form of patriotism, an image of pre-modern ways, of knowing one's social place and duties.[50]

LOSS OF REFLECTION

A strange story from Lincolnshire, in England, provides a fitting conclusion to this chapter. It tells of a time long ago when the extensive bog-land was inhabited on moonless nights by dreadful spirits, creeping and crawling horrors.[51] The Moon heard about these things and set out to have a look, wrapping herself in a black cloak and hood. As she went deeper into the bogs, she saw more and more grotesque creatures. Then she stumbled and grasped a root with both hands. Suddenly she found herself trapped as the root twisted itself firmly around her wrists. Nearby she heard a piteous cry from a man, lost in the bog, who was being tormented by the malevolent bog-creatures. Angrily, the Moon struggled to free herself, and her hood slipped back so that the light streamed out from her face, throwing a bright silver clarity over the landscape. The bog-creatures retreated in confusion, and the man joyfully escaped. The demonic spirits then buried the Moon under a large, heavy rock. As dark night followed dark night, the malevolent creatures gained in confidence and started to venture right up to the doors of the humans' houses. Deeply concerned, some people went to consult a Wise Woman who gave them instructions on how to protect themselves against the encroaching bog-creatures. Eventually, the man who was saved on the night that the bog suddenly lit up deduced that the light must have come from the trapped Moon. A group of humans set out, advised by the Wise Woman to keep total silence and to have a stone in their mouths and a hazel twig in their hands. After a dreadful journey they found the Moon and released her.

Importantly, in this ancient story the bogs were not drained, reclaimed, or pacified, just kept to within their established bounds. Without the Moon there could be no vegetative reflection. The people are not so naive as to believe that Nature has only their best interests at heart. Without periodic nighttime reflection, they can only become literally bogged down, swallowed up by a barely differentiated mass of vegetate life.

CONCLUSIONS

While I have scarcely attempted any full-scale reading of these stories, I hope at least to have shown the ubiquity of the vegetable imagination in European folklore. These tales reveal a peasant's world of intimate daily association with, and dependence on, the vegetable kingdom. Like the vegetables themselves, peasant culture has long been at the very bottom of any cultural hierarchy. Vegetables therefore provide a fitting metaphorical field for this group's aspirations, wisdoms, and pathologizings, whether these be individual, political, or spiritual. The peasant seems to be well aware of the ambiguities and dangers inherent within the social, psychological, and vegetable worlds. Images from each weave and intertwine inseparably. Through the vegetable the "peasant" imagines how to deal with both the "King" and the "Devil." The "peasant" is, therefore, a crucial imaginal character in our involvement with the vegetable world.[52] These tales map out the phenomenology of such a root metaphor and as such help to reanimate contemporary vegetable imaginings.

CHAPTER SEVEN
Vegetables and Modernism

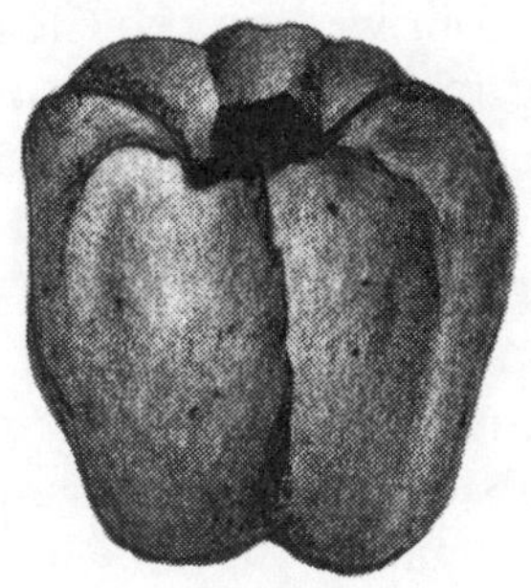

PART ONE: VEGETABLES IN ART

A painting by the Victorian English artist Blandford Fletcher portrays a poor but proud woman accompanied by her young daughter as they are forced to leave their home in an English country town. Suitably titled *Evicted* (1887), it shows sympathetic but powerless neighbors watching their tragic departure, perhaps worried themselves about who will be next. The entire foreground of the painting is taken up with a bare, rough courtyard or street, across which the presumably widowed or abandoned mother and child walk into homelessness. Significantly, also located in this bleak foreground, just at the point where the sympathetic but frightened neighbors hesitate, is a sizable cane basket with a lid. Lying on the ground next to it is a large green cabbage. This vegetable is no mere embellishment. The cabbage is located at a crucial place in the picture's composition, connecting the evicted family with their old home and community. The cabbage, that most basic and traditional of vegetables for the English peasant, is shown itself to be homeless; the plight of the vegetable, of the whole metaphorical domain of vegetableness, echoes the human tragedy being played out around it. Within this painting we can find most of the themes that have come to dominate vegetative imaginings over the past one hundred years.

In the nineteenth century in Europe and America, the effects of rapid industrialization and urbanization wreaked havoc on the old established rural traditions. Enclosures in eighteenth-century England were followed by the Clearances in the Scottish Highlands and famine in Ireland. All across Europe the mainly peasant population were thrown into turmoil and uncertainty. We have clearly entered a very different world than that from which traditional folktales arose.

All the hopes and concerns of what has come to be called modernity weave themselves through the nineteenth- and twentieth-century portrayals of vegetableness: the loss of rural roots and the associated nostalgia for these by a growing urban population; the rise of intense nationalism and global aspirations; a loss of religious faith and a deepening of existential doubt; widespread exile and migrations, accompanied by feelings of homelessness and rootlessness; the dawning of an ecological awareness caused by the rapidly deteriorating quality of the environment; the development of political sophistication and militancy among the dispossessed peasantry and factory workers; the rise of vast state bureaucracies and totalitarian governments; the invention of new sciences and technologies. All of these events provoked a widespread sense of depersonalization, anomie, and alienation, as well as utopian hopes of an end to human suffering and for the birth of a new era.

Just eight years before *Evicted* was painted, the French artist Ernest Hebert had completed his work *La Mal'aria*. It shows a forlorn group of peasants—three women, two men, and a baby—drifting aimlessly in an open boat. The primitive craft floats on a scarcely moving, reed-lined river that is sunk down beneath the surrounding bleak earth bank. Propped up in the rear of the boat is a small image of the Madonna and child, while in the prow lies a heap of fresh vegetables: cabbages, onions, turnips. One of the young men stands in a heroic posture gazing out across the vegetables toward the small piece of horizon that presents itself in the extreme distance. What a powerful metaphor for a dispossessed peasantry struggling to throw off a soporific malaise and find new meanings in a disenchanted world. They carry with them not only the new generation and their ancient faith but also a symbol of their previous rootedness: the vegetables. These are not just physical provisions for the journey but soulful, ancestral icons, reminders of their past and, because the vegetables are significantly placed in the prow of the vessel, of their hope for the future.

In the Bottom Corner

We have already seen how vegetables tend to quietly state their presence from the corners in dreams and folktales, from small, seemingly insignificant places. Western painting over the past one hundred fifty years provides no exception to this phenomenon. In *The Blind Fiddler* (1806) by Sir David Wilkie, a poor family crowd into a gloomy room to be entertained by an itinerant musician. The family group occupies the entire righthand two-thirds of this extremely influential painting, while the fiddler sits by himself on the left. Beneath him, in the foreground, taking up the entire bottom lefthand corner, is a profusion of humble objects, particularly baskets and vegetables: cabbages, onions, swedes. Under the influence of Wilkie's work, J. M. W. Turner painted *The Blacksmith Disputing the Price of Iron* (1807). In this work the vegetables lie conspicuously strewn in the bottom righthand corner of a poor, but picturesque, village smithy. In *The Itinerant Artist* (1825–1830) by the American painter Charles Bird King, the motif is repeated: a poor interior, a family group, and basic vegetables placed in the bottom corner.[1] There are numerous other examples of this theme, but one more will suffice. *The Sleeping Hermit* (*L'ermite Endormi*), by the French artist Joseph Vien (1716–1809), shows an old hermit asleep by the roadside, violin laid carelessly across his lap. In one bottom corner lie a number of ancient, weighty books, while in the other, tumbling from an old straw basket, are turnips, onions, celery, and fennel.

So pervasive is this motif, across a wide range of painting

styles, that it is surely more than just a conceit or an attempt at realism. The vegetables signify a basic, humble honesty. They are images of certainty and rootedness; they confirm an acceptance of the established social hierarchy which in reality was undergoing marked, stressful, and frequently violent changes.[2] Vegetables, like 'good' peasants, know their place—at the very bottom of the "picture." On the other hand, by occupying these otherwise unwanted corners, vegetables draw our attention downward; they keep the floor and foreground cluttered and busy. They imaginally populate it.

Still Life: Beneath the Table

In fact, this lowly placing of vegetables has a long history in the popular genre of still life painting. Frans Snyders's *Still Life with Fruit and Vegetables* (early sixteenth-century Flemish) shows an array, a veritable abundance. But closer inspection reveals that, while all of the fruit is stacked on the large, solid wooden table, all of the vegetables are placed beneath, on the floor.[3]

When vegetables do manage to reach the surface of the table, it is generally in the kitchen and in conjunction with 'gross' objects such as hunks of raw meat, as in Richard Waitt's *Still Life with a Leg of Mutton* (1706–1726), Monet's *Nature Mort* (showing raw beef with garlic cloves), or Baltasar Gomez Figueira's *Oranges, Onions, Fish and Cucumber* (1561–1627). Only exceptional vegetables join fruits and flowers on the tops of elegant tables in the drawing rooms of wealthy families: asparagus (Louise Moillon, 1609–1696, *Still Life with Asparagus*), artichoke (Maurice Vlaminck, 1876–1958, *Bottles and Artichoke*), aubergines (Matisse, *Yellow Pottery from Provence*, 1906; Renoir's *Fruit from the South*), and mushrooms.

Of course, single vegetable types have frequently been portrayed: *Broad Beans* (Giovanna Garzoni, 1600–1670), *Gourds* (David-Alfaro Sigueiros, 1898–1974), *Still Life with Mushrooms* (Sir William Nicholson, 1872–1949). These paintings show a profound respect for vegetable aesthetics. But with Cezanne's *Pink Onions*, or Van Gogh's *Onions* (1889), or *Still Life with Rhubarb, Flowers and Vegetables*, by James Ensor (1860–1949), the vegetable takes its place alongside other objects on top of the table.[4] In Van Gogh's picture, the onions are an integral part of a tableau of pipe, book, candle, letter, teapot, and wine bottle that has deeply intimate associations for the artist.[5] But the vegetable has not just been accepted into the bourgeois space: this space has itself been transformed. A process of imaginal democratization has occurred. Vegetableness, with all its metaphorical connotations, is not simply admitted as a literal, somewhat basic, bottom layer, but is allowed a more pluralistic sensual play at the very heart of daily life. This is particularly the case in Matisse's *Still Life with Egg Plant* (1911–1912), in which three shiny aubergines take their purple place atop a table set in a lounge that vibrates with swirling patterns, colors, and textures.

Peasants and Vegetables

One would expect Van Gogh to have a deeply sympathetic attitude to vegetables. He was a man who devoted himself toward a truly empathic understanding of peasant life. Indeed, the artistic portrayal of vegetables is profoundly connected to the corresponding imaginal attitude toward the rural worker. As peasant life came under threat, and in many cases began to disappear, in much of Western Europe and as country-folk flooded the swelling urban centers, "The Peasant" became a crucial imaginal character in nineteenth- and twentieth-century art. Around this character clustered the most diverse sentiments, spanning the complete political spectrum, embracing all social classes, and expressing most of the nostalgic fantasies held by a disenchanted, often rootless urban population.

Georgic: Social Harmony and Seasonal Certainty

The paintings of John Constable's middle years epitomize what has come to be called the Georgic vision: a productive farming landscape of social and natural harmony, in which the seasonal rhythms echoed the stability of an almost feudal social order. In

Landscape, Ploughing Scene in Suffolk (1814), the peasant is merely an anonymous figure in the landscape, a signifier of seasonal labor and harmony. In *View of Dedham* (1814), two farm laborers shovel manure from a large heap onto a cart. To one side we can see it being ploughed into the field. In the far distance, at the very center of the painting, the tower of Dedham church gives divine sanction to the mundane activity in the foreground. Vegetable soulfulness, nature's seasons, agricultural rhythms, social and divine order are all brought into intimate alignment. The picture is painted in such a way that the viewer occupies precisely that vantage point that a landowner would take up to survey his domain and reassure himself that all was well.[6]

Turner's *Ploughing up Turnips* (1809) portrays a similar fantasy: the center of the painting shows a group of peasants collecting turnips, and vegetables are stacked to the right in a large basket at which a black cow is cautiously sniffing. Hovering over this scene of rustic contentment and productive labor, shimmering in the distant background, is Windsor Castle, the royal residence. During the Napoleonic Wars, agricultural production in Britain was viewed as a patriotic act.[7] In this painting Turner relates the most basic of vegetables to the highest patriotic sentiments; turnips and royalty are directly connected.

As a portrayal of contemporary social reality, both Turner's and Constable's paintings are utterly misleading, highly conservative, and quite repressively nostalgic. Farm workers were suffering great hardships and expressing often violent dissatisfaction. Agriculture was experiencing a massive upheaval, and the rural population was in decline.[8] But on a more symbolic, almost alchemical level, these paintings express the individuals' desire to anchor their "highest," almost spiritual, beliefs and aspirations in the firm vegetative ground, particularly in these times of great insecurity and change.[9] The "problem" with these paintings is the way in which they are presented and read as literal, naturalistic statements, as social documentation, rather than as expressions of the imaginal. Unfortunately, vegetable life (including farmers, peasants, etc.) often functions in modern culture as a profound signifier of the "natural," of a down-to-earth truth that lies outside the paradox and ambiguity of fantasy-making.

Basic Honest Toil

A World War II poster, from the London Underground, shows a sturdy looking costermonger (someone who sells fruit and vegetables from the street). He stands tall, legs firmly apart, with a steady, worldly-wise gaze, in front of a row of busy shops. With one large hand he holds the reins of his trusty donkey that pulls his barrow, while with the other he cradles a large cabbage, almost to his heart. The caption reads "London Characters—The Coster: The Anti-Profiteer." Clearly, the cabbage confirms the integrity of this wise city "peasant." Patriotically content with his basic but meager income, he serves as an example to possibly profit-hungry, self-centered shopkeepers suggested by the busy background.[10]

In Western culture throughout the nineteenth and twentieth centuries, city life has constantly been contrasted unfavorably with that of the countryside.[11] While this recurring motif led into the extremes of Nazi and Fascist idealization of the rural patriot—earthy, honest, pure—it can also be found in less sinister, but no less nationalistic fantasies. The English painter George Clausen, for example, believed rural areas provided a morally healthier climate than the city, one that still embodied 'true' values: *In the Fields in June* (1914) shows muscular, clean-limbed young men at work in open fields under sweeping skies. Their pose is full of a heroic nostalgia. In *Harvest—In the Bean Field* (1904), a group of sturdy farm laborers are busily engrossed in their work. There are no hints of complaint, no suggestions of the spreading mechanization. In his *Morning—Decoration in Hall at High Royd, Honley* (1919), the idealization is complete: a rural family—cleanly dressed in homespun medieval clothes, stoutly built, fresh, open-faced—are contentedly gathered together in a neat, orderly, and productive landscape. A young man, stripped to the waist, muscles rippling, feet bare, concentrates his whole being into digging the soil.[12]

Another direction taken by this motif leads into the portrayal of the proud, militant peasant. A painting by Jules Breton, *Le rappel des glaneuses (Artois)* (1859), shows a group of clean, strongly built women and girls, heads held high, walking firmly and purposefully toward the viewer. It is dusk, and they have reached the end of their day's work of binding and gathering sheaves of wheat.[13]

The Picturesque Peasant Idyll

At a far remove from such vegetable patriotism and moral earnestness are those paintings which depict peasant life as bounteous, carefree, sensual delight amid picturesque landscapes. This was a popular fantasy among late Victorian painters such as Richard Redgrave, with his *The Valleys Also Stand Thick with Corn* (1865), or James Clarke Hook with his portrayal of *The Mushroom Gatherers*: country waifs wandering freely along a richly vegetated but precipitous cliff-edge in search of wild mushrooms.[14] There is a sense of sexual titillation about many of these paintings, as well as a vague hint of danger. Country life and the vegetable soul both express sensual fantasies that otherwise remained repressed and embody many of the characteristics that Freud was to label polymorphous perversity.[15]

Piety and Community

A famous painting by Jean-Francois Millet, *L'Angelus* (1857–1859), shows a poorly dressed peasant couple with heads bowed in prayer, standing beside their wheelbarrow in the middle of a vast, bleak field. On the ground between the husband and wife is an old basket containing potatoes, some of which still lie on the dark earth next to the man's pitchfork. The whole scene speaks of hardship, poverty, and struggle but also of a quiet, pious dignity. Van Gogh's *The Potato Eaters* (1885), which shows a dark interior of a poor house with a family of exhausted looking peasants seated around a bare table on which is a plate of cooked potatoes, follows a similar theme. Of this picture he wrote: these people have dug the earth with those very hands they put into the dish. It was, he piously exclaimed, "honest labor."[16]

In his sketch *Work in the Fields*, Van Gogh depicts an old peasant couple sowing potato seeds. As the husband laboriously digs the hard ground, the wife throws down the seed, which is shown in midair. Both man and woman are painfully bent over in a habitual, almost permanent stoop. In his *Peasant Woman Put-*

ting Corn into Sheaves (1885), Van Gogh sketches an old woman almost totally bent double as she binds up the grain. Both pictures uncompromisingly direct the whole attention and orientation downward toward the earth. The peasants embody this earthboundness of the vegetable soul, sharing in its suffering, as well as in its dark, underrated divinity.[17]

In these paintings we can also detect the ritual power of the vegetable soul to foster community. This need not always be portrayed so somberly. The American artist Eastman Johnston, in his painting *Corn Husking Bee* (1876), shows two rows of men and women seated on the ground amid a carpet of discarded corn husks. In his painting *October* (1867), another American, John Whetten Ehninger, depicts a group of prosperous farmers helping each other to gather up pumpkins and corn.[18]

The Vegetable Market

Vegetables achieve their most public celebration at the market. Time and again, paintings portray this rough abundance, this proliferation of coarse, earthy sensuality. Here the vegetable is center-stage, and, unlike Turner's *Ploughing up Turnips*, aristocracy and peasantry mingle. The marketplace is the most democratic and most socially pluralistic location in eighteenth- and nineteenth-century towns. Partly hidden are both the exhausting labor of the fields and the oppressive opulence of the mansions. In his mid-nineteenth-century painting *Covent Garden with Saint Paul's Church*, Balthazar Nebot shows a group of 'ladies' and 'gentlemen' gaily approaching a vegetable stall. The setting is spacious, surrounded by the elegant order of neo-classical buildings. This is a most cautious acceptance of the democratic role of vegetables, one in which so-called 'refined' society dominates.

In Michele Graneri's *Turin: Piazza San Carlo* (1752), the vegetables take over the city center; the balance is on the side of the lower classes. Dominating the central foreground is a splendid mound of cabbages with a peasant woman plying a busy trade. There is a sense of carnival about this and many other paintings of vegetable markets, a robust exuberance in the air, an earthy promise of freedom. Potential anarchy is held in check only by the presence of the vegetables. In Gustave Bauernfeind's *Jaffa Street Scene* (1890), such vegetative musings take on an oriental guise.[19] The scene is one of ruined splendor as a colorful procession advances through an ancient market. Along one side vegetable stalls witness the display. Decadence, power, and sexuality pervade the fantasy.

A market filled with an abundance of healthy vegetables signifies that all is well with the world. Social divisions are suspended; culture is grounded in the fruits of the earth. This is surely a breeding ground for nostalgia. In Henry Bryant's late-nineteenth-century painting *The Vegetable Market*, the fantasy is complete: rosy cheeks and full, rounded vegetables abound.[20]

Vegetable Gardens

A fresh-faced old woman sits by the backdoor of her white-washed cottage; washing is on the line; sunflowers grow amid other bright, homely blooms. She is peeling large yellow pumpkins on an old wooden bench. Beside her stands a large, brown earthenware pot. In another painting, two slender women in homely long dresses and white aprons are gathering fruit from a tree in the back garden. Washing is on the line; green vegetables are growing all around.[21] In another rustic back garden cottage scene a woman is shown tending her rows of cabbages and other green vegetables.[22] Paintings of vegetable gardens, perhaps like no other paintings, evoke sentimental reveries of "home." Not the home of one's childhood but of an idealized, 'lost' childhood of our culture—one that is grounded, supportive, intimate, nourishing, enclosed, secret.[23]

Alone in the Kitchen

In his painting *Woman Peeling Potatoes* (1883), Van Gogh captures an essential existential aspect of the vegetable soul. A tired-looking woman sits upright with knife in her hand and plate of potatoes in her lap, an old bucket on the floor beside her to catch the peelings. She is almost in meditation. While the kitchen can be a place of family conviviality, all too often it has been the site of a woman's loneliness, solitude, and labor—whether for love, duty, or necessity. *Girl Shelling Peas*, by W. K. Bigg (1755–1825), though a less somber expression of this theme, still shows the same ritual.[24] The Australian artist Joshua Smith's *Peeling Vegetables* (1939) reiterates, even celebrates, the same solitary domestic ritual, the same direct handling of the individual vegetable, the concentrated, familiar attention: a middle-aged woman sits alone on an upright chair, feet firmly and squarely placed on the floor, enamel bowl filled with basic vegetables on her lap, a sharp knife in her hand.[25]

Existential Vegetables

While we have encountered the existential downwardness of the vegetable soul in some of Van Gogh's portrayals of peasant life or in the solitary women peeling vegetables, nowhere does it reach such bleakness as in Millet's *Crows in Winter* (1862). Agricultural implements lie scattered and abandoned over an unrelentingly bare dark-brown plain. The only life is provided by numerous black crows, on the ground and in the air. In this portrayal of vegetative absence, there is scarcely any hint of a future resurrection. Vegetative death is experienced as absolute, and we follow its retreat inexorably downward.

Octave Fassaert's mid-eighteenth-century painting *In the Studio* brings us back to the surface: a poor, struggling young artist sits with his cat on the bare floor and huddles up against the fireplace for warmth. A simple black pot is on the fire, while beside him, almost blending in with his painting implements, are strewn a dozen or so potatoes. Despite the painting's sentimentalized romanticism, the humble vegetable here takes its rightful place in the work of artistic creation. It is what supports the process at its most fundamental level, when all else seems hopeless.

The painting *Now or Never* (1849), by the American Tompkins Harrison Matteson, draws many of these threads together and at the same time takes us back to *Evicted* discussed at the beginning of this chapter. An attractive, young, intelligent-looking woman sits by an open window gazing out thoughtfully. Partly kneeling on a chair, standing almost bent over her, cap in hand is a rather slick and somewhat shallow-looking young man who seems comfortably well-off. He is clearly proposing to her. A small curtain flaps gently in the window just by the young woman's serious face as reminder both of a possible but precarious freedom and of a secure but loveless confinement. For women of her era and station there was really little choice. Just as the woman's gaze is directed outward, the man's focuses inward into the interior of the room, drawing our attention to a cluster of vegetables on the floor, beneath a simple table in the bottom corner of the picture. A paradoxical connection is thereby made between the fate of the young woman and that of the vegetables.

Surreal Vegetables

In his painting *The Explanation* (1952), Rene Magritte shows a tall, long-necked, brown glass bottle standing side-by-side with what appears at first to be a rather large carrot. But second glance reveals that the bright red flesh at the top of the vegetable merges into bottle-shaped brown glass at the base. Lying horizontally between bottle and hybrid is an ordinary carrot. Magritte invites us to play with the vegetable form, to whimsically deepen our appreciation of vegetable aesthetics. In Max Ernst's *The Joy of Living* (1936), the surrealist delight in an ambiguity of form results in a complex metamorphosis. Tangled, dense green vegetation seems inseparable from strange insect and human shapes. We are drawn into a deeply attentive looking just in order to see exactly what transformations could be taking place in the vegetative darkness.

Such a playful attitude toward vegetable forms can of course be traced back to Giuseppe Arcimboldo's bizarre, often grotesque, portraits. In *Summer* (1573), fruit and vegetables are grouped in such a way as to invite the viewer to see the profile of a rosy-cheeked, rather jolly young man. In fact, 'his' nose is a zucchini, 'his' ears a combination of corncob, aubergine, and garlic cloves, while 'his' mouth is a half-open pea pod.

Sexual Vegetables

This polymorphous aspect of vegetables also contains a rather earthy and humorous sexuality. Alvan T. Fisher's *The Corn Husking Frolic* (1828–1829) shows the inside of a large American barn. Hay is piled up high all around while the floor is covered in corn husks. The atmosphere is warm and playful. Family groups are gathered, and a young man, holding a corncob aloft, flirts suggestively with a young woman. In another American painting, Lilly Martin Spencer's *Kiss Me and You'll Kiss the Lasses* (1856), a saucy-looking young woman turns from her cooking, vegetables piling in abundance out of a large basket at her feet, to smile invitingly over her shoulder at the viewer.[26]

In *We Are What We Eat* (1981), the contemporary British "Primitivist" Barry Castle shows a giant naked man walking firmly toward the viewer across rich brown soil. But instead of a penis he has a large, bright red, pointed carrot, and in front of his face, or perhaps instead of his face, he holds a large flat basket neatly filled with rows of colorful carrots. Vegetable humor is rarely subtle and seems to delight in crude visual punning.

Conclusions

While vegetables perhaps have not seen their Georgia O'Keeffe, whose immensely intimate portraits of flowers have celebrated their every sensual line, the humble vegetable has by no means been ignored in Western art of the past two hundred years. In fact, whether quietly sustaining their presence in the odd corners or steadily moving into the very center of the picture, vegetables have become a persistent signifier of modernity's most pressing concerns. Paintings, unlike most literary expression, allow us a visual play with vegetable aesthetics, reminding us of a polymorphous complexity in our vegetable imaginings.[27]

It is crucial that any image be related to its imaginative context, rather than somehow interpreted in isolation. For example, the concerns imbedded in the word *ecology*, which appeared in the English language in 1873, have proved congenial soil for political orientations ranging from Fascism to Communism, rural Conservatism to urban Liberalism. (Many interested in organic farming in Britain in the 1930s were drawn to far-right politics.)[28]

During this time, the portrayal of vegetables in art underwent a marked shift. At the beginning of the modern era, they signified the transition from a social structure founded upon rural production to one based more upon urban living. Condensed into the vegetable was therefore a debate about the status of the peasantry, as well as a concern about the new, emerging social order and about threatened identities and privileges. Midway through this era, by the end of the nineteenth century, this new order—industrial capitalism—was unquestionably in place. Vegetables then came to connote a nostalgia for lost, imagined communities, for bygone certainties and beliefs: *gesellschaft* versus *gemeinschaft*. The end of this two-hundred-year span, sometime in the mid-twentieth century, was marked by the emergence of an ecological concern, by a deep disillusionment with society's relationship to the "natural" world. Vegetables suddenly aligned themselves with a new wisdom, one that manifested itself in issues as diverse as habitat conservation and health diets.

Of course, each of these attitudes still lingers on, as layers in an imaginal archeology, waiting to be invoked. Within these fantasies, as in myths and folktales, are crucial root metaphors of our culture. But, for some reason, twentieth-century painting has failed to utilize the imaginal power of vegetables, a power we have seen consistently expressed in artists throughout the nineteenth century, from Constable and Turner to Millet and Van Gogh. A more complete view of modernity's relationship with vegetables is only obtained if we turn our attention toward literature.

Blandford Fletcher, British (1858–1936), *Evicted*, 1887, oil on canvas, 122.9 × 185.5 cm, Purchased 1896, PT0015, Collection of the Queensland Art Gallery

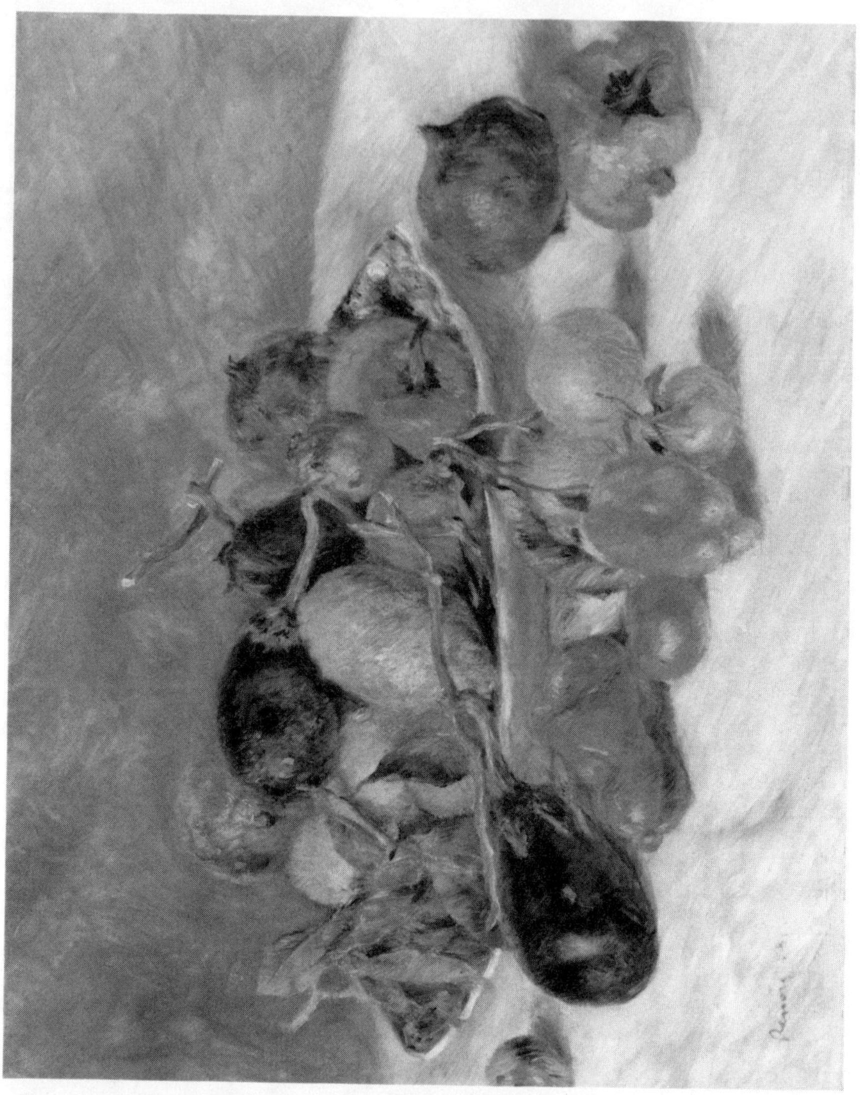

Pierre Auguste Renoir, French (1841–1919), *Fruits from the Midi*, 1881, oil on canvas, 50.7 × 65.3 cm, Mr. and Mrs. Martin A. Ryerson Collection, 1933.1176.. Photograph © 1990 The Art Institute of Chicago, All Rights Reserved

E. A. Cox, *The Coster*, Copyright London Transport Museum

Vincent Van Gogh, *The Potato Eater*, F82, painting, Vincent Van Gogh Foundation/National Museum Vincent Van Gogh, Amsterdam

Vincent Van Gogh, *Peasant Woman Picking a Sheaf of Grain*, F 1266, drawing, Vincent Van Gogh Foundation/National Museum Vincent Van Gogh, Amsterdam

PART TWO: VEGETABLES IN MODERN LITERATURE

Roots and Mobility: A Parable

On a small planet far away, evolution followed a very different path than that which occurred on Earth, due to the high levels of light and heat cast on it by a very large sun. Animal and plant life were not as sharply separated as on Earth; indeed, every organism was simultaneously both animal and vegetable. The higher forms of life carried immense foliage on slender green bodies. Because violent storms and floods, which were common on this small hot world, caused rapid changes to the soil, plants had to be able to move to the most suitable location.

Some plants would just withdraw their simple roots and move by means of a caterpillar-like action. Others would spread their foliage and allow the ever present wind to carry them. But perhaps the most remarkable means of solving this question of how to combine roots with mobility belonged to an organism whose upper portion would detach itself from its embedded roots in order perhaps to locate fresh roots elsewhere. When this new site had subsequently exhausted its fertility, the upper half would either seek out a new place to establish its roots or return to its original bed if that had recovered its vitality. The mobile part would then attach itself and arouse its old dormant roots.

Due to its small size, this planet gradually lost its atmosphere. Life was only possible due to sealed reservoirs that had been constructed in nearly all of the valleys. All around the vast reservoirs were clustered the lower halves of these highly intelligent and resourceful organisms. During the day, the mobile upper halves of these plant-people sat on their root parts, foliage spread to the sun. Then at night, they became active, busy with machines or moving around pursuing their various aims.

By day, therefore, their life was static, mainly vegetable, whereas by night it was mobile and mainly animal. During the day, the plant-people would sleep in a trance, a contemplative reverie with deep mystical and meditative qualities. Sap would journey up and down the trunk, bringing oxygen and also purifying the system. As the sun set, the population would awake, fold up their leaves, close up the entrances to their roots, then detach themselves and go about the business of active, "civilized" life.

At one point in its history, this advanced civilization was caught in a terrible spiritual crisis, one that reflected the tension between the two sides of the plant-people's nature, the animal and the vegetable. One was extrovertedly curious and assertive, while the other was receptive and meditative. The domination and practical exploitation of its world was primarily due to the animal half, whereas the vegetable part provided a direct contact with the vital source of cosmic Being. This part directly absorbed the essential elixir of life and therefore bathed in a mystical and sensual ecstasy that was almost sexual. The relationship between these two parts was crucial to the success of the civilization. The one provided action and ingenuity, the other reflection and ecological contemplation.

Over the centuries, the active, mobile aspect invented various energy sources, communication systems, luxuries, and so on. The demands of social life, reforms, and revolutions became of uppermost concern. Gradually, the time spent in contemplation was resented, its importance devalued and even forgotten as ways were discovered to do away entirely with these seemingly non-productive periods of sleep. The products of artificial photosynthesis were simply injected daily into the body. Virtually the whole day could then be spent in activity and work.

It was not long before the root parts were being dug up and used as raw material in manufacture. However, gradually a disease of the spirit began to permeate the population, a mechanical, soulless attitude to life. Although physically vigorous, the plant-people lacked reflection, depth, a sense of authentic meaning to their now busy, almost all-consuming materialistic lives. Wars vied with the pursuit of worldly success and shallow pleasures.

After much suffering, they began to realize that their whole way of life was alien to their essential plant nature. Nearly all the ancient roots of the race had been destroyed, but the achievements of their biological sciences were redirected into generating, from the few roots remaining, new roots for everyone. Slowly the entire population, exhausted and desperate for inner peace, returned to natural photosynthesis. Industrial culture went into decline and eventually vanished. The contrast between the organisms' former restless, aggressive lives and the regained ecstasy of their vegetal nature merely heightened their remorse and determination. A new plane of spiritual awareness and lucidity was quickly reached by this culture.

But the rejection of their animal nature became so pronounced that they slowly sank into a vegetal life just as onesided as their overly active period. Eventually, even the nights were spent in vegetable contemplation, and the assertive animal intelligence became lost forever. For a while the population continued on in a vague, totally passive reverie, but gradually the life-support structures of their civilization fell into disrepair and broke down. The reservoirs dried up. The harsh conditions of the planet reasserted themselves, and the entire population succumbed, one by one.

This "parable" is a small extract from Olaf Stapledon's massively influential work *Star Maker.* First published in 1937, it is typical of Stapledon's unique brand of philosophical-cosmological fiction.[29] The metaphorical power of his imagery is quite transparent, as is its relevance for the modern era. The vegetable aspect is concerned with being, not doing, with vertical contemplation, not horizontal, worldly achievements. The vegetable soul takes us into deep reverie, into the immobility of meditation. Stapledon's vegetables do not lack wisdom or intelligence. They are deep listeners, soulful digesters. But Stapledon, a concerned socialist, was critical of otherworldly spirituality. In his story there is a crucial balance between contemplation and action, a balance whose loss results in individual and social disaster.

This tension between roots and mobility is almost a leitmotif of modernism. Having roots, belonging to a place, can easily merge into a stuckness, parochialism, an imaginal stagnation; but, on the other hand, being mobile can so easily merge into shallowness, restlessness, and superficiality, in an imaginal exile and alienation. As we have seen in paintings, vegetables have been forced to carry this nostalgic desire for dwelling. In John Wyndham's classic 1960s fantasy thriller *The Day of the Triffids*, a particular kind of vegetable is discovered that produces a substitute for petroleum.[30] To a society that worships speed and physical mobility, the promise of cheap, readily available fuel is irresistible. In addition, it also allows Britain to achieve independence from Middle Eastern supplies and so circumvent the complexities of its post-imperial identity. Vast acres of this vegetable are planted before anyone realizes, perhaps too late, that it can move, think, and communicate with its fellows. It also hunts and kills humans. The dream of cheap mobility turns into a nightmare. The vegetable refuses to be sacrificed to the god of manic restlessness, refuses to meekly allow its sap to become the blood for machines. The repressed, the supposed "immobility" of vegetative life, returns with a vengeance. Appropriately, the plant's aggressive technique is to accurately shoot a blinding liquid into the eyes, thereby gradually immobilizing the entire human population which then becomes easy prey for the vegetable killers.

Vegetable Madness and the Foundation of Things

Unlike painting, literature has provided an outlet for disturbing, fearful images of the vegetable soul. In addition to Stapledon's plant-people and Wyndham's triffids, we can point to the horror of the plant-pod births in *The Invasion of the Body Snatchers* (1951); to the Gothic melancholy of Edgar Allan Poe's "Silence—A Fable," with its "pale desert of gigantic water-lilies . . . [that] sigh one unto the other" and where "strange poisonous flowers lie writhing in perturbed slumber"; and to the vegetable fecundity and ferocity in Brian Aldiss's futuristic novel *Hothouse*.[31]

If one had to select the arch-symbol of modernity's malaise, it would have to be the "city." Often portrayed in terms of superficial materialism, crass acquisitiveness, and heartless greed, the "metropolis" has, for over one hundred years, been constantly contrasted unfavorably with the countryside. As one of the most important of all cities for much of the modern era, London has been the focus of considerable vegetative revenge by those authors who yearn for a civilization built on deeper, more "organic" values than those provided by industrial capitalism.

In his fantasy novel of 1885, *After London*, Richard Jefferies, the well-known nature mystic and commentator on rural life, imagined the sprawling metropolis to be completely swallowed-up by the vegetable world. This vegetable apocalypse was triggered by a great, prolonged flood: "It became green everywhere in the first spring, after London ended. . . . So that there was no place which was not more or less green. . . ."[32] Jefferies went into minute botanical detail of how the vegetable kingdom reclaimed the city, driving out its human inhabitants, reducing civilization to another Dark Age. Adventurers subsequently returned to the "vast stagnant swamp" that covered London, looking for treasures of a lost age. But the vapor from this "oozy mass" was deadly: "For all the rottenness of a thousand years and of many hundred millions of human beings is there festering. . . ." But Jefferies knew too much about the hardships and meanness of rural life to counterpose a naive picture of a country idyll. With his image of a green Armageddon he was trying to neutralize the immense symbolic power that London exerted, a power that he saw as largely negative: spiritually shallow, imaginatively monotheistic, aesthetically numbing, and alienated from the natural world.

The vegetable soul is about the organic foundation of things. In Iain Sinclair's powerful poem/narrative *Lud Heat*, he delved into the substratum upon which London, as the spiritual and financial power center of empire, is founded.[33] Lud was the Celtic God of the underworld, and upon his ground was unwittingly built the cathedral of St. Paul's, the symbol of reason, order, and enlightenment. But at the same time that Sir Christopher Wren reigned as supreme architect, Hawksmoor was creating his own series of rival churches, based on occult and Hermetic principles. Arranged in geomantic patterns, these churches were designed to act as geological acupuncture needles, located at vital power centers in London's occult "body": the ancient ground upon which the "temples to reason" presume to stand. These churches summon up the demons of the deep, reminding the city of its dark, primeval roots.

Sinclair's work is a complex mix of autobiography (he is

employed as a gardener by the city), poetry, history, and Hermetic speculation. London's roots lie among its ancient, numberless dead: Sinclair draws our attention to a famous vegetable market that is built on the site of a medieval hospice which in turn was built over an ancient burial ground; St. Luke's church, he points out, is built near Bunhill Fields, the site of a plague-pit—a mass grave for victims of London's Great Plague. Blake, Defoe, and Bunyan are buried here. He delights in telling us that the Romans regarded East London as a necropolis, a city for the dead. He associates the churches with rites of autopsy: a macabre way that the living can communicate with the dead. For Sinclair, London's roots go much deeper than those of mere literal history: "And this goes back, once more, to Egypt—not by direct route, carried in migration, the plodding cultural transfer theory—but by sap connection . . . —it is the essential shape of a particular kind of fear."[34]

Sinclair's work in the municipal gardens is an apt metaphor for the vegetative invocation he attempts with the dark foundations of London's soul: "He feels the weakness enter the plates of his feet. The charge in his bone marrow sustains a field of deformed mushrooms."[35] The earth itself is charged with ancient occult forces: "it is a field of memory/ out of reach/ drawn up through the prongs/ as the rake drags over the ground."[36] London is founded on ancient sickness, as well as on death: "What has been held down will flower in this form. Plant birth. Each disease discovering its own markings. A garden of dividing songs and repeated chants."[37] The vegetable roots return to the surface, questioning and deforming the shape of orderly civic society: "the bicycle/ bucks over lime roots/ they have turned the tarmac apron into a wave sequence."[38] He writes of "a chaos of plant life loosed to discover its own parliament."[39] "Rain brings relief in the night/ dusty soil drinks a preparation for cabbages. . . ."[40]

But these dark vegetative roots so often remain unseen, below the surface of daily life. The plague-pits and pagan sites are forgotten: "These facts fade. The big traffics slam by. A work ethic buries ancient descriptions."[41] The poet's task is to delve deep into *memoria*, and Sinclair gives a wonderful image of how the *prima materia* is gathered. He recounts a tale told by Herodotus of the Egyptian ruler Asychis, who built a pyramid of bricks.

These were made from the material gained by pushing a pole to the bottom of a sacred lake and then bringing up to the surface the mud that clung to it. The poet's task is also to overcome the cultural vegetal amnesia:

> So again we service the dead,
> complete the stifled gesture,
> grasp at the arm raised in
> salute from the choked ground.[42]

Politics and the Vegetable Soul

The political equation, implicit in the work of Sinclair, Stapledon, and Jefferies, comes to the fore in Raymond William's novels. In *Second Generation*, for example, the tension between a national and global struggle for social justice and an intensely local sense of place and belonging is played out around the image of gardening. Sweeping ideals clash with sensual, earthy details; complex class allegiances vie with loyalties of family and community. "I'll soon have to choose between being a teacher and a gardener," says one of the characters; "One can hardly be both for long."[43] To become a teacher means leaving the locality, moving not just to another location, but to another level of living, adopting another set of values. Throughout such decisions runs the question of guilt. To stay, as a "gardener," may satisfy the need for roots but ignores the call for involvement in wider social struggles; to leave, as a "teacher," could involve co-option into a professional career and hence a betrayal of one's class. "We get misled by the metaphors of gardening and so on," warns one character; "Often it's no more, really, than the child's sandpit. It's very nice but we don't want to make an issue of it."[44] But in a world filled with doubts, disappointments, social injustices, and betrayals, gardening provides some individuals with just a corner of their lives without contradictions, a small part that they can actually make work. Nevertheless, Williams still leaves us in doubt about whether even this intimate concern is a palliative, an escape from the modern world.

While Williams hesitates about trusting the political nature of the vegetable soul, merely contrasting it oppositionally with concerns for social justice, the South African writer Coetzee, in his novel *The Life and Times of Michael K*, plunges straight into vegetative politics.[45] The result is an extraordinary vision of the world, a vegetable-eyed view of the turmoil and oppression of Black South Africa.

Michael K. is a simpleton caught up in grinding poverty, ignorance, and totalitarian control. A civil war rages all around him as he pushes his dying mother in a wheelbarrow from the city back to the farm where she said that she had been born. But her memory is vague, and we seem to move in a landscape of dream and nightmare. After his mother's death on the road, Michael takes her ashes to where he thinks she was born. Her description fits the windswept, dusty plain backed by a few hills. But the farm is deserted and derelict. "The time came to return his mother to the earth. . . . This was the beginning of his life as a cultivator."[46]

This is his homeland. The first part of the vegetable alchemy is complete: returning the mother's dust to the Mother dust. The next task is to cultivate something from what has become a desert. He takes little from the abandoned farm buildings of the white owners: just a few pumpkin seeds, a maize kernel, and a solitary bean. This cultivation has to be done circumspectly both so as not to be detected by the authorities and also so as to get as close to the ground, as close to a new beginning, as possible.

"The impulse to plant had been reawoken in him; now in a matter of weeks, he found his waking life bound tightly to the patch of earth he had begun to cultivate and the seeds he had planted there."[47] Through intense imagination, Michael begins to enter the world of the new shoots pushing their way through the earth. He struggles with this "cord of tenderness," for it is all that holds him to the earth, to life. His intense labor of watering, night after night, fearful of discovery, leaves him "with a strange green glow behind the eyes."[48] Gradually, apart from the slow care for his few vegetables, he becomes almost totally inactive, lying below the ground in his shelter. "It is not hard to live a life that consists merely of passing time," he muses, almost in a vegetative trance.

He experiences a "yielding up of himself to time, to a time flowing slowly like oil from horizon to horizon over the face of the world. . . ."[49] "Then the melons ripened. . . . Their flesh was the colour of orange river-silt, but deeper. He had never tasted fruit so sweet. How much of that sweetness came from the seed, how much from the earth?"[50] But with the final ripening of melons and pumpkins, Michael descends deeper into the vegetative state, being drawn to a silent depth where decision, action, protest, and possibly renewal occur totally independently of the social authority on the surface and beneath even the level that social conditioning can reach.

A white man sympathetically contemplates Michael's state: "As time passed . . . I slowly began to see the originality of the resistance you offered. You were not a hero and did not even pretend to be. . . . In fact you did not even resist at all." The garden, he continues in his imaginary dialogue with Michael, "is another name for the only place where you belong, . . . where you do not feel homeless." Yet the white man is unsure. He urgently needs Michael's response; he yearns for Michael's unfathomable intimacy with the earth: "Am I right? . . . Have I understood you? If I am right, hold up your right hand, if I am wrong hold up your left!" The Black African, like the Indian of America or Aboriginal of Australia, has, to a large extent, supplanted the "peasant" in modern times, as Western culture desperately searches for an exemplary symbol of dwelling close to the "earth."[51]

In a poignant final passage, comprehensible only in a state of absolute oppression, Michael reflects on how he will obtain water in the desolate countryside for his seeds:

> He would produce . . . a teaspoon and a long roll of string. He would clear the rubble from the mouth of the [abandoned well] shaft, he would bend the handle of the teaspoon in a loop and tie the string to it, he would lower it down the shaft deep into the earth, and when he brought it up there would be water in the bowl of the spoon; and in that way, he would say, one can live.[52]

The vertigo of Michael K.'s descent into vegetable life is perhaps unparalleled in modern literature.

Vegetable Humor

Vegetable politics and modernism's apparent alienation from the "natural" world also find expression in humor. Italo Calvino's collection of short stories *Marcovaldo* tells of a former peasant of the same name who is forced, along with his family, to live and work in one of the large industrial cities. Poor and feeling out-of-place, he is constantly on the lookout for signs of his rural origins: "a leaf yellowing on a branch, a feather trapped by a roof-tile, . . . a fig-peel squashed on the sidewalk. . . ."[53] On a narrow strip of unused ground alongside a busy freeway, Marcovaldo, on his way to work, sees the faint early signs of wild mushrooms. Jealously he guards his secret, sharing it only with his wife and children, reminiscing nostalgically of home, promising the children a taste of true living. Each day on his way to work in the factory he watches the mushrooms' growth. "To Marcovaldo the gray and wretched world surrounding him seemed suddenly generous with hidden riches; something could still be expected of life, beyond the hourly wage of his stipulated salary, with inflation index, family grant, and cost-of-living allowance."[54] In the hilarious harvesting scene, Marcovaldo is unable to keep his secret and invites passers-by, passengers queuing for a tram, etc., to join in the feast. Being city-dwellers they are unsure about which fungi are safe to eat. Marcovaldo, the peasant, proudly reassures them. But that evening they all find themselves recovering in the hospital, after having their stomachs pumped out.

But nothing deters Marcovaldo's rural nostalgia and his search in the heart of the city for traces of his roots. On one occasion, "when the simplest foods contained threats" and the sight of his wife's shopping-bag, "which once had given him such joy with its celery and eggplant," filled him with distrust, he determinedly set out to find some pure food from the wild.[55] Of course, his pure, natural food ends up being even more polluted than that bought from the shops. At another time, when he insists on caring for the only potted plant at his factory, even to the point of taking it home for weekends or moving it around the city on the back of his motorbike so as to catch any sun or rain that is around, it grows so large that it no longer fits into the office.[56]

Calvino's humorous vegetables are deeply political and existential. They mirror the plight of many millions of rural migrant workers throughout, not just Italy, but the whole of Europe. Marcovaldo's quixotic quest for vegetable life in the city also echoes the wider search for roots in a restless age of mass displacement and exile. Perhaps through the cracks, in the odd, unproductive corners of the modern world, one can catch glimpses of another, more fundamental order of life. In fact, perhaps this whimsical sideways glance is more applicable to most people than the thaumaturgical solemnity of Sinclair or the vegetable apocalypse of Jefferies.

Listening to the Vegetable

In his poetry anthology *News of the Universe*, Robert Bly suggests that the past two hundred years have seen a movement away from isolated subjectivity, with its estrangement from nature, toward a type of consciousness that locates itself in the world "out there."[57] But how can we listen to the things of the world and to vegetables in particular? Quite clearly, this is an imaginal project, not one of somehow trying literally to hear the "authentic" vegetable voice. Organic empathy and bio-technology have their place as yet other modes of fantasy-making.

Although vegetables consistently embody a dark vision in modern literature, serving as symbols of the struggle for a deeper connectedness with Nature, they have also, from time to time, intimated another style of consciousness. This move, from subject to object, involves careful attention to the vegetable's aesthetics, its sensual presentation. In his essay "Fantasia of the Unconscious," D. H. Lawrence writes: "I would like to be a tree for a while. The great lust of roots. Root-lust."[58] Like Dylan Thomas's famous line "The force that through the green fuse drives the flower/ drives my green age," Lawrence's vegetable imaginings have a blatantly erotic urgency about them. He celebrates "the powerful sap-scented blood roaring up the great columns" and confesses: "I used to fear their lust, their rushing black lust. But now I like it."[59]

Pablo Neruda's "Ode to the Tomato" reiterates the eroticism of Lawrence and Thomas but in a less desperate, more playful manner. "The street/ drowns in tomatoes . . .," he writes, "and the streets/ run/ with juice. . . ." Neruda sings of the watermelon: "the green whale of summer . . . / firmament of coolness . . . / jewel box of water. . . ."[60]

"Listening to the vegetable" implies, not just a turnip to human rap session, but an imaginal appreciation of vegetableness in as pluralistically full a context as possible. By this I mean that vegetables are not just "natural" things, to be found in their pristine truth in "natural" surroundings. They are imaginal beings that are "authentically" located in art and poetry, dreams and literature, as much as in fields or gardens.

CONCLUSIONS

In the face of the vegetable, modern culture stands questioned, its fundamental notions of human identity and consciousness in disarray. Attention to the vegetable undermines our view of Nature. The idea of "landscape," for example, with its connotations of detached overview, of visual contemplation, of mastery and control is thrown into doubt once the vegetable is heeded. Close attention to the potato or cabbage scarcely engenders a sense of sweeping vistas. One must get close to the ground. Similarly, theory cannot sustain its pretensions to occupy a privileged site based on its abstractions, generalizations, and overviews. Theory too, as we saw in earlier chapters, must be re-vegetated, taking its place alongside other ways of fantasy-making.[61] A "green psychology" is less a new body of concepts and theories than a returning of the old ones to their vegetable roots, an imaginal vegetative insighting of them.

In this book I have deliberately concentrated on sources that arise, albeit often at the fringe, from within what could be called the mainstream Western cultural tradition: scientific and psychological theories, myths and folktales, dreams, art, and literature. To this extent, alternative expressions of vegetable life—for example, from eco-feminism or non-Western cultures—have really only been considered to the extent that they are implicitly present in the general philosophy of "Deep Ecology" or in the revisioning initiated from within Archetypal Psychology. Such a decision was not made for pragmatic reasons, but in order to reveal the capability of a vegetative remetaphorizing from within. This is not to deny the crucial place of such alternative views: indeed, it is only in an imaginatively pluralistic dialogue that any body of myth can reveal its depths, its limits, and the richness of its paradoxes.

Vegetables can bring a deeper sense of the vegetable soul at work, both within ourselves and within the world—a certain kind of psychological life, a particular kind of "green" alchemy. As we have seen, weaving their way through the vegetable soul are ideas about the body and nervous system; nourishment, digestion, circulation, and reproduction; a fundamental substratum of consciousness; a sense of dwelling, of having roots, of being grounded; a reverie and repose that take us back to childhood, to the beginning of things; an anima involvement in the sensual world; an all-pervading cosmic life-energy, and so on. But running through all of these images, sometimes in the foreground, elsewhere just as background, has been a profound melancholy. This question of melancholy not only returns us downward into our own root concerns, or just to the Renaissance as historical home of the "vegetable soul" as a notion, but also to the vegetative tragedy facing the world today.

APPENDIX

Freud's Vegetable Dream

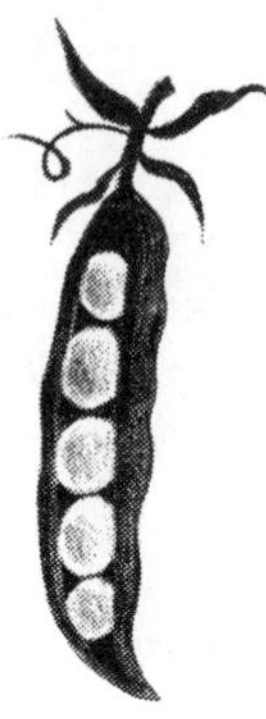

One of the most seminal and often referred to examples in Sigmund Freud's classic study *The Interpretation of Dreams* is thoroughly permeated by vegetableness—"The Dream of the Botanical Monograph."[1]

> I had written a monograph on a certain plant. The book lay before me and I was at the moment turning over a folded coloured plate. Bound up in each copy there was a dried specimen of the plant, as though it had been taken from a herbarium.

At the time of writing his study (1900), Freud had reached a crucial moment in the development of his vision and was highly sensitive to any professional, medical and scientific, recognition of his theories. His monumental work on dreams was also a response to the death of his father—a personal self-analysis.

In the dream, the vegetable world is subject to the scrutiny of scientific abstraction. Removed from its original, organic matrix, the plant has been transformed into a specimen: isolated, dried, preserved, categorized. As such, it is laid at the altar of the senex.

The elusive and complex vitality of the plant has been replaced by the power/knowledge both of sight (the colored plate) and of systematic naming (the herbarium). Thus tamed, the vegetable world lies passively before the dreamer's examination. But there is also movement in the dream, a fulcrum, as it were. At the moment the dreamer turns the colored plate, the bound and dried specimen that corresponds to the image is revealed. This action of turning the page signifies a mobilization of the dreamer's fantasy of power and authority over the vegetable kingdom. But what he is perusing at his leisure is, in fact, his own fiction, for he is the author of this text. What is revealed, on the other side of the illustrated page/text, is dried and bound. This is a vegetable image of the underworld: bloodless, sapless, and bound.[2]

Freud overlooked this shadow-side to his theorizing, ignored the vegetable call that announces the presence of death and the underworld. In 1900 he wanted to redeem his father's death, reclaim something from it. It would be over twenty years before he finally acknowledged the primacy of both vegetality and the death-instinct.[3] From that moment the optimistic confidence in his dayworld theorizing was permanently edged with the blackness of pessimism and limitation.

The dream shows images as vegetables: bound, dried, and laid out in Freud's "herbarium," his dream book. Instead of descending into these images, Freud drew them to the surface as specimens to illustrate his theories. As James Hillman stresses, to forcibly bring images into the light of day and analysis takes away their color, and "they expire in psychiatry's labeled baskets. . . ."[4]

This dream invites many kinds of approach, especially when read in conjunction with Freud's own lucid associations and, as always, his brilliant analysis. The dream, the associations, the analysis, and the theoretical reflections can all be taken as a whole within the context of Freud's book, his "herbarium." It is surely worth pondering over this dream, for here, at the very beginning of the twentieth century's psychological engagement with dream and the imaginal, we encounter both a profound vegetableness and its rejection.

Freud remembered that on the morning of the dream he

had seen a monograph with the title *The Genus Cyclamen*. Cyclamens were his wife's favorite plant, and he reproached himself for failing to bring her these flowers. Freud had previously used this phrase "bringing flowers" in a discussion to support his theory about the meaning of forgetfulness. He associated the monograph with the one he had in fact written himself on the coca-plant, drawing our attention to the importance of this work in the anesthetic use of cocaine in medicine. At this point, Freud whimsically digressed, in a self-satisfied way, upon the possibility of his needing such an anesthetic if he should suffer from glaucoma and require an eye operation. Indeed, his own father had needed this operation, and Freud's vital role in the introduction of cocaine had been acknowledged by the anesthetist. Following on from this, Freud recalled looking at a *Festschrift*, a book of essays in honor of a well-known teacher, written by his grateful students.

As Freud skillfully unraveled the associations, he remembered an awkward conversation with his friend, the eye surgeon who had operated on his father. This had touched upon the sensitive topic of Freud's tendency to become over-absorbed in his favorite hobbies, in particular a passion for owning and collecting books. The conversation with the eye surgeon was interrupted by a Professor Gartner (Gardener) and his wife. Freud congratulated them on their blooming looks. Gartner was one of the authors of the aforementioned *Festschrift*.

The herbarium in the dream reminded Freud of an incident from his school days. The headmaster had instructed some of the students to look through and clean the school's herbarium, which was riddled with bookworm. Freud was only assigned a minor role, as if the head lacked confidence in him. The few sheets he was given to work on included some Crucifers. Indeed, Freud recalled both his lack of intimacy with botany and his failure to identify a Crucifer during an examination. Only his theoretical knowledge had saved the day. From Cruciferae Freud had moved on to the Compositae, such as artichokes, and recalled that these were his favorite "flowers." Given his own lack of consideration about his wife's choice of flowers, he felt a bit guilty that she often brought artichokes home for him.

Freud wrote that as a medical student "he was enthralled by coloured plates." He valued the prestige of monographs and felt intellectually superior due to his own thoroughness in single-mindedly learning from them. However, his own success at publishing papers had exposed him to a colleague's ridicule when he had attempted to illustrate one of them with his own drawings. From this embarrassingly painful memory, Freud moved to a much earlier one when his father had given him and his sister a book recounting a journey through Persia. This book had contained colored plates, and for some reason they were told to destroy it. Freud had gained such pleasure from this destruction (to pull it apart "leaf by leaf, like an artichoke") that he credited this incident with initiating his passion for collecting and owning books, a passion that was to take him into debt by the age of seventeen and require the assistance of his aggrieved father. Reflecting on this passion for devouring books, including a precious Bible given to him by his father, Freud joked that in many ways he was himself a bookworm.

Freud believed this dream was "in the nature of a self justification," that beneath the surface calm lay "a passionately agitated plea on behalf of my liberty to act as I chose to act and to govern my life as it seemed right to me and me alone." However, Freud used the dream primarily to illustrate his theories: the relation of a dream's content and the experiences of the previous day; the ideas of overdetermination, condensation, and displacement; the method of untangling the various disguised threads of the dream and following them to their most basic source. The vegetative content of this dream was simply discarded as a signifier. He wrote: "The element 'botanical' had no place whatsoever in this core of dream thoughts. . . ."[5]

But quite clearly, there is an exact parallel between the reduction of the living dream-content to a mere example for supporting his psychological theories and the reduction of a living plant to a mere specimen in order to illustrate botanical classification. The crucial tensions in the dream and in his associations are between theory and vegetal substantiality. For example, his lack of intimacy with botany and his failure as a student to identify a particular plant are redeemed by his theoretical ability; his failure to buy the actual flowers that his wife likes is excused because of his knowledge of the underlying psychodynamics and even becomes yet another illustration of his brilliant theorizing; an involved conversation that has manifold associations with the prestige of his theories is interrupted by a Professor Gardener, and so on. Underlying this tension is a deep anxiety about the status and recognition of his theoretical ability, from the self-reassuring anecdote of his youthful pride in monographs, to the self-congratulatory retelling of his discovery of cocaine, even assuring himself and the reader that subsequent crucial developments in the use of cocaine had in fact been foreseen by him but omitted due to lack of thoroughness. This question of thoroughness surfaces again with his recollection that as a college student he took pride in only studying monographs. His anxiety also shows itself in a nervously playful reference to Wilhelm Fliess and to the status of the crucial work on dreams. Behind each of these anxieties lurks the presence of the Father/Senex and the question of recognition: headmaster, the *Festschrift*, his own father.

He associates his childhood destruction of the illustrated travel book (sanctioned by his father) with the leaf by leaf dissection of the artichoke, whose aim is to reach the soft, succulent center. "Collecting and owning" books, artichokes, dreams, anecdotes about forgetting—all are for the sole purpose of supporting his theories and gaining recognition from the Father. The colored pages of the travel book or the outer leaves of the artichoke, like the dried plant specimen in the dream, are expendable.

A Lacanian interpretation that reads the dream in terms of Freud's incestuous desire for his mother (by virtue of the father's comment that the Bible he gave his son was second in value only to his spouse) is not necessarily challenged by my more vegetable reading. Itself a complex symbol, "Mother" in our culture is replete with common associations of "Nature," "body," "earth," "vegetation," and so on.

In the dream, the monograph "lay before" him, open to his gaze, but there was also a seed of doubt. Perhaps Freud's work is "lying" before him?[6] Where is the truth of the matter? On turning the illustrated page (with the expressed connotations of a failure to connect with the actual thing in itself), Freud is confronted with a lifeless, bound, and dried plant, a specimen. The bookworm is devouring and destroying the "herbarium," the abstraction, the Latin classification. But this seems to be less the penetrative, phallic worm than the mulching, digestive (earth-) worm. On the shadow side of Freud's senex theorizing is the sacrificed plant, plus the worm of doubt keeping his psyche in direct contact with the imaginal earth. Senex and worm have an archetypal relationship, the one burrowing ever deeper as the theorizing of the other becomes more abstract. The senex finds its "earth," keeps its vegetative connection, through the morbid fantasy of the worm.

Two other associations within Freud's *Die Traumdeutung* reinforce the essential vegetative aspect of this dream. Freud recalled that when he was three he snatched some yellow flowers from his sister and then gleefully bit into a slice of wholemeal bread.[7] Also, it is perhaps significant that immediately preceding the botanical monograph analysis, Freud recounted a dream of a digestive disturbance and a dietary cure.[8] The vegetative imagination, the vegetable soul, is not ignored but sacrificed. Held prisoner to the panoptican of psychological theory, it still works away in the depths.[9]

NOTES

PROLOGUE

1. See B. Devall and G. Sessions, *Deep Ecology: Living as if Nature Mattered* (Salt Lake City: Peregrine Smith Books, 1985); also, M. Tobias, *Deep Ecology* (San Marcos: Avant Books, 1988); and my paper, "Facing the World: Depth Psychology and Deep Ecology," forthcoming in *Harvest* (1990).

2. On the idea of an imaginal fiction, see J. Hillman, *Healing Fiction* (Barrytown, NY: Station Hill Press, 1983); for a discussion of the crucial imaginal fiction of the Whole Earth image, see my "Shadows of the Holistic Earth," *Spring 1986*.

3. E.g., R. Coward, in *The Newstatesman*, 15 December 1989, p. 48; also, P. Wright, *On Living in an Old Country* (London: Verso, 1985), p. 109.

4. J. Hillman, "Silver and the White Earth (Part One)," *Spring 1980*: 24.

5. I use the term *Nature* in the sense established in the European Enlightenment, as a reality different and even oppositional to *Culture, Spirit, Imagination*, and so on. In fact Culture, Spirit, and Imagination are anything but "unnatural." See S. Moscovici, *Society against Nature* (London: Harvester Press, 1977).

6. E.g., see B. Berlin and P. Kay, *Basic Color Terms* (Berkeley: University of California Press, 1969); and C. Rowe, "Concepts of Colour and Colour Symbolism in the Ancient World," in *Color Symbolism: Excerpts from Eranos Yearbook 1972* (Spring Publications, 1977), pp. 35–42; and E. Irwin, *Colour Terms in Greek Poetry* (Toronto: Hakkert, 1974).

7. Rowe, "Colour in the Ancient World," p. 58; also R. Huyghe, "Color

and the Expression of Interior Time in Western Art," in *Color Symbolism*, p. 143, points out how the colors blue and green virtually "disappeared" in the "violent and somber" fifteenth century. As colors associated with love, they were out of place in an era that favored black clothing with only violet and crimson, "denoting tragic feeling," being truly acceptable.

8. On green and the functions, see C. G. Jung, *Collected Works,* trans. R. F. C. Hull, Bollingen Series XX, vols. 1–20 (Princeton: Princeton University Press and London: Routledge and Kegan Paul, 1953 ff.), vol. 9,i, §§581–82, vol. 14, §390, hereinafter cited by volume and paragraph numbers; on Ficino, see M. Ficino, *The Book of Life*, trans. C. Boer (Dallas: Spring Publications, 1980).

9. E.g., on "red" as a vegetable color see Huyghe, "Color and Interior Time," pp. 134, 140; also, R. Grinnell, *Alchemy in a Modern Woman* (Spring Publications, 1973), pp. 75, 77.

10. See Irwin, *Colour Terms in Greek Poetry*, pp. 29, 31–78.

11. C. G. Jung, *CW* 14, §623; *CW* 13, §§193 ff., 215 ff.; J. Hillman, "The Thought of the Heart," *Eranos Yearbook 48–1979* (Frankfurt a/M: Insel Verlag, 1981), p. 177.

12. A. Marvell, "The Garden," in H. Gardner, ed., *The Metaphysical Poets* (Harmondsworth: Penguin, 1963).

13. C. G. Jung, *The Visions Seminars: Book Two* (Spring Publications, 1976), p. 497.

14. M. Detienne, *The Gardens of Adonis* (London: The Harvester Press, 1977), pp. 158n66.

15. Jung, *CW* 12, §491.

16. Jung, *CW* 9,i, §§581–82.

17. Jung *CW* 12, §498.

18. For more on this imagery of unicorns, see T. Moore, "The Virgin and the Unicorn," in *Images of the Untouched*, ed. J. Stroud and G. Thomas (Dallas: Spring Publications, 1981).

19. Rowe, "Colour in the Ancient World," p. 34; also Irwin, *Colour Terms.*

20. E. Benz, "Color in Christian Visionary Experience," in *Color Symbolism*, p. 106.

21. C. Burland, *The Arts of the Alchemists* (London: Weidenfield and Nicolson, 1967).

22. Jung, *CW* 14, §§136–37, 140n, 392–95.

23. Benz, "Color in Christian," p. 99.

24. Huyghe, "Color and Interior Time," p. 139.

25. Ibid., p. 163.

26. D. Thomas, *The Poems* (London: J. M. Dent, 1979).

27. Marvell, "To His Coy Mistress," in *Metaphysical Poets.*

28. Jung, *CW* 9,ii, §§57, 386; *CW* 12, §319; *CW* 13, §§102, 415.

29. Jung, *Visions: Book Two*, p. 352.

30. H. Conklin, "Hanunoo Color Categories," *Southwestern Journal of Anthropology* 11 (Winter, 1955): 339–44.

31. Jung, *Visions: Book One*, p. 151; see also Irwin, *Colour Terms*, p. 33.

32. Jung, *CW* 11, §118; *CW* 13, §§102, 415.

33. See chapter two of this volume.

34. Jung, *Visions: Book Two*, p. 402.

35. Jung, *CW* 12, §§198–99.

36. Ibid., §§207–08.

37. J.-P. Sartre, *Nausea* (Harmondsworth: Penguin, 1970).

38. Jung, *CW* 5, §§677–79.

39. L. Wimberly, *Folklore in the English and Scottish Ballads* (New York: Dover Publications, 1965), p. 176.

40. Ibid.

41. Ibid., p. 177.

42. Ibid., p. 241.

43. Ibid.

44. Ibid., pp. 242–43; cf. Jung, *Visions: Book One*, pp. 99, 105, 114; and *Book Two*, pp. 455–56.

45. Jung, *Visions: Book One*, p. 207.

46. Jung, *CW* 12, §498; *CW* 13, §§273n, 319; *CW* 11, §151; *CW* 9,ii, §386. He also relates Mercurius and the "Eleusinian" corn to the always tricky Proteus in *CW* 9,ii, §339.

47. C. Kerényi, *The Gods of the Greeks* (London: Thames and Hudson, 1976), p. 128.

48. Jung, *CW* 12, §519; *CW* 11, §157n; *CW* 9,i, §§581–82.

49. M.-L. von Franz, *A Psychological Interpretation of the Golden Ass of Apuleius* (Spring Publications, 1980), p. 143.

50. Hillman, "Heart," p. 140.

51. Ibid.

52. Ibid., p. 177.

53. See J. Hillman, "Silver and the White Earth: Part Two," *Spring 1981*, on other ways of "whitening."

54. Hillman, "Heart," pp. 178–80.

55. Hillman, "Silver: Part One," p. 32.

56. E. Kessler, *Images of Wallace Stevens* (New Brunswick: Rutgers University Press, 1972), p. 215.

57. Ibid., p. 216.

58. Ibid., p. 219.

59. Jung, *Visions: Book Two*, pp. 334–35.

60. Ficino, *Book of Life*, p. 61.

61. Ibid.

62. Ibid., p. 62.

63. Ibid., p. 63.

64. Ibid., pp. 63, 153.

65. Jung, *CW* 14, §§622–24.
66. Ibid., §§393–95.
67. Ibid., §394.
68. Kessler, *Images,* pp. 173–220.
69. Grinnell, *Alchemy,* p. 75.
70. Ibid., p. 76.
71. Ibid., pp. 77–78.
72. Hillman, "Silver: Part Two," p. 46.
73. Kessler, *Images*, p. 207.
74. Ibid.
75. Irwin, *Colour Terms*, pp. 53, 59, 63.
76. See J. Hillman, *The Yellowing of the Work,* a paper first presented in Paris, 1989, at the International Congress of the International Association for Analytical Psychology.
77. G. Adler, *The Living Symbol* (London: Routledge and Kegan Paul, 1976), p. 326; Jung, *CW* 12, §420; J. Cirlot, *A Dictionary of Symbols* (London: Routledge and Kegan Paul, 1976), pp. 52–56.
78. Hillman, "Heart," p. 177.
79. Cirlot, *Dictionary*, pp. 52–55.
80. C. R. Leslie, *Memoirs of the Life of John Constable* (1843) (London: John Lehmann, 1949).
81. Wright, *On Living*, p. 109.
82. Hillman, "Silver: Part Two," p. 54n58.

CHAPTER ONE

1. P. Suskind, *Perfume* (Harmondsworth: Penguin, 1986), p. 22.
2. Takahashi, quoted in R. Bly, *Leaping Poetry* (Boston: Beacon Press, 1975).
3. J. Ortega y Gasset, *Meditations on Quixote* (New York: W. W. Norton & Co., 1963), pp. 41, 67–68.
4. E.g., on Descartes' corporeal imagination, see E. Michael and F. Michael, "Corporeal Ideas in the Seventeenth Century," *Journal of the History of Ideas* 50/1 (1989): 31–48.
5. R. Burton, *The Anatomy of Melancholy* (London: Chatto and Windus, 1881), pp. 98–100.
6. See also J. Bremmer, *The Early Greek Concept of the Soul* (Princeton: Princeton University Press, 1983), pp. 125–27; E. Mahoney, "Lovejoy and the Hierarchy of Being," *Journal of the History of Ideas* 48/2 (1987); A. Lovejoy, *The Great Chain of Being* (1933) (Cambridge: Harvard University Press, 1966).
7. See Plato's *Timaeus* in *Dialogues of Plato*, trans. B. Jowett (Oxford University Press, 1964), III. 89e.

8. See N. Kretzmann et al., eds., *The Cambridge History of Late Medieval Thought* (London: Cambridge University Press, 1982), pp. 612–17.

9. See the extensive references in *The Complete Oxford English Dictionary* (Oxford: The Clarendon Press, 1961), vol. 12, under "vegetable," "vegetate," and so on; see also Lovejoy, *Great Chain of Being*.

10. See Mahoney, "Lovejoy," p. 222.

11. Lovejoy, *Great Chain of Being*, p. 56.

12. Ibid., p. 82.

13. See J. Hillman, "Anima Mundi," *Spring 1982*; also, F. Yates, *Giordano Bruno and the Hermetic Tradition* (London: Routledge and Kegan Paul, 1977).

14. See A. Jacob, "Henry Moore's *Psychodia Platonica* and Its Relationship to Marsilio Ficino's *Theologia Platonica*," *Journal of the History of Ideas* 46/4 (1985): 503–22; also, M. Ficino, *The* Philebus *Commentary*, trans. and ed. M. Allen (Berkeley: University of California Press, 1975), pp. 198, 316–18.

15. W. Pater, *The Renaissance* (London: Macmillan, 1913), p. 42; also see Yates, *Bruno* and P. French, *John Dee* (London: Routledge and Kegan Paul, 1972).

16. R. Southwell (1574), quoted in *The Complete Oxford English Dictionary*, vol. 12, p. 74; and J. Comenius, *Orbis Sensualium Pictus* (1658) (Sydney: Sydney University Press, 1967).

17. Burton, *Anatomy*, pp. 98–100.

18. Jacob, "Henry Moore," p. 511.

19. Ibid.

20. Ibid., p. 514.

21. Burton, *Anatomy*.

22. M. Ficino, *The Book of Life*, trans. C. Boer (Dallas: Spring Publications, 1980), pp. 20–21, 42–43.

23. Ibid.

24. R. Kugelmann, "Hammering Metaphor from Metal," *Spring 1982*.

25. E. Partridge, *Origins* (London: Routledge and Kegan Paul, 1979). All etymologizing in my book is taken from this volume.

26. W. Evans-Wentz, *The Tibetan Book of the Dead* (New York: Oxford University Press, 1974).

27. H. Corbin, *Spiritual Body and Celestial Earth* (Princeton: Princeton University Press, 1977), p. 215.

28. J. Hillman, *Re-Visioning Psychology* (New York: Harper & Row, 1975).

29. Quoted in *The Complete Oxford English Dictionary*, p. 74.

30. See ibid., pp. 74–76.

31. On the vegetable stone, see M. Junius, *Practical Handbook of Plant Alchemy* (New York: Inner Traditions International, 1985), pp. 183 ff.; also, E. Edinger, *Ego and Archetype* (Harmondsworth: Penguin, 1980), pp. 262, 264, 272, 274; A. Dillard, *Teaching a Stone to Talk* (London: Picador, 1984).

32. F. Ponge, "Fauna and Flora," in *The Random House Book of Twentieth Century French Poetry*, ed. P. Auster (New York: Vintage, 1984), pp. 315–21.

33. G. Bachelard, *The Poetics of Reverie* (Boston: Beacon Press, 1971), pp. 82–83.

34. R. Sardello, "The Cancerous Body of the World," in *Stirrings of Culture*, ed. R. Sardello and G. Thomas (Dallas: The Dallas Institute Publications, 1986), pp. 215 ff.; see also E. Newton, *This Bed My Centre* (Melbourne: McPhee Gribble, 1981).

35. P. Berry, "Stopping: A Mode of Animation," *Spring 1981*.

36. Ponge, "Fauna and Flora."

37. Ficino, *Book of Life*, pp. 18, 46.

38. *The Complete Oxford English Dictionary*, vol. 12, pp. 73, 76.

39. Ibid., p. 76.

40. Ibid., p. 75.

41. Ibid., p. 76.

42. C. G. Jung, *C. G. Jung Speaking*, ed. W. McGuire and R. F. C. Hull (London: Picador, 1980), pp. 200–01; C. G. Jung, "Mind and Earth," in *CW* 16.

43. Corbin, *Spiritual Body*, p. 90.

44. R. Bly, "The Glimpse of the Waterer," in *Selected Poems* (New York: Harper & Row, 1986); see also C. Dunne, "The Roots of Memory," *Spring 1988*, which traces the mythic and etymological "ground" of memory.

45. J. Grayson, *Nerves, Brain and Man* (London: Phoenix House, 1961), pp. 114–15.

46. See P. Ucko and G. Dimbleby, eds., *The Domestication of Plants and Animals* (London: Gerald Duckworth, 1969); L. Brockway, *Science and Colonial Expansion* (New York: Academic Press, 1979).

47. See J. Platts, *The Manners and Customs of All Nations* (London: Henry Fisher, 1827), p. 777; J. Borges, *The Book of Imaginary Beings* (Harmondsworth: Penguin, 1974), pp. 28, 96–98.

48. Brockway, *Science*.

49. *The Complete Oxford English Dictionary*, vol. 8, p. 1184.

50. For the story of sugar, see the brilliant study by S. Mintz, *Sweetness and Power* (Harmondsworth: Penguin, 1986).

51. E.g., on rainforest degradation see C. Caulfield, *In the Rainforest* (London: Picador, 1986); on land degradation in Australia, see E. Rolls, *They All Ran Wild* (Sydney: Angus and Robertson, 1969).

52. *Seeds* (London: Friends of the Earth Trust Ltd., 1986).

53. G. Hobson, "How the Tomato Lost Its Taste," *New Scientist*, 29 September 1988, pp. 46–50.

54. See S. Connor, "Genes Defend Plant Breeding," *New Scientist*, 27 November 1986, pp. 33–35.

55. Ibid.; also *Seeds*. Of course, "new" vegetables are also being "discovered" by the West; for example, many old, traditional Inca vegetables, just as ancient and versatile as the potato, are being studied for their potential.

Isolated groups of Indians have kept these crops going since the days of the Spanish invasion and conquest (see P. de Groot, "New Life in Old Crops," *The New Scientist*, 7 April 1988, pp. 44–48).

56. See Mintz, *Sweetness*, pp. 187–214.

57. See R. Alberts, *The Good Provider* (Boston: Houghton Mifflin, 1973), for a biography of H. J. Heinz and the early years of food canning and bottling.

58. J. Hillman, "The Animal Kingdom in the Human Dream," in *Eranos Yearbook 51—1982* (Frankfurt a/M: Insel Verlag, 1983), p. 304.

59. K. Thomas, *Man and the Natural World* (London: Allen Lane, 1983), pp. 209 ff.

60. E. Sewell, *The Orphic Voice* (London: Routledge and Kegan Paul, 1955).

61. Ibid., pp. 171 ff.

62. Thomas, *Natural*, p. 66.

63. Ibid.

64. Ruskin, quoted in Sewell, *Orphic,* p. 253.

65. See D. Dombrowski, *Vegetarianism* (Wellingborough: Thorsons Publishers Ltd., 1985).

66. E.g., vegetarians seldom like to mention Hitler's consuming interest in not eating meat or vegetarianism's connection with eating disorders such as anorexia. See J. Barkas, *The Vegetable Passion* (New York: Charles Scribner's Sons, 1975); also, a study undertaken at Sydney's Royal Prince Alfred Hospital between 1982–1986 found that of 116 patients suffering anorexia nervosa 54.3% were vegetarians.

67. On the question of diet and the vegetable soul, see my "Oat Cuisine: No(a)tes Towards a Post-Modern Diet," forthcoming in *Sphinx* 4.

68. On the medieval gardening advice, see M. Baker, *The Gardener's Folklore* (Newton Abbot: David and Charles, 1977).

69. Burton, *Anatomy*, p. 492; L. Watson, *Supernature* (London: Coronet, 1974); P. Tompkins, *The Secret Life of Plants* (Harmondsworth: Penguin, 1974).

70. Burton, *Anatomy,* p. 492.

71. See the comments on imagination as an aesthetic phenomenon rather than a purely experiential one in J. Hillman, "Anima Mundi," *Spring 1982*.

72. A. Huxley, *Plant and Planet* (Harmondsworth: Penguin, 1987), p. 16.

73. W. Reich, *The Function of the Orgasm* (London: Souvenir, 1975).

74. C. G. Jung, *CW* 13, §§243, 459; Bachelard, *Poetics of Reverie*, p. 134.

75. A. Marvell, in H. Gardner, ed., *The Metaphysical Poets* (Harmondsworth: Penguin, 1963); D. Thomas, *The Poems* (London: J. M. Dent, 1979).

76. See Huxley, *Plant*, pp. 53–55; also Erasmus Darwin in Sewell, *Orphic*, p. 200.

77. G. Bachelard, *Water and Dreams* (Dallas: The Pegasus Foundation, 1983), p. 28.

78. C. Lévi-Strauss, *Totemism* (Harmondsworth: Penguin, 1969), especially the introduction.

79. M. Heidegger, *Poetry, Language, Thought* (New York: Harper & Row, 1970).

80. Lévi-Strauss, *Totemism*.

81. F. Waters, *Book of the Hopi* (Harmondsworth: Penguin, 1978).

82. See L. Gordon, *Green Magic* (London: Ebury Press, 1977).

83. Corbin, *Spiritual Body*, p. 5.

84. See Ad. de Vries, *Dictionary of Symbols and Imagery* (London: North Holland Publishing, 1984); Baker, *Gardener's Folklore*, p. 138.

85. Baker, *Gardener's Folklore*, p. 64.

86. On Paracelsus, see C. G. Jung, *CW* 13.

CHAPTER TWO

1. E.g., for a discussion of "instinct" as an imaginal concept, rather than either a literal physical, biological drive or a philosophical idea, see R. Severson, "Titans under Glass: A Recipe for the Recovery of Psychological Jargon," *Dragonflies* (Fall 1978).

2. On the crisis facing Hermetic philosophy during the eighteenth century, see C. G. Jung, *CW* 12, §§332, 502, 514; *CW* 13, §482.

3. See J. Hillman, "The Imagination of Air and the Collapse of Alchemy," in *Eranos Yearbook 50—1981* (Frankfurt a/M: Insel Verlag, 1982); C. Wilson, "Visual Surface and Visual Symbol: The Modern Microscope and the Occult in Early Modern Science," *Journal of the History of Ideas* 49/1 (1988).

4. See the comments by C. G. Jung, *CW* 12, §§332, 502, 514; *CW* 10, §471.

5. B. Rosner, "Recovery of Function and Localization of Function in Historical Perspective," in *Plasticity and Recovery of Function in the Central Nervous System*, ed. D. Stein, J. Rosen, and N. Butters (New York: Academic Press, 1974), p. 11.

6. E.g., see Hillman, "Imagination of Air."

7. E.g., M. Burman, *The Reenchantment of the World* (Ithaca: Cornell University Press, 1981).

8. See C. G. Jung, *CW* 10, §471.

9. For a recent attempt to ground the idea of archetypes in biology and brain functioning, see A. Stevens, *Archetype* (London: Routledge and Kegan Paul, 1982).

10. For modern examples of "brain" or "nerve" mythologizing, see J. Jaynes, *The Origins of Consciousness in the Breakdown of the Bicameral Mind* (London: Allen Lane, 1979); also Stevens, *Archetype*. For a biological reading

of Freud and Jung, see F. Sulloway, *Freud: Biologist of the Mind* (London: Burnett Books, 1979).

11. Rosner, "Recovery of Function," p. 10; J. Hillman, *The Myth of Analysis* (New York: Harper & Row, 1978), p. 139.

12. J. Miller, "History of Hypnotism," in R. Williams, *Nervous Insights* (Sydney: A.B.C., 1976), p. 47.

13. See *The History and Philosophy of Knowledge of the Brain and Its Functions* (Amsterdam: B. M. Israel, 1983).

14. W. Pagel, "Medieval and Renaissance Contributions to Knowledge of the Brain and Its Functions," in ibid., p. 108.

15. W. Riese, "Descartes' Ideas of Brain Function," in *Brain and Its Functions*, p. 119.

16. Ibid., p. 121.

17. H. Ellenberger, *The Discovery of the Unconscious* (New York: Basic Books, 1970), pp. 62 ff.

18. Ibid., p. 78.

19. Ibid., pp. 207 ff.; C. G. Carus, *Psyche (Part One)* (Spring Publications, 1970).

20. Ellenberger, *Discovery*, p. 218.

21. W. James, *A Pluralistic Universe* (1909) (Cambridge, MA: Harvard University Press, 1977).

22. On Stapledon and de Chardin, see P. Bishop, "The Mysticism of Immensity," *Colloquium* 18/2 (October 1986); G. Bachelard, *The Poetics of Reverie* (Boston: Beacon Press, 1971); B. Devall and G. Sessions, *Deep Ecology* (Salt Lake City: Peregrine Smith Books, 1985).

23. See Jung's reference to Fechner's ideas on plurality, *CW* 12, §272n.

24. James, *Pluralistic Universe*, pp. 64, 72, 80.

25. Riese, "Descartes' Ideas of Brain Function," p. 129.

26. For a contemporary example of "brain mythologizing," see Jaynes, *The Origins of Consciousness*.

27. J. Hillman, *Emotion* (London: Routledge and Kegan Paul, 1962), p. 119.

28. See J. Strachey's introduction to S. Freud, *The Interpretation of Dreams* (London: George Allen and Unwin, 1971); also, Ellenberger, *Discovery*, pp. 477–80.

29. Freud, *Interpretation*; S. Freud, *Three Essays on the Theory of Sexuality* (London: Hogarth Press, 1970).

30. Freud, *Interpretation*, p. xvi.

31. Ibid., p. xviii; Sulloway, *Freud*, pp. 121–22, 130–31.

32. S. Freud, *Beyond the Pleasure Principle* (London: Hogarth Press, 1971), p. 3.

33. Ibid., pp. 2, 3, 20, 22, 23, 45, 51, 57.

34. W. Reich, *The Function of the Orgasm*, rev. ed. (London: Panther, 1972), p. 143. Reich dropped the notion of vegetotherapy in 1948, replacing

it with his new "discovery" of orgone energy and its related therapy of "orgonomy" (D. Broadella, *Wilhelm Reich and the Evolution of His Work* [London: Arkana, 1985]).

35. Reich, *Function*, p. 31.
36. Ibid., p. 334.
37. Ibid., p. 332.
38. Ibid., p. 80.
39. Ibid., p. 85.
40. Ibid., p. 371.
41. Ibid., pp. 339–40.
42. Ibid., p. 339.
43. Ibid.
44. Ibid., p. 350.
45. Jung, *CW* 16, §§84–85.
46. M. Brazier, "The Evolution of Concepts Relating to the Electrical Activity of the Nervous System, 1600–1800," in *Brain and Its Functions*, pp. 202–03.
47. Reich, *Function*, pp. 278–83.
48. Ibid., p. 280.
49. Ibid., p. 46.
50. Ibid., p. 360.
51. Ibid., p. 361.
52. Miller, "History of Hypnotism," p. 51.
53. Jung, *CW* 8, §658.
54. Ibid., §657.
55. Ibid., §232.
56. Ibid.
57. Ibid., §268.
58. Ibid., §657.
59. Jung, *CW* 10, §1056; *CW* 11, §489.
60. Jung, *CW* 11, §491.
61. Jung, *CW* 13, §76n2.
62. Jung, *CW* 12, §400.
63. Jung, *CW* 10, §780.
64. Jung, *CW* 11, §§489–90.
65. Ibid., §496.
66. Jung, *CW* 8, §678.
67. Ibid., §§367–68.
68. Ibid., §380.
69. Jung, *CW* 11, §494.
70. Jung, *CW* 4, Foreword to "Significance of the Father in the Destiny of the Individual."
71. Jung, *CW* 10, §780.
72. Jung, *CW* 8, §642.

73. Ibid., §729.
74. Jung, *CW* 12, §399; *CW* 8, §380.
75. Jung, *CW* 8, §947.
76. Ibid., §957.
77. Ibid.
78. C. G. Jung, *The Visions Seminars: Book Two* (Spring Publications, 1976), p. 403.
79. Jung, *CW* 8, §§388–96. On the idea of multiple souls, see *CW* 8, §§217–18, 365–70, 577, 587.
80. Ibid., §388.
81. Ibid., §§217–18, 365–67, 577, 587.
82. Ibid., §393.
83. E.g., Jung, *CW* 14, §374.
84. Jung, *CW* 11, §152.
85. On Mercurius, see Jung, *CW* 13, §§243, 250, 408; on the "blessed greenness," see Jung, *CW* 12, §319; *CW* 13, §§102, 415; *CW* 11, §151; *CW* 9,i, §386.
86. Jung, *Visions: Book One*, p. 100.
87. Jung, *CW* 13, §242.
88. Ibid., §374.
89. Ibid., §§406–08.
90. Jung, *CW* 12, §§198–99; *Visions: Book Two*, p. 335.
91. Jung, *CW* 5, §615; *CW* 9,i, §226; *CW* 13, §§239 ff., 433.
92. Jung, *Visions: Book One*, p. 100.
93. Ibid.; on "greenness," see note 85, above.
94. Jung, *CW* 13, §§304–482; *CW* 10, §§49–103.
95. Jung, *CW* 13, §482.
96. Ibid., §354.
97. Ibid., §304.
98. M.-L. von Franz, *C. G. Jung: His Myth in Our Time* (Boston: Little Brown and Co., 1975), p. 267.
99. B. Hannah, *Jung: His Life and Work* (London: Michael Joseph, 1976), p. 271.
100. G. Bennet, "Domestic Life with C. G. Jung: Taperecorded Conversations with Ruth Bailey," *Spring 1986:* 185–86.
101. C. G. Jung, *C. G. Jung Speaking*, ed. W. McGuire and R. F. C. Hull (London: Picador, 1980), pp. 200–01.
102. C. G. Jung, *Memories, Dreams, Reflections* (New York: Vintage Books, 1963), p. 189.
103. Jung, *CW* 5 (Foreword to 4th edition).
104. E.g., see Jung, *CW* 5, §§213, 215, 220, 226, 671; *CW* 9,i, §§224, 226n; *CW* 12, §171; *CW* 13, §§128, 130n14; *CW* 14, §162n.
105. Jung, *CW* 10, §§103, 969, 979.
106. Ibid., §§18, 19, 68, 968.
107. Ibid., §103.

108. Ibid., §909.
109. Ibid., §1001.
110. Jung, *CW* 8, §815; *CW* 16, §98; *Visions: Book One*, p. 151.
111. Jung, *CW* 11, §767.
112. Jung, *CW* 10, §44.
113. Jung, *CW* 13, §355.
114. Jung, *CW* 5.
115. E. Neumann, *The Origins and History of Consciousness* (1949) (Princeton: Princeton University Press, 1970); see also W. Giegerich, "Ontogeny = Phylogeny? A Fundamental Critique of Erich Neumann's Analytical Psychology," *Spring 1975*.
116. Neumann, *The Origins*, p. 42.
117. Ibid., pp. 296–97.
118. Ibid., pp. 306–07.
119. Ibid., p. 307.
120. Ibid., p. 30.
121. Ibid., p. 29.
122. Ibid., p. 47.
123. Ibid., p. 49.
124. Ibid., p. 40; E. Neumann, *The Great Mother* (Princeton: Princeton University Press, 1974), p. 149.
125. M.-L. von Franz, *The Problem of the Puer Aeternus*, 2d ed. (Santa Monica, CA: Sigo Press, 1981); G. Adler, *The Living Symbol* (London: Routledge and Kegan Paul, 1961), p. 110.
126. Jung, *CW* 5 (Foreword to the 4th edition).
127. R. Grinnell, *Alchemy in a Modern Woman* (Spring Publications, 1973).
128. Ibid., p. 89.
129. Ibid.
130. Ibid., pp. 77, 119, 164.
131. Ibid., p. 164.
132. Ibid., p. 19.
133. Ibid., p. 77.
134. Ibid., pp. 162–63.
135. R. Grinnell, "Reflections on the Archetype of Consciousness: Personality and Psychological Faith," *Spring 1970*; E. Edinger, *Ego and Archetype* (Harmondsworth: Penguin, 1980), p. 98.

CHAPTER THREE

1. See J. Hillman, *Re-Visioning Psychology* (New York: Harper & Row, 1975).

2. J. Hillman, *The Myth of Analysis* (New York: Harper & Row, 1978), p. 53; J. Hillman, "An Essay on Pan," in *Pan and the Nightmare* (Spring Publications, 1972), p. xxvi.

3. J. Hillman, *Insearch* (Dallas: Spring Publications, 1979), p. 120; also, *Re-Visioning Psychology,* p. 21.

4. Hillman, *Myth of Analysis,* p. 259.

5. Hillman, "Pan," pp. xxvi, lii.

6. See H. Corbin, "Mundus Imaginalis: or the Imaginary and the Imaginal," *Spring 1972.*

7. Hillman, *Myth of Analysis,* p. 284; *Re-Visioning,* p. 89.

8. Hillman, *Insearch,* pp. 120–21; also, "On the Necessity of Abnormal Psychology: Ananke and Athene," in *Facing the Gods,* ed. J. Hillman (Dallas: Spring Publications, 1980), pp. 16–17.

9. Hillman, *Insearch,* p. 123.

10. J. Hillman, "Going Bugs," *Spring 1988*: 55.

11. J. Hillman, "Therapeutic Value of Alchemical Language," *Dragonflies* 1/1 (1978): 37.

12. Ibid., p. 39.

13. Hillman, *Re-Visioning,* p. 88.

14. Hillman, *Myth of Analysis,* p. 290.

15. J. Hillman, "The Animal Kingdom in the Human Dream," *Eranos Yearbook 51—1982* (Frankfurt a/M: Insel Verlag, 1983).

16. J. Hillman, *The Dream and the Underworld* (New York: Harper & Row, 1979), p. 34.

17. J. Hillman, "Anima Mundi," *Spring 1982*: 77.

18. Ibid., pp. 82–84.

19. Hillman, "Animal Kingdom."

20. Ibid.

21. F. Ponge, "Fauna and Flora," in *The Random House Book of Twentieth Century French Poetry* ed. P. Auster (New York: Vintage, 1984), pp. 315–21.

22. On the idea of "epistrophé," see Hillman, *Dream and the Underworld,* pp. 4, 100, 198, 199.

23. See J. Grigson, *Jane Grigson's Vegetable Cookbook* (Harmondsworth: Penguin, 1984).

24. Hillman, "Going Bugs," p. 54.

25. Ibid., pp. 67–68.

26. Ibid., pp. 54–55.

27. Ibid., p. 58.

28. Hillman, *Re-Visioning,* p. 88.

29. Ibid., pp. 84–86.

30. Hillman, *Dream and the Underworld,* pp. 172–73.

31. Hillman, *Re-Visioning,* p. 124.

32. J. Hillman, "Natural Beauty without Nature," *Spring 1985*: 51.

33. A. Ziegler, "Rousseauian Optimism, Natural Distress, and Dream

Research," *Spring 1976*: 55; see also S. Grof, *Realms of the Human Unconscious* (New York: E. P. Dutton, 1976), pp. 181–83, on claims of human empathy with plant consciousness, a deep, ecological layer of the human unconscious.

34. Hillman, *Dream and the Underworld*, p. 36.

35. Ibid., pp. 136–37; see also his reflections on alchemy's "Silver and the White Earth (Part One)," *Spring 1980*; or "Part Two," *Spring 1981*: 23–26, where he writes of the "Celestial" Earth and the "terra alba," the psychological soil. Similarly, roots do not have to be envisaged as going into the "earth" but can, as in alchemy, reach upward into the sky ("Part One," p. 24).

36. J. Hillman, *Suicide and the Soul* (Spring Publications, 1976), p. 58.

37. G. Bachelard, *The Poetics of Reverie* (Boston: Beacon Press, 1971), p. 190.

38. Hillman, "Animal Kingdom."

39. G. Bachelard, *Water and Dreams* (Dallas: The Pegasus Foundation, 1983), pp. 3, 10.

40. S. Simmer, "The Academy of the Dead," *Spring 1981*: 89.

41. Ibid., pp. 99, 103.

42. Ibid., p. 91.

43. Bachelard, *Poetics*, pp. 82–83.

44. E. Casey, "Getting Placed: Soul in Space," *Spring 1982*: 23.

45. See M. Heidegger, *Poetry, Language, Thought* (New York: Harper & Row, 1970). He suggests that "things" express their essence by "gathering" the world: earth, sky, humans, and Gods. See also my "Habits," *Sphinx* 2 (1989).

46. Bachelard, *Water*, p. 2.

47. C. G. Jung, *CW* 13, §§375, 409.

48. Jung, *CW* 12, §19.

49. G. Bachelard, *Air and Dreams* (Dallas: The Dallas Institute Publications, 1988), pp. 203–24.

50. P. Furst, *Hallucinogens and Culture* (San Francisco: Chandler & Sharp Publishers, 1976), p. 16. See also his discussion of the relation between plant, shaman, and animal, especially the jaguar and frog.

51. Ibid., pp. 24–25.

52. For a full discussion of such contradictions, see my "Singing the Land: Australia in Search of Its Soul," *Spring 1989*.

CHAPTER FOUR

1. J. Hillman, *The Dream and the Underworld* (New York: Harper & Row, 1979), p. 70.

2. E.g., C. G. Jung, *CW* 13, §164n; also, M. Ficino, *The* Philebus *Commentary*, trans. and ed. M. Allen (Berkeley: University of California Press, 1975),

pp. 136, 240; and J. Hillman, *Re-Visioning Psychology* (New York: Harper & Row, 1975), p. 85.

3. Jung, *CW* 5, §§526 ff.; also, C. G. Jung and C. Kerényi, *Essays on a Science of Mythology* (Princeton: Princeton University Press, 1973).

4. Kerényi, "Kore," in *Essays on a Science*, pp. 114–15, 182.

5. P. Berry, "The Rape of Demeter/Persephone and Neurosis," *Spring 1975*: 187.

6. Hillman, *Dream and the Underworld*, p. 49.

7. Kerényi, "Kore," p. 120.

8. Ibid., p. 136.

9. Hillman, *Dream and the Underworld*, pp. 49–50.

10. Berry, "Rape of Demeter/Persephone," p. 197.

11. Ibid., p. 198.

12. T. Traherne, *Centuries* (Leighton Buzzard: The Faith Press, 1975), p. 110.

13. E. Herzog, *Psyche and Death* (London: Hodder and Stoughton, 1966; rept. Dallas: Spring Publications, 1983), pp. 69, 85, 120, 128, 139–40, 173–76.

14. C. Ponce, *Papers towards a Radical Metaphysics: Alchemy* (Berkeley: North Atlantic Books, 1983), p. 7.

15. Ibid., p. 25.

16. Kerényi, "Kore," p. 118.

17. E.g., Jung, *CW* 5, §§530–35; E. Neumann, *The Origins and History of Consciousness* (Princeton: Princeton University Press, 1970), p. 46.

18. M. Detienne, *The Gardens of Adonis* (London: The Harvester Press, 1977).

19. Ibid., p. 68.

20. J. Hillman, "Anima Mundi," *Spring 1982*: 84.

21. W. F. Otto, *The Homeric Gods* (London: Thames and Hudson, 1979), p. 100.

22. J. Hillman, *The Myth of Analysis* (New York: Harper & Row, 1978), pp. 69, 101–03.

23. Otto, *Homeric Gods*, p. 63.

24. Ibid., p. 81.

25. T. Moore, "Artemis and the Puer," in *Puer Papers*, ed. J. Hillman (Dallas: Spring Publications, 1979), p. 174.

26. Ibid.

27. Hillman, *Myth of Analysis*, p. 275.

28. Ibid., pp. 279–80.

29. Ibid., p. 285.

30. J. Hillman, "Dionysos in Jung's Writings," in *Facing the Gods*, ed. J. Hillman (Dallas: Spring Publications, 1980), p. 203.

31. W. F. Otto, *Dionysus: Myth and Cult* (Dallas: Spring Publications, 1981), pp. 121–22.

32. Ibid., pp. 138–39.

33. See Hillman, *Re-Visioning*, pp. 95–99, on the fantasy of resurrection.

34. Otto, *Dionysus*, pp. 141–42.

35. Ibid., p. 155.

36. Ibid., p. 96; C. G. Jung, *The Visions Seminars: Book One* (Spring Publications, 1976), p. 151.

37. C. Kerényi, *The Gods of the Greeks* (London: Thames and Hudson, 1976), pp. 260–61.

38. Otto, *Dionysus*, pp. 136–37.

39. Ibid., p. 95.

40. F. Maraini, *Secret Tibet* (London: Hutchinson, 1972), p. 46.

41. Kerényi, *Gods of the Greeks*, p. 273.

42. Otto, *Dionysus*, pp. 159–61.

43. Kerényi, *Gods of the Greeks*, p. 262; Euripides, *The Bacchae* (Harmondsworth: Penguin, 1979).

44. J. Hillman, "An Essay on Pan," in *Pan and the Nightmare* (Spring Publications, 1972), pp. xvii–xviii.

45. Ibid., pp. xx–xxi.

46. Ibid., p. xxii.

47. Ibid., pp. xxvii–xxviii.

48. Ibid., p. lx.

49. Ibid., p. lxii.

50. See Otto, *Homeric Gods*; and Kerényi, *Gods of the Greeks*.

51. Kerényi, *Gods of the Greeks*, pp. 139–41.

52. Hillman, *Myth of Analysis*, p. 259.

53. Of course, it is vital that the shadows specific to all the Gods are recognized. For discussion of Apollo's shadow, see C. Boer, "In the Shadow of the Gods: Greek Tragedy," *Spring 1982*; also, I. Mitroff, "Science's Apollonic Moon," *Spring 1974*; also, Hillman, *Myth of Analysis*.

54. Kerényi, *Gods of the Greeks*, p. 140.

55. Ibid., p. 141.

56. Ibid., p. 142.

57. Ibid., p. 140.

58. Jung, *The Visions Seminars: Book One*, pp. 100–01.

59. Jung, *CW* 13, §304; also, his *Visions Seminars: Book One*, pp. 99, 105.

60. Maraini, *Secret Tibet*, p. 46.

61. In some ways, the story of Frankenstein carries this Apollonic shadow. See B. Easlea, *Fathering the Unthinkable* (London: Pluto Press, 1983).

62. Quoted in H. Krips, "After Nature," *Arena* 84 (1988): 49.

CHAPTER FIVE

1. F. Ponge, "Fauna and Flora," in *The Random House Book of Twentieth Century French Poetry*, ed. P. Auster (New York: Vintage, 1984), p. 321.

2. J. Hillman, "On Culture and Chronic Disorder," in *Stirrings of Culture*, ed. R. Sardello and G. Thomas (Dallas: The Dallas Institute Publications, 1986).

3. J. Hillman, "White Supremacy," *Spring 1986*.

4. J. Hillman, "Going Bugs," *Spring 1988*: 51, 57.

5. Ibid., p. 60.

6. See C. Pye-Smith and C. Rose, *Crisis and Conservation* (Harmondsworth: Penguin, 1984), pp. 76–123.

7. See my paper "Habits," *Sphinx* 2 (1989).

8. On puer phenomenology, see J. Hillman, ed., *Puer Papers* (Dallas: Spring Publications, 1979).

9. E. Relph, *Place and Placelessness* (London: Pion, 1976).

10. The Islamic mystic Shaikh Ahmad Ahsa' I quoted in H. Corbin, *Spiritual Body and Celestial Earth* (Princeton: Princeton University Press, 1977), p. 90.

11. This connection with history, the past, is frequently an expression of the anima; see J. Hillman, *Anima* (Dallas: Spring Publications, 1986). On the theme of exile, see my "David Malouf and the Language of Exile," *Australian Literary Studies* 10/4 (1982) and "Singing the Land: Australia in Search of Its Soul," *Spring 1989*.

12. S. Freud, "The New Introductory Lectures," in *The Complete Introductory Lectures on Psychoanalysis* (London: George Allen and Unwin, 1974), p. 544.

13. For two very contrasting imaginal approaches to water, see G. Bachelard, *Water and Dreams* (Dallas: The Pegasus Foundation, 1983) and I. Illich, *H_2O and the Waters of Forgetfulness* (Dallas: The Dallas Institute of Humanities and Culture, 1985). Illich, in particular, captures much about vegetable water.

14. It is crucial to deliteralize images such as the "farmer" or "forester," which have such archaic roots in our mythologizing. Farmers and foresters are rarely the earthy representatives of a traditional, harmonious relationship to the land. In fact, today the opposite seems to be the case: farmers and foresters include some of the worst environmental offenders. Yet many persist, most effectively in their publicity, in drawing upon these ancient imaginal associations to rally public sympathy for their indifferent, or even anti-, conservation stance (Pye-Smith and Rose, *Crisis and Conservation*).

15. For an imaginal discussion of salt, see J. Hillman, "Salt: A Chapter in Alchemical Psychology," in *Images of the Untouched*, ed. J. Stroud and G. Thomas (Dallas: Spring Publications, 1981).

16. See Jung's essay on "The Philosophical Tree," *CW* 13. For too long the only archetypal study of trees, this seminal, spiritually inclined essay has by this dominance obscured the soulful plurality of possible readings.

17. On the harmfulness of planting inappropriate trees in sensitive ecological environments, see the debate about conifer plantations in bog-lands (Pye-Smith and Rose, *Crisis and Conservation*; also D. Thompson, "Battle of the Bog," *New Scientist*, 8 January 1987, pp. 41–48).

18. In his *Alchemy in a Modern Woman*, Robert Grinnell discusses at some length a dream that a woman has about the healing effect of red tomato pulp. He associates it with the " 'red balsam' of a positive 'red sulphur', a positive solar-masculine consciousness" that "is correlated to a soothing activity in the neuro-vegetative nervous system." In the dream, the color red manifests "in its cool, soothing vegetable aspect." For Grinnell this indicates a deep inward turning, a healing process taking place at the mysterious levels of the autonomic nervous system ([Spring Publications, 1973], pp. 75–77, 89, 116).

19. Takahashi, quoted in R. Bly, *Leaping Poetry* (Boston: Beacon Press, 1975).

20. See chapter one of this volume for discussions of "totemism" and the "gathering" power of vegetables.

21. C. G. Jung, "The Philosophical Tree," in *CW* 13; M. Eliade, *Rites and Symbols of Initiation* (New York: Harper Torchbooks, 1965); D. Davies, "The Evocative Symbolism of Trees," in *The Iconography of Landscape*, ed. D. Cosgrove and S. Daniels (Cambridge: Cambridge University Press, 1989).

CHAPTER SIX

1. P. Colum, ed., *The Complete Grimm's Fairy Tales* (New York: Pantheon Books, 1972), pp. 121–27. While no mention of the pumpkin occurs in this version of the story, it has become well established subsequently, particularly through Perrault's retelling.

2. For example, compare with Bettelheim's neo-Freudian comments on both "Cinderella" and "Jack and the Beanstalk," in which the vegetable is pushed to the very edge of the interpretation (B. Bettelheim, *The Uses of Enchantment* [New York: Vintage Books, 1977]).

3. L. Degh, ed., *Folktales of Hungary* (London: Routledge and Kegan Paul, 1965).

4. I. Calvino, *Italian Folktales* (New York: Harcourt Brace Jovanovich, 1980).

5. Ibid.

6. G. Bachelard, *Water and Dreams* (Dallas: The Pegasus Foundation, 1983), p. 12.

7. E.g., for a Jungian reading, see M.-L. von Franz, *An Introduction*

to the Interpretation of Fairytales (Spring Publications, 1975); *Problems of the Feminine in Fairytales* (Spring Publications, 1972); *Shadow and Evil in Fairytales* (Spring Publications, 1974). For influential "revisionist" Freudian readings, see Bettelheim, *Uses of Enchantment*, and E. Fromm, *The Forgotten Language* (New York: Grove Press, 1978).

8. See C. Lévi-Strauss, *The Raw and the Cooked* (New York: Harper & Row, 1969); also, V. Propp, *Morphology of the Folktale* (Bloomington: Indiana University Press, 1968).

9. For an insightful Marxist-oriented reading of fairytales, see J. Zipes, *Breaking the Magic Spell* (London: Heinemann, 1979).

10. For a detailed study of the social rituals of story-telling, see L. Degh, *Folktales and Society* (Bloomington: Indiana University Press, 1980).

11. G. Bachelard, *The Poetics of Reverie* (Boston: Beacon Press, 1971), p. 124.

12. *The Complete Grimm's.*

13. Ibid.

14. See also "Rosina in the Oven" and "The Golden Ball," from Calvino, *Italian Folktales*; and "The Buckwheat," in *Tales and Stories by Hans Christian Andersen* (Seattle: University of Washington Press, 1980).

15. Calvino, *Italian Folktales.*

16. C. G. Jung, *The Visions Seminars: Book Two* (Spring Publications, 1976), p. 403.

17. One of the best discussions of such an alchemy can be found in R. Grinnell, *Alchemy in a Modern Woman* (Spring Publications, 1973).

18. M. Foss, ed., *Folk Tales of the British Isles* (London: Macmillan, 1977). See also "Bone-meal in the Flour," in K. Briggs, *A Dictionary of British Folktales*, Part B, vol. 2 (Bloomington: Indiana University Press, 1970).

19. "Animal Talk and the Nosy Wife," in Calvino, *Italian Folktales.*

20. Calvino, *Italian Folktales.*

21. Ibid.

22. See M.-L. von Franz, *A Psychological Interpretation of the Golden Ass of Apuleius* (Dallas: Spring Publications, 1980).

23. Calvino, *Italian Folktales.*

24. On this "night journey" of the hero, see Jung, *CW* 5, and J. Campbell, *The Hero with a Thousand Faces* (Princeton: Princeton University Press, 1968).

25. Briggs, *A Dictionary,* Part A, vol. 1.

26. Calvino, *Italian Folktales.*

27. Ibid.

28. *The Complete Grimm's.*

29. R. Ratcliff, *Scottish Folktales* (London: Frederick Muller, 1976).

30. Calvino, *Italian Folktales.*

31. See the comments by Reich, Jung, and Grinnell in chapters two and three of this volume.

32. Calvino, *Italian Folktales.*

33. "The Ear of Corn," in *The Complete Grimm's*; "That's Enough to Go On With," in Foss, *Folk Tales of the British Isles.*

34. *The Complete Grimm's.*

35. Calvino, *Italian Folktales.*

36. J. Hillman, *Healing Fiction* (Barrytown, NY: Station Hill Press, 1983), p. 37. On the sense of the uncanny when these vegetable "laws" are broken, see "Crossed Corn," in Briggs, *A Dictionary*, Part B, vol. 2.

37. Briggs, *A Dictionary*, Part B, vol. 1; see also "The Peasant and the Devil," in *The Complete Grimm's.*

38. For examples of vegetable humor, see "The Straw, the Coal and the Bean," in *The Complete Grimm's;* "The Pancake," in S. Thompson, ed., in *One Hundred Favorite Folktales* (Bloomington: Indiana University Press, 1975); "A Giant Cabbage," "The Giant Parsnip," "The Great Turnips," "Growing the Church," "King Edward VII and the Salad," "The Three Turnips," "The Little Cake," in Briggs, *A Dictionary*, Part A, vol. 2.

39. See R. Burton's description of the vegetable soul in chapter one of this volume and other, clinical assessments in chapter two.

40. "Rosemary," in Calvino, *Italian Folktales.*

41. See my discussion in chapter three of this volume.

42. Calvino, *Italian Folktales.*

43. On the theme of a vegetable birth, see also "Rosemary" and "The Handmade King," in Calvino, *Italian Folktales*; "Calabash Children," in K. Arnott, ed., *African Myths and Legends* (London: Oxford University Press, 1972); "Gallant Szerus," in Degh, *Folktales of Hungary.*

44. *The Complete Grimm's.*

45. See von Franz, *The Golden Ass.*

46. "The Princess and the Pea," in *Hans Christian Andersen.*

47. See also "The Crumb in the Beard," in Calvino, *Italian Folktales.* Also in "The Twelve Huntsmen," from *The Complete Grimm's*, peas are used as a truth tester.

48. Calvino, *Italian Folktales.*

49. In *Hans Christian Andersen*; see also "The Little Gardener with the Golden Hair," in Calvino, *Italian Folktales.*

50. On this patriotic appeal to a sentimentalized image of the gardener, see R. Samuels, ed., *Patriotism* (London: Routledge and Kegan Paul, 1989), pp. xxv, xxxvi. For another view, see D. Crouch and C. Ward, *The Allotment* (London: Faber and Faber, 1988).

51. "The Dead Moon," in Foss, *Folk Tales of the British Isles.*

52. The fantasy image of "The Peasant" is, of course, complex and needs careful study. See E. Wolf, *Peasants* (Englewood Cliffs, NJ: Prentice-Hall, 1966).

CHAPTER SEVEN

1. See P. Hills, *The Painters America (1810–1910)* (New York: Praeger, 1974); and also J. Rothenstein and M. Butlin, *Turner* (London: Heinemann, 1964).

2. J. Barrell, *The Dark Side of the Landscape: The Rural Poor in English Painting, 1730–1840* (Cambridge: Cambridge University Press, 1980).

3. C. Sterling, *Still Life Painting* (New York: Harper & Row, 1981).

4. For excellent paintings of vegetables as food, see C. Clifton, *The Art of Food* (Sydney: Collins, 1988); and E. David, *Italian Food* (London: Barrie and Jenkins, 1987).

5. M. Tralbaut, *Vincent Van Gogh* (London: Macmillan, 1969).

6. M. Rosenthal, *Constable* (New Haven: Yale University Press, 1983).

7. See H. Prince, "Art and Agrarian Change, 1710–1815," in *The Iconography of Landscape*, ed. D. Cosgrove and S. Daniels (Cambridge: Cambridge University Press, 1988).

8. See Barrell, *Dark Side of the Landscape.*

9. See A. Bermingham, *Landscape and Ideology: The English Rustic Tradition, 1740–1860* (London: Thames and Hudson, 1986).

10. M. Levey, *London Transport Posters* (London: Phaidon, 1976).

11. E.g., see R. Williams, *The Country and the City* (London: The Hogarth Press, 1985).

12. See M. Rosenthal, *British Landscape Painting* (Oxford: Phaidon, 1982); and K. Bazarov, *Landscape Painting* (London: Octopus Books, 1981). Especially significant are the many different moods portrayed in innumerable ploughing and harvesting scenes.

13. Another popular painting in this genre is *The Fourth Estate*, by Giuseppe Pellizza Da Volpedo (1868–1907).

14. G. Reynolds, *Victorian Painting* (London: Studio Vista, 1966).

15. Another example with this strong sexual undertone is William Holman Hunt's *The Hireling Shepherd*.

16. Tralbaut, *Van Gogh.*

17. See also *Farm Labourers* (1883), which shows a man ploughing a potato field as a woman follows along picking up the few potatoes that are left.

18. See Hills, *The Painters America*; also, *The Pea Gathering* (1913) by the Italian/Australian artist Anthony Dattilo Rubbo, which shows a family at work in the fields.

19. M. Verrier, *The Orientalists* (London: Academy Editions, 1979).

20. See the modern Primitivist painting *Cross of York* (1979), by Richard Parker, which shows a vegetable simplicity and naivete in its depiction of a local market: E. Lister, *British Primitive Fantasists* (New York: Alpine Fine Arts Collection, 1982).

21. Edmund Blair Leighton (1853–1923), *September*; also, Cecil Gordon Lawson's *The Minister's Garden*, in Reynolds, *Victorian Painting*; see also *A*

Flemish Garden by Henri de Braekeleer (1840–1888), with its portrayal of huge cabbages tended by a woman.

22. Myles Birket Foster (1825–1899), *A Cottage Garden*.

23. Compare these naively romantic sentiments with the more basic portrayals of urban back gardens: e.g., W. Baron, *The Camden Town Group* (London: Scolar Press, 1979).

24. See also *The Kitchen Maid* (anon. seventeenth-century Dutch, in Clifton, *The Art of Food*).

25. There are, of course, many other kitchen images, from Willem Kalf's mid-seventeenth-century *Interior of a Rustic Kitchen* (which shows a bare, dark room with two very large cabbages, a pumpkin slice, and a straw broom in the bottom corner, all lit up by a single shaft of light); or Antoine Raspail's (1738–1811) *The Provencal Kitchen*, with its well-mannered and orderly portrayal of the preparation of vegetables. There are many kitchen scenes in David's *Italian Food*.

26. Hills, *The Painters America*.

27. Although vegetables have not had their Georgia O'Keeffe, the voluptuous paintings by Bartolemo Bimbi (1648–1730) and Giovanna Garzoni (1600–1670) come close (see David, *Italian Food*, pp. 54–59). Some of Cedric Morris's twentieth-century paintings begin to explore the sensuality of vegetables. See, for example, his *Still Life in a Summer Garden* (1963) (R. Morphet, *Cedric Morris* [London: The Tate Gallery, 1984]).

28. For an astonishingly detailed study of the complex roots of ecological activism in the twentieth century, many of them extreme right-wing, see A. Bramwell, *Ecology in the Twentieth Century* (New Haven: Yale University Press, 1989); also, C. Spretnak and F. Capra, *Green Politics* (London: Paladin, 1985); U. Knoepflmacher and G. Tennyson, eds., *Nature and the Victorian Imagination* (Berkeley: University of California Press, 1977). On the origins of ecology, see my "Shadows of the Holistic Earth," *Spring 1986*. On the importance of contextualizing, see C. Shaw and M. Chase, eds., *The Imagined Past* (Manchester: Manchester University Press, 1989); also my *Myth of Shangri-La* (London: Athlone, 1989) is a detailed case study of shifts in imaginal contexts of landscape appreciation.

29. O. Stapledon, *Star Maker* (London: Methuen, 1979); see also my "The Mysticism of Immensity," *Colloquium* 18/2 (October 1986), for a fuller discussion of Stapledon's work.

30. J. Wyndham, *Day of the Triffids* (Harmondsworth: Penguin, 1977).

31. E. Allan Poe, *Complete Stories and Poems of Edgar Allan Poe* (New York: Doubleday and Co., 1966); B. Aldiss, *Hothouse* (London: Victor Gollancz, 1990).

32. R. Jefferies, *After London (or Wild England)* (Oxford: Oxford University Press, 1980); see also his autobiography, *The Story of My Heart* (London: Quartet Books, 1979).

33. I. Sinclair, *Lud Heat* (Uppingham: Goldmark, 1987); Sinclair's book

was the inspiration behind P. Ackroyd's best-selling novel *Hawksmoor* (London: Abacus, 1988).

34. Sinclair, *Lud Heat*, p. 20.

35. Ibid., p. 84.

36. Ibid., p. 57.

37. Ibid., p. 53.

38. Ibid., p. 55.

39. Ibid., p. 80.

40. Ibid.

41. Ibid., p. 16.

42. Ibid., p. 111.

43. R. Williams, *Second Generation* (London: Chatto and Windus, 1964), p. 73.

44. Ibid., pp. 81, 84.

45. J. M. Coetzee, *The Life and Times of Michael K* (London: Secker and Warburg, 1983).

46. Ibid., p. 81.

47. Ibid.

48. Ibid., p. 142.

49. Ibid., p. 158.

50. Ibid., pp. 156, 162.

51. Ibid., pp. 223, 229.

52. Ibid., p. 250.

53. I. Calvino, *Marcovaldo (or The Seasons in the City)* (London: Secker and Warburg, 1983), p. 1.

54. Ibid., p. 2.

55. Ibid., p. 67.

56. Ibid., pp. 77–83.

57. R. Bly, ed., *News of the Universe* (San Francisco: Sierra Club Books, 1980).

58. D. H. Lawrence, *Fantasia of the Unconscious and Psychoanalysis and the Unconscious* (London: Heinemann, 1971), p. 39.

59. Ibid., pp. 38–39; Dylan Thomas, *Collected Poems 1934–1952* (London: J. M. Dent and Sons, 1967), p. 9.

60. N. Tarn, ed., *Pablo Neruda: Selected Poems* (Harmondsworth: Penguin, 1985), pp. 161–65; R. Bly, *Neruda and Vallejo: Selected Poems* (Boston: Beacon Press, 1971), pp. 146–51. See also E. Jong, *Fruits and Vegetables* (London: Secker and Warburg, 1971); or R. Bly, "Glimpse of the Waterer," in his *Selected Poems* (New York: Harper & Row, 1986); and F. Ponge, "Fauna and Flora," in *The Random House Book of Twentieth Century French Poetry*, ed. P. Auster (New York: Vintage, 1984), pp. 315–21; or W. Berry, *Farming: A Handbook* (New York: Harcourt Brace Jovanovich, 1970).

61. Also see the Appendix to this volume.

APPENDIX

1. For references to the dream of the botanical manuscript, see S. Freud, *The Interpretation of Dreams* (London: George Allen and Unwin, 1971), pp. 169–76, 282–84, 305, 467. See also the "Lacanian" rereading of this dream in A. Lemaire, *Jacques Lacan* (London: Routledge and Kegan Paul, 1977), pp. 171–73.

2. On "binding" and the underworld images of "Ananke," see J. Hillman, "On the Necessity of Abnormal Psychology: Ananke and Athena," in *Facing the Gods*, ed. J. Hillman (Dallas: Spring Publications, 1980); for images of a "bloodless" underworld, see J. Hillman, *The Dream and the Underworld* (New York: Harper & Row, 1979).

3. On Freud's "death instinct" and its relation to the metaphor of the neuron, see chapter two of this volume.

4. See J. Hillman, *The Myth of Analysis* (New York: Harper & Row, 1978), p. 174.

5. Freud, *Interpretation*, p. 305.

6. In a letter to Freud, Fliess wrote that he could see Freud's completed book on dreams "lying" before him. Freud wished that he, too, could see it finished (*Interpretation*, p. 172).

7. Lemaire, *Jacques Lacan*, p. 173.

8. Freud, *Interpretation*, p. 168.

9. For other "vegetable" dreams in *Interpretation*, see pp. 183–185, 374–77, 406–07. In each of these the "vegetableness" is reduced to a mere signifier. See also E. Edinger's highly spiritual interpretation of a garden dream (*Ego and Archetype* [Harmondsworth: Penguin, 1980], pp. 208–09). In its own way, this is just as reductive as Freud's sexual interpretations. Both miss the vegetableness of the image.

INDEX

OTHER VALUABLE TITLES

GOD IS A TRAUMA
Vicarious Religion and Soul-Making
Greg Mogenson

"Here is a book that does not fear to look the Devil in his face and to embrace what there it sees" (Marion Woodman). Many books have attempted to bring religion and psychology together but usually fail because they assume religion is an affair only of the spirit. Greg Mogenson approaches the issue more radically by presenting a theology of soul. By valuing the soul's language—images—this theology protects the soul from the sadism of the spirit. Faithfulness to the soul shifts our focus from the overwhelming nature of whatever functions as "God" to the small scale of daily soul-making. (167 pp.)

OVID'S METAMORPHOSES
Charles Boer, tr.

All the classic tales of Western mythology come to life in a striking new translation. Ovid's *Metamorphoses* has always been recognized as the greatest single narration of what the myth world of antiquity looked, thought, and felt like at its climax. Boer's rendering brings the reader a fuller-bodied Ovid, one closer to the Ovid of Dante or Shakespeare or Ezra Pound. Faithful to the poet's literal level, Boer parts company with the standard American versions of the fifties. Extensive glossary. (ix, 359 pp.)

THE CULT OF CHILDHOOD
George Boas

Could our fascination with our early years and the issues of child abuse and abortion—and even developmental psychology—be recapitulations of what Boas calls "cultural primitivism," that theory which holds earlier states are better, purer because more innocent? Innocence, rather than the primary characteristic of children, may be a fond fantasy about them. By examining the *idea* of childhood from Plato to Norman O. Brown, Boas exposes the buried assumptions that continue to influence nearly everything we do and say about children. Index. (120 pp.)

ON POETIC IMAGINATION AND REVERIE
Selections from Gaston Bachelard
Colette Gaudin, tr.

Bachelard's books on the psychoanalysis of fire and the poetics of air, water, earth, and space—excerpted here—are indispensable for the study of dreams, poetic images, alchemical symbols, and all forms of reverie. His genius has produced the single most important body of thought in the rehabilitation of imagination in this century. Bibliography and a new preface by Colette Gaudin supplementing her introduction of 1970. Index. (lviii, 112 pp.)